Leading for Positive Impact

Today's business leaders know that creating social impact while leveraging updated technology and effective leadership is critical for success; their challenge is how to do it and how to strike this balance.

The book's step-by-step, visual approach makes it easy to grasp even complex concepts, and the model presented has been designed so you can use it immediately with your teams, for your own development path, and within organizations. It can be applied no matter the industry you are in or size of the organization you either own, work for, or work. Based on research, real-world experience, and fascinating stories by the people who have risen through the organizations, it highlights the role of digital technology in enhancing business and social results as a core part of doing business. The book also blends real action with insights from management and sustainability to address the growing trend of emphasizing actual positive impact on business and social results. It offers hands-on strategies on how to achieve this, rather than engaging in empty social washing or greenwashing communication and promises that never come to life and never make an impact beyond fancy slogans and illusions.

This book's holistic and dynamic approach to leadership in an ever-evolving world will appeal to established and next-generation leaders, aspiring business leaders, sustainability professionals, strategic consultants, business students, and researchers.

Kristian Pultz Schlosser grew up in a working-class family in Denmark, starting on the floor, and working his way up, enabled by people showing him how to get things done. Today a director level professional, strategic leadership expert, and researcher, he holds a PhD from a European university and has led large-scale digital transformations across Europe, Asia, South America, and the United States. His work bridges people, technology, and impact, helping leaders turn purpose into real results.

Leading for Positive Impact

A Practical Guide for Next Generation Leaders

Kristian Pultz Schlosser

Routledge
Taylor & Francis Group
NEW YORK AND LONDON

Designed cover image: Getty

First published 2026
by Routledge
605 Third Avenue, New York, NY 10158

and by Routledge
4 Park Square, Milton Park, Abingdon, Oxon, OX14 4RN

Routledge is an imprint of the Taylor & Francis Group, an informa business

Library of Congress Cataloging-in-Publication Data
Names: Schlosser, Kristian P. author
Title: Leading for positive impact : a practical guide for next generation leaders / Kristian P. Schlosser.
Description: New York, NY: Routledge, 2026. | Includes bibliographical references and index.
Identifiers: LCCN 2025052755 (print) | LCCN 2025052756 (ebook) |
ISBN 9781041070498 hardback | ISBN 9781041070481 paperback |
ISBN 9781003638551 ebook
Subjects: LCSH: Leadership
Classification: LCC HD57.7 .S3545 2026 (print) | LCC HD57.7 (ebook) |
DDC 658.4/092—dc23/eng/20260304
LC record available at https://lccn.loc.gov/2025052755
LC ebook record available at https://lccn.loc.gov/2025052756

ISBN: 9781041070498 (hbk)
ISBN: 9781041070481 (pbk)
ISBN: 9781003638551 (ebk)

DOI: 10.4324/9781003638551

Typeset in Perpetua
by codeMantra

Contents

Acknowledgments

My first jobs weren't driving global, large-scale transformations; they were hands-on. Sweeping factory floors after school, scrubbing restaurant toilets, cleaning the gym long after everyone had gone home, and working full-time as a carpenter and repairing houses in the middle of winter storms.

Those years taught me about life and people, earning the trust of construction crews on cold mornings after a night in the site's camper, sharing laughs with janitors after midnight shifts. I learned that respect is built eye-to-eye through action, not top-down, and that wisdom can come from the calloused hands as much as from any boardroom. Today, working across cultures in every corner of the world, it's those early lessons that guide me.

I didn't write this book alone. Whether we're still in touch or not, I haven't forgotten what you gave me along the way.

Special thanks go to Jens Husted, who has believed in me before I was even considered to be a leader, who understood how to move me forward, who taught me how to keep focus and do it, and who is a lifelong friend and mentor who continues to elevate me in life and business.

Special thanks also go to Martin Lindberg, Dr. Scott Roach, and Michael Clarke, whose advice showed up in moments I didn't even realize I needed it, to Tom Johnston for years of mentorship and buying into my wild transformation ideas when we worked together, and to Aythami Thaifon and Mariana, my first friends when I moved abroad, who helped me understand the value of emotional awareness when facing unfamiliar customs and culture. Despite our limited ability to communicate verbally, you welcomed me with endless hospitality while I was finding my way in a new country.

Special thanks also go to my PhD supervisors, Prof. Tatjana Volkova and Prof. Aivars Spilbergs, for challenging me and helping shape the research behind this book. Your guidance made it stronger, and I'm grateful for every conversation.

Hanne Møller is a creative Art Director and UX Designer with a background in graphic design and branding. She takes a people-driven approach to developing solutions and brings design to life with clarity and empathy. It's a pleasure working with you on the book. Hanne, you knew exactly how to give this book an identity through your designs! Thank you for taking on this project with me and I look forward to what comes next. I would like to acknowledge my wider book team, Robert from Highline Editorial, NYC, and James Bullivant at Margin Editorial, for copy editing and my partnership with Meredith and Bethany from Routledge.

Special thanks go to the key voices in this book, Lucy Blount, Michael Olesen, Esben Thorup, Nis Alstrup, and Claudio Caputo – your stories gave this work its heartbeat and inspiration to our readers, just as you are an inspiration to me!

Special thanks also go to the Horizon56 team, and especially Michael, for backing this project while we were deep in the middle of various global projects.

I would like to express my special thanks to my family and all the rest of you in Denmark and abroad for the patience, the push, and the quiet support provided by them when needed. Even if I didn't always show it, I noticed. You taught me how always to be kind, be the diplomat, be useful and engage with people on all levels of society with respect, curiosity, and trust. Special thanks go to the people I met while living and working abroad – you changed how I see the world. You taught me that leadership is much more than what any business school can teach, more than the inspiring quote we read when scrolling on our phone, and that it is deeply rooted in culture and it is all about people.

Finally, a Danish version for my closest family and friends, both in Denmark and abroad:

> Til slut en dansk version til min nærmeste familie og venner som både er i Danmark og i udlandet. Selvom jeg bor ude i verden, og vi kun ser hinanden få gange om året, mærker jeg altid jeres nærvær. Jeg ved, at I har været nysgerrige på, hvad jeg kaster mig ud i, og det har betydet mere, end I aner. Mest af alt har jeres støtte, som har givet mig en tryghed og styrke til at fortsætte. At vide, at I er der, uanset hvor jeg befinder mig, er noget jeg aldrig tager for givet.
>
> [Even though I live out in the world and we only see each other a few times a year, I always feel your presence. I know you've been curious about what I've been getting myself into, and that has meant more than you can imagine. Most of all, your support has given me the sense of security and strength to keep going. Knowing that you are there for me, no matter where I am in the world, is something I never take for granted.]

About the Author

Kristian Pultz Schlosser is a strategic leadership expert, researcher, and lecturer motivated by one thing: making a positive impact on people. He grew up in a working-class, fishing family in Esbjerg, Denmark. He first trained as a carpenter, learning the value of hard work, craftsmanship, and a hands-on approach. Those beginnings shaped how he leads and connect him with people from every layer of business and society.

Over the past decade, Kristian has led digital transformation projects in some of the world's largest companies, across Europe, Asia, South America, and the United States. His leadership has been tested in boardrooms and in the field, often in high-stakes environments where technology, safety, and people all had to align to deliver results.

Academically, Kristian earned his PhD (*summa cum laude*) and MBA (*with distinction*), focusing his research on the intersection of leadership, technology, and positive social impact. He is recognized for his ability to bridge theory and practice, turning research into actionable strategies that leaders can apply in real-world settings.

What drives him today is passing that experience forward. Through his teaching, public speaking, and his book *Leading for Positive Impact*, Kristian is committed to inspiring the next generation of leaders, equipping them to act with purpose, clarity, and confidence and to build businesses that deliver results while making a lasting difference for people and society.

Foreword

Over the course of a long career working in both small and large companies, leading more than 700 employees, managing projects in over 25 countries worth more than 120 million dollars, founding and selling businesses, and running my own company for more than 30 years, I have met an incredible number of people.

Some stand out, for better or worse. And then, there are those who stand out so quickly that you know at once they have far more to offer than they let on. That was my first impression of Kristian. Within a very short time, I knew he was someone with unusual abilities, perhaps not even fully aware of himself of how his life experiences had shaped him into someone with a remarkable and still-unrealized potential. Kristian managed, in his own humorous, unique, and humble way, to present himself and his background in such a way that I quickly saw that what he needed was not talent; he already had that. He needed someone who could enable him, a sparring partner, and guide to help him unlock his potential.

Our paths first crossed through music. Alongside my professional career, music and entertainment have always been passions of mine. I have spent a lifetime playing and performing, and those lessons – communicating, attracting attention, bringing people together, and doing so with credibility, have served me well in business. For the past 17 years, I have been a singer in a band where Kristian's father, Per, plays the drums. In 2018, Per asked me to meet Kristian, believing I might be someone who could guide him. Since then, it has been a great pleasure and inspiration to coach, advise, and collaborate with Kristian, both in Denmark and abroad, and to watch how, with his own abilities and only a few nudges, he has been able to release a potential I have rarely seen.

From a winding path, including a well-executed leadership role in Barcelona in 2018, to a strong position in Riga, the founding of several companies, a successful leadership role in a large international company with travel across the globe, the completion of a PhD with highest possible distinction, and now the publication of this book on strategic leadership, it is clear to me that Kristian understands what it means to turn theory into practice.

Music offers a fitting parallel to leadership. You can be the best singer or band leader, have read everything about music, and still fail if you can't make it sound good together. To start right, keep the rhythm, and finish in a way that leaves the audience delighted requires that everyone can play and wants to play. Perfection is not necessary every time, but you must believe in the lyrics, sing them with joy, and deliver them so that the audience feels and enjoys them. And you must be willing to step up and perform whenever asked, without showing fatigue.

Leadership, in my view, is the same. It rests on personal connection, an understanding of people's differences, and the ability to handle those differences calmly, while also daring to make the hard calls. "It is better to make a bad decision than none at all." Turning theory into practice requires patience, talent, and experience, whether in leadership, in your own business, or in writing a book. And that is precisely what Kristian has managed to capture in these pages.

A good friend and mentor once told me, many years ago: "*No one ever insulted their way to a good friendship or a good business.*" That thought has stayed with me throughout my career as a business leader.

I wish you great enjoyment and learning in reading this book.

Jens Husted

Jens Husted is a Danish business leader and entrepreneur with more than 30 years of international experience founding companies, leading large organizations, and managing projects around the world. Known for valuing people above all else, he leads with his heart, whether he is enabling future leaders, or solving highly complex semi-submersible drilling-rig crane projects between Trinidad, United States, China, and Australia, or performing as a lifelong musician and bandleader. His belief in turning theory into practice and creating trust through human connection has shaped both his career and his approach to leadership.

Introduction

This book is built on high-quality research and first-hand experiences of failures and successes of executives, leaders, managers, and frontline employees. Told through data, real-world case studies, and hard-earned insights, this book serves as the foundation for your practical guide on how to create and sustain a positive impact.

As Lucy said during lunch, 18 months into a global digital transformation, when we talked about driving change across continents.

"It's almost like running a campaign, you have to meet people where they are. The hard truth? It takes a marathon level of empathy that most struggle to sustain until the end." – Lucy Blount

HOW TO GET THE MOST OUT OF THIS BOOK

This book gives you the *how*.

How to navigate the tension – and strike the balance – between technology, sustainability, innovation, and day-to-day operations, while building confidence and credibility as a leader. Once that balance is in place, the book shows how to scale and amplify impact, delivering results that strengthen business performance, people empowerment, and societal outcomes at the same time.

To support this, the book introduces a practical, step-by-step leadership model – *The Enablers*. Co-developed with executives, managers, and frontline staff, *the Enablers* function as both a leadership model and a practical toolbox you can lean on to make confident decisions when the pressure is on.

Most business books focus on the *why* and the *what*. The real challenge today is the *how* – how leaders enable impact when execution begins.

That's what this book delivers.

I want you to think that you're stepping into a classroom taught by world-class leaders, backed by quality research.

***

DOI: 10.4324/9781003638551-1

Think of it as an advanced MBA in leadership, delivered through lived cases, engaging diagrams, and custom tools that reflect the actual choices leaders face when the pressure is on.

This book was built to answer the questions that no one else could answer for me, the ones I kept hearing in classrooms, in project meetings, at the coffee machine, in boardrooms, and in team meetings.

I challenge readers to read it cover to cover; however, I'm a realist, and I'll readily admit that readers are often sure busy, so I've also structured it for chapter skippers: each chapter stands on its own.

***

I interviewed global leaders, so you'll understand what happened when a health executive launched an augmented reality app that let users preview cosmetic surgeries on their own body, a decade before regulators approved it.

In another chapter, I interview a post-merger leader who mapped every real decision path, not based on titles, but on influence, value add, and team diversity.

Plus, you'll get the insights of a project and leader who was tasked with delivering a multi-billion-euro offshore energy project in a high-pressure political environment, through ecosystem thinking.

I asked two leaders with opposite instincts how they learned to balance speed and structure, and what it takes to shift from a spinout innovation team to a global digital enabler.

Finally, you'll meet a leader who started working as a petroleum engineer, spent years working offshore, and now drives digital transformation across one of the world's most complex industries. She does it by meeting teams face to face, listening first, adapting second.

The book is not overloaded with theory, and I'm sure you'll quickly discover that I'm offering real-world application, and have combined their stories with years of quality research, so you will understand *how* to make a sustained positive impact!

This book is both **educational** and **experiential**.

Being *educational* means you'll understand how leadership actually works, not just in theory, but through step-by-step frameworks that simplify complexity.

Being *experiential* means you'll work with the material directly. You'll write. Sketch. Map decisions. Adapt tools to your own team or context. You'll use this book the way great leaders learn, by doing, not just reading.

That means you'll learn, and then immediately apply. Think of it as a hexagon, or six-sided power block, where you can plug in your own ideas. I've designed this model around six leadership enablers: **Empowerment, Structure, Ecosystems, Technology, Transformation, and Scalability.**

For the chapter skippers, look for the parts marked with 'Key Takeaways' – these are the high-leverage moves. And if something challenges your thinking, that is exactly what this book aims to do. Therefore, the book requires something from you. Not just your attention, but an emotional investment. I want you to reflect, challenge your assumptions, and confront uncomfortable truths about what it really takes to lead for impact.

This isn't a book you finish – I hope that it's one you'll return to over and over, and that it will become a powerful action tool that will drive transformation and innovation, whatever size business you are operating.

The timing couldn't be more relevant: leaders today are tasked with driving social impact while delivering business results. This book shows you how to leverage technology, innovate disruptively, and utilize tested ideas on how to lead with authenticity without falling into the trap of social greenwashing. Or worse, ending up in a mission-drift situation, where your aim was to drive both the social and business agenda, but you lacked the right leadership traits. Without them, you start drifting toward business goals, only left to write about the good you are doing (intended to do) while harvesting the profit.

Sustainability trends and digital transformation are reshaping all industries, and the urgency for meaningful leadership is at an all-time high. This book is designed to help you navigate these challenges and turn them into opportunities for positive impact. The very core of this book is centered around the Enablers. *These are a framework of six strategic dimensions that equip leaders to balance and integrate core business operations with future opportunities, creating positive impacts on both business and social results.*

To get the most out of this book, whether you're strategizing for your organization or using it for academic purposes, you should follow the model, engage with the case studies, and apply the actionable strategies in your own work.

My extensive research has proven that good intentions alone are insufficient in today's business world. Strategic leadership without contextual understanding is also insufficient – good projects and companies without profits will struggle to sustain their positive impact, and good companies without a social impact will struggle to attract employees, funding, and reputation.

Before you plunge into Chapter 1, I should remind you: no single leader can embody every trait and master all the complexities of technology, plus drive transformative change, while being a visionary leader. However, the good news is – you don't have to. What you're about to discover is how you, as a nascent or experienced leader, *can enable these traits in yourself and others*, navigate technology with purpose, and ensure real, measurable results. One person can't do it all – but you will learn how to create lasting impact in a business world where uncertainty, regulation, market demands, and customer needs and wants are changing faster than ever.

This book cover is green on purpose. It's not meant to blend in. Neither are you. Dive in and you will understand how to enable impact.

Chapter 1

The Enablers Part I

Operations and Innovation, Transparency, and Structure

The Enablers are six essential strategic dimensions that will help you balance today's operations with tomorrow's opportunities. *They don't just describe how to lead, they show you how to do it*.

This hands-on section could be described as a shortcut to dive directly into the toolbox for an early understanding of the Enablers framework.

TIP

If you do not want to read the whole book now but want to get hands-on and enable success, stick to this chapter! The Enablers have been split into three parts: Enablers 1–3 in this chapter, 4–6 in Chapter 4, and finally the remaining Enablers and results in Chapter 5.

Disclaimer: Shortcuts can lead to dead ends, so reader beware!

Each section in the chapter features one Enabler with three subsections. First you will find a short description of the Enabler followed by some considerations for you to discuss. Lastly, you will be presented with key takeaways.

Your objective is to understand how to cope with the challenges that every organization faces: balancing stability with innovation, to ensure that today's operations run efficiently while simultaneously preparing for future opportunities. The Enablers provide strategic dimensions that help navigate this balance, ensuring both business success and social impact (Figure 1.1).

DOI: 10.4324/9781003638551-2

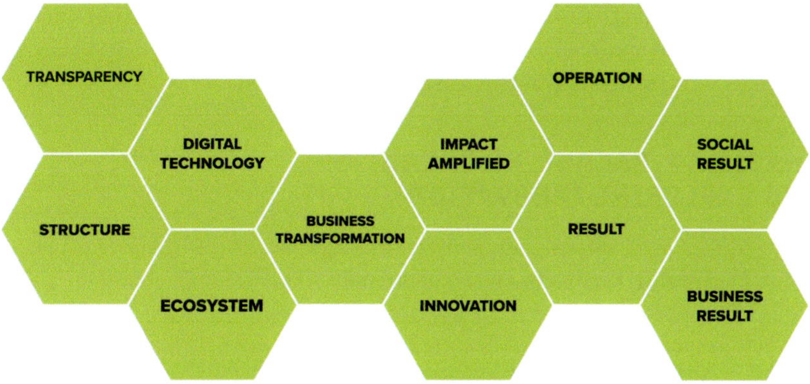

Figure 1.1 Enablers: Your Leadership Model That Will Show You "How" to Make a Positive Impact

UNDERSTANDING ENABLERS – YOU WILL LEARN HOW TO

- Find out how the Enablers are interconnected, how they impact each other and how you can use them independently based on the opportunity or challenge in front of you.
- Spot the gaps before they spread, learning how to ask the right questions in the right context.
- Detect the subtle signals: slowing momentum, growing inefficiencies, or innovation roadblocks that could derail your progress.

Related to the above, you will learn how to unlock enhanced collaboration with your team, clients, and stakeholders by learning how to ask the right questions in the right context.

PUTTING THE ENABLERS TO WORK

You can use this powerful framework to fine-tune your organization's balance between today's execution and tomorrow's breakthroughs. As an elaboration of the work by Michael Tushman and Charles O'Reilly on structural ambidexterity,[1] I am adding a social responsibility element to go beyond "just" competitive advantage.

How? By turning strategy into action: master proven tools to unleash your team's potential, streamline operations, and forge alliances that magnify both business success and social impact.

Lead with intent: Confidently navigate transformation, scale your impact, and ensure every move aligns with your purpose, whether you're driving change internally or across several ecosystems.

ENABLER 1: BALANCING OPERATIONS AND EXPLORING INNOVATION

First and foremost, the paradox is that it's not just about this balance; it's about doing it faster than ever before to avoid disruption and becoming obsolete. Companies' lifespans are shorter than ever, with an average of 15 years, which used to be 67! Very few companies have been able to manage both existing operations and explore future opportunities.

Understanding the balance is one defining trait of a successful leader and is not just about strategy, *it's about enabling others*.

However, when you become aware that tasks cannot be mastered all at once, but you know how and what steps to take, that is the real game changer. You will enable your team, build the right traits at the right time, and allocate resources effectively between two opposing but interconnected forces (Figure 1.2):

- **Operations**: Optimizing current assets, capabilities, and offerings.
- **Explorer Innovation**: Identifying trends, entering new markets, and innovating.

Resources can be human (specialized skills, designers, engineers, etc.), physical (offices, hardware, logistics infrastructure, etc.), financial (cash, credit structure, etc.), and intellectual (brand, copyright, etc.).

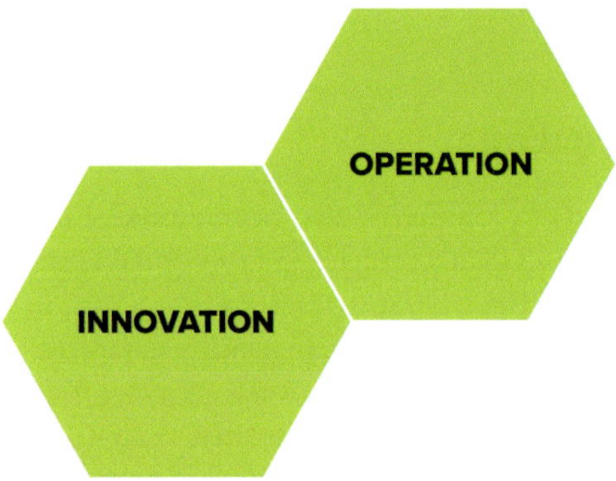

Figure 1.2 Operations and Innovation Balancing Act

Operations: Stability and Efficiency

Operations focus on exploiting existing strengths to maximize performance. It involves:

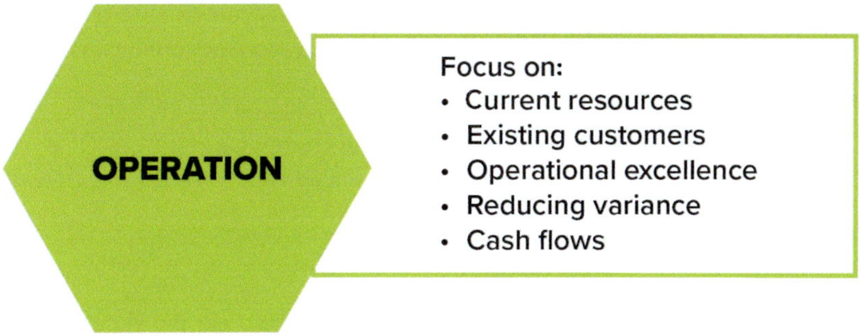

Figure 1.3 Operations and Your Core Business Activities

- Using current resources.
- Serving existing customers.
- Maintaining operational excellence.
- Reducing variance through efficiency methods (e.g., Lean Six Sigma).
- Focusing on cash flows. Your cash will enable your future and keep you afloat.

Remember, you have to be willing to spend that cash on research and innovations and you must stay profitable, unless potential investors give you a time range where you can experiment before making a profit. So, while it's necessary to focus on profitability, an overemphasis on operations can lead to stagnation and thus expose you to disruption. As leading business leaders and researchers, your best practices will lead you to a dead end.

Exploring innovation is about looking ahead, driving change in the market, and capturing new opportunities. Key focus areas include:

- Tracking trends and market disruptions. Exploring technology, people trends, and client needs. Do your clients want you to develop new features, products, or to integrate with their other vendors?
- Expanding into new customer segments *or* identify or create additional needs within your current segment. This can be related to your existing offering, where you develop it through exploration and by using the other enablers.
- Aligning innovation with operations capabilities.

Figure 1.4 Innovation and Your Future Business

- Increasing variance to foster creativity (e.g., you use the design thinking method).[2]
- Cash flow: you should expect not to generate cash flow, rather you will be burning through cash until your exploration efforts identify your next cash flow opportunity.

However, without the right balance, innovation efforts can lack direction or fail to translate into business success.

Exploring innovation requires you to actively track trends, expand customer value, align innovation with operational capabilities, and embrace creative variance, while accepting that cash flow may initially suffer as you search for the next opportunity to scale impact. If you want to lead tomorrow's business, this is your blueprint – not for survival, but for impact at scale.

The Leadership Challenge of Balance

Leadership today is about navigating the fine line between operational stability and disruptive innovation. To thrive, you must tackle tough questions: Should stability and innovation be managed by the same team, split into separate units, or spun off entirely?

This book doesn't just ask these questions, it shows you how to answer them. *Each of the Enablers in the following chapters offers practical guidance to help you find the right balance for your context.*

Practical Steps for Leaders

- *People:* Who thrives in maintaining day-to-day stability? Who excels in driving change and embracing uncertainty? Identifying these strengths is critical to placing the right people in the right roles.

- *Capital:* Where will financial resources deliver the most value, securing operational efficiency or seeding future opportunities?
- *Decision-Making Autonomy*: How much control does each group need to ensure agility without creating misalignment?
- *Culture:* Recognize that operations and innovation teams may need distinct values and behaviors. A culture rooted in stability won't necessarily nurture creativity, and vice versa. Leaders must foster alignment without forcing homogeneity.
- *Foster Empowerment*: Build a culture where employees confidently contribute to both stability and growth. Empower them with decision-making autonomy and a clear vision of their role in the larger mission.
- *Cultivate Ecosystems*: Strengthen relationships with stakeholders, customers, and partners to unlock synergies that amplify both operational success and innovation.
- *Lead with Emotional Intelligence (EQ)*: Navigate uncertainty with empathy and adaptability, ensuring trust and resilience within your teams and networks.[3]

The challenge isn't just about balancing two opposing forces, it's about structuring, enabling, and empowering teams and ecosystems to thrive.

Considerations Related to Operations and Innovation

- Does your team culture favor stability or innovation? Do you have the right balance of people who thrive on efficiency vs. those who embrace uncertainty and risk?
- Who in your organization naturally drives change? Are your explorers empowered to experiment, or are they held back by rigid structures?
- Are you leveraging both types of employees effectively? How do you create an environment where those who prefer stability support innovative efforts rather than resist them and vice versa?
- How adaptable is your leadership team? Are key decision-makers comfortable balancing both operational excellence and future exploration? Is your team and leadership aware of how these opposing mechanisms impact?
- Does your company culture encourage risk-taking? Or are new ideas dismissed because they don't fit existing structures?
- How do you prevent "innovation fatigue"? Are employees being asked to innovate while still being evaluated based on efficiency and predictability?

Empower teams and build cultures to drive long-term success. *Remember, culture is referred to as a social control system, were you break it down on a behavioral level. What behaviors are expected in operations and what are expected in your innovation?*

KEY TAKEAWAYS:

- Balance: striking a balance does not mean equal focus on each side, in most cases, means imbalance, and it's up to you to enable the right balance at the right time based on your context.
- Operations: Optimize existing strengths, reduce variance. Build a culture of continuous improvement for example.
- Explorer Innovation: Capture future opportunities, increase variance.

Leaders must allocate resources wisely between the two.

ENABLER 2: EMPOWERMENT IN ACTION – THE ROLE OF EXTREME TRANSPARENCY

This section serves as a quick, actionable reference for creating a culture where transparency leads to empowerment, and ultimately, lasting business success.

Experts and current research confirm that when employees understand the company's vision, feel empowered, and see opportunities for development, both business and social results improve.[4] As a colleague and business partner said, "When employees know where the organization is heading and why, they are more likely to feel motivated and committed to contributing to its success".

We can conclude that transparency builds trust, drives engagement, and ensures that employees feel aligned with the company's mission rather than just following orders. Consider this scenario: Have you been left out from emails and meetings that actually impacted you, but you were not included? Or have

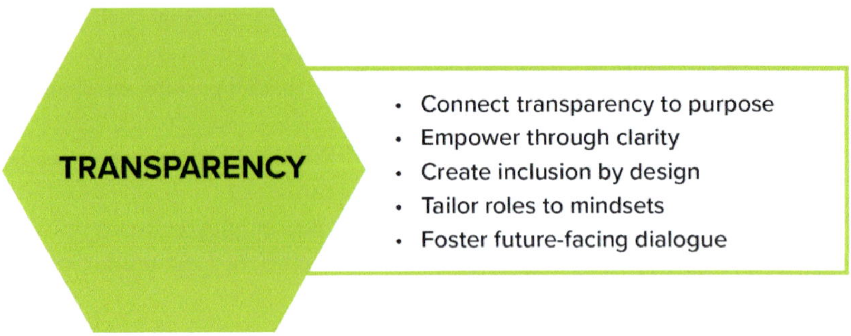

Figure 1.5 Transparency and Empowerment Enabler

they been included for visibility on emails and meetings? How did it feel being included vs excluded?

Practical Steps for Leaders

✓ Share Your Vision Clearly: Regional Level, Team Level, Project Level

Communicate the goals and strategic direction, with tactical steps at all levels. Employees need to see how their work connects to the bigger picture.

✓ Empower Employees Through Decision-Making

Encourage employees to take ownership of their work. Give them the autonomy to make meaningful contributions rather than micromanaging every step.

✓ Invest in Employee Development

Foster a learning culture where employees continuously develop new skills, preparing them for the current situation (it might read current, but always evolving) and future roles.

✓ Identify Who Thrives in Operations vs. Innovation

Not all employees are wired the same way. Some excel in structured, efficiency-driven environments (operations), while others thrive in innovation and experimentation (explorer innovation). Identify these strengths and place people accordingly.

Considerations Related to Empowerment and Transparency

- Are you clearly communicating the difference between operations and exploring roles?

  Do employees understand where they fit best, whether in efficiency-driven operations or future-focused innovation? Not everyone is suited for disruptive innovation, just as not everyone thrives in routine execution. Are you placing and developing employees where they can succeed?
- Do employees see how their work connects to long-term business goals?

  Are they aware of how their contributions impact both current stability and future opportunities?
- Do your managers enable open conversations about the future?

  Beyond daily operations, do leaders create space for discussing trends, disruptions, and the company's strategic direction? Employees need clarity on where the business is going.
- Are employees empowered to make decisions within their roles?

  Transparency is not just about sharing information; it's about giving employees the trust and autonomy to act on it. Are leaders delegating decision-making effectively?

KEY TAKEAWAYS:

- Transparency fuels motivation, trust, and alignment.
- Some employees stay when they see a future within the organization, and others stay when they can see stability.
- Leaders must communicate vision, empower decision-making, and invest in growth.
- Placing the right people in operations vs. exploration roles enhances both stability and innovation.

ENABLER 3: STRUCTURES FOR SUCCESS – SEPARATING AND ALIGNING OPERATIONS AND INNOVATION

Your internal structure will directly impact how well you can run existing operations while exploring future opportunities. Without the right structure, decision-making slows, accountability blurs, and innovation stalls. You must design for both stability and agility, ensuring that operations and innovation each have the right level of autonomy, resources, and alignment (Figure 1.6).

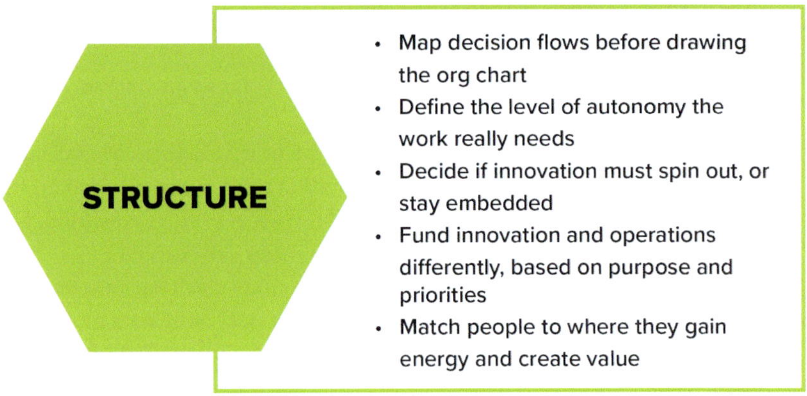

Figure 1.6 Structure Enabler

Questions That Need Answers

- How will your structure enable current operations and your innovation?
- What kind of structure or structures do you need? How do you facilitate operations and innovation?
- How do you empower people and enable the right level of decision-making?

Practical Steps

✓ *Separate or Integrate?*

Should innovation be a separate unit, a spin-off, or embedded within operations? Some organizations create dedicated innovation teams, while others integrate future-focused projects across functions. As either or both areas grow, you must make decisions on how to structure your team/business. Failing to do so will choke one or the other.

✓ *Matrix vs. Hierarchy?*

Rigid hierarchies can slow decision-making, while complex matrix structures can create confusion. The key is balancing agility and accountability to ensure clarity in roles and faster execution. In many cases, you may use several in combination; have agile teams for your development, hierarchy for your operations, and matrix when you engage in projects.

✓ *Resource Allocation: Balancing Stability and Growth*

Are financial and human resources distributed effectively between operations and innovation? Underfunding exploration limits growth, while excessive focus on the future can weaken stability, as you won't have the resources to deal with day-to-day tasks.

✓ *Autonomy and Decision-Making Power*

Who has the authority to act? Teams should have enough autonomy to move quickly without creating misalignment or inefficiencies. Leaders must ensure the right level of control vs. flexibility. Remember that delegating decision-making authority puts a huge responsibility on the employee/team. Have you trained them? Are they comfortable taking on this responsibility? Did you empower them?

✓ *Avoiding Complexity Traps*

Overly complicated structures slow decision-making, innovation, and create bottlenecks. Streamline layers, simplify decision processes, and clarify accountability to maintain both speed and agility.

KEY TAKEAWAYS:

- Structure must enable both stability and adaptability.
- Decide whether to separate or integrate innovation.
- Balance agility with accountability, avoid rigid or overly complex structures.
- Empowered teams make better, faster decisions.
- Clear roles and streamlined processes drive execution and innovation.

In the next chapter, you will be presented with Enabler 4 (Ecosystems), focusing on stakeholders and how you will enable these to balance your operations and innovation, and Enabler 5 (Digital Technology) that will show you how to use digital technology and the consequences – good and bad – by executing different strategies. Finally, Enabler 6 (Business Transformation) will enable you to bridge all Enablers in a way to create a lasting positive impact. Let's dive in.

NOTES

1 This extends the work of Michael Tushman and Charles O'Reilly on structural ambidexterity – particularly their synthesis in *Organizational Ambidexterity: Past, Present and Future* (2013), which outlines how firms can balance exploitation and exploration by designing dual structures, processes, and leadership systems to manage both simultaneously.
2 Design thinking offers a powerful methodology for business leaders to develop impactful products, services, and processes. By focusing on human needs, design thinking ensures that solutions are technologically feasible, economically viable, and deeply relevant to the people they serve. Visit https://www.ideo.com/thinking for more information.
3 In high-stakes environments, your ability to read the room, stay composed under pressure, and respond with empathy matters as much as your strategic judgment. EQ isn't soft, it's a core leadership skill. If you want to go deeper, Daniel Goleman's *Emotional Intelligence* and Annie McKee's *How to Be Happy at Work* are great places to start.
4 This insight is supported by my own research on strategic leadership and shared value, based on survey data from over 400 leaders and in-depth interviews across sectors. For a summary of findings and practical tools, visit www.docschlosser.com.

Chapter 2

The Enablers Part II

Ecosystems, Technology, and Transformation

ENABLER 4: ECOSYSTEMS

The success and social impact of your business depend on how well you engage the right partners.[1] Mapping your ecosystem is not just about relationships; it's about strategy. Leaders must identify, engage, and leverage the right partners to unlock growth, innovation, and long-term success (Figure 2.1).

How will your ecosystem enable current operations and your innovation? What players do you want/need in your ecosystem? What kind of structure or structures do you need? To facilitate operations and innovation. Empowerment of people, enable the right level of decision-making?

Key Players in Your Ecosystem

Government Agencies

Government entities can be partners, regulators, or enablers. Engaging with them proactively ensures compliance, unlocks funding opportunities, and helps navigate policy landscapes that affect your industry.

Figure 2.1 Ecosystems for Lasting Partnerships Enabler

DOI: 10.4324/9781003638551-3

Private Companies

Strategic business partnerships with technology providers, suppliers, financial institutions, and service firms can enhance operations, drive innovation, and expand market reach.

Investors

Whether internal or external, investors provide capital, strategic guidance, and governance. Aligning with investors who support both business and social impact goals is crucial for long-term success.

Regulators

Regulatory bodies ensure compliance with industry standards, legal frameworks, and operational guidelines. A strong relationship with regulators can mitigate risks, prevent disruptions, and provide a competitive edge.

Advisors and Specialists

Legal, financial, and industry-specific advisors provide critical insights, risk management, and specialized expertise. They help navigate complex challenges and ensure strategic decision-making is well-informed.

Practical Steps

- Map key stakeholders and understand their role in business growth and social value creation.
- Develop strategic partnerships to complement internal capabilities and enhance reach.
- Integrate external expertise to navigate industry shifts and regulatory landscapes.

Considerations Related to Your Ecosystem

Who Are Your Critical Stakeholders?

Identify which government agencies, private companies, investors, or advisors are essential to your business. Are they required for compliance, strategic growth, or operational support?

What Is the Role of Government in Your Business?

Governments can be enablers or barriers. Understanding regulatory frameworks and proactively engaging with policymakers is crucial for industries like healthcare, energy, and finance.

Which Private Sector Partnerships Create Value?

Technology providers, financial institutions, legal experts, and other specialists can help you scale and enhance both operational efficiency and future innovation.

How Do You Use Advisory and Specialist Support?

Environmental specialists, legal advisors, and industry experts can help navigate risks, ensure compliance, and provide insights that sharpen strategic decision-making.

Are Your Investors and Shareholders Aligned with Your Vision?

Whether internal or external, investors and board members should align with your strategic direction and support both business and social impact goals.

KEY TAKEAWAYS:

- A well-structured ecosystem amplifies both business success and social impact.
- Stakeholders may be required (legislation and compliance) or strategic (growth and innovation).
- Government relations can be a competitive advantage; remember to engage proactively.
- Private sector partnerships unlock expertise, technology, and market access.
- Advisors and investors shape strategic decisions and align them with your vision.

ENABLER 5: LEVERAGING DIGITAL TECHNOLOGY FOR BUSINESS AND SOCIAL IMPACT

As Lucy Blount said, “It’s almost like running a political campaign, you have to meet people where they are, listen to their concerns, and explain how you’re going to address them.”

A successful digital strategy isn’t just about adopting technology; it’s about putting people at the center and ensuring when, where, and how it’s deployed. This serves both business and employees, *enabling* a positive impact. The right balance between efficiency and innovation, gradual vs. concurrent adoption, and workforce readiness determines success:

> If you align technology with business needs, employee empowerment, and social impact, your technology adoption will create lasting value – those who ignore these nuances risk failure. The key to a thriving, future-ready organization is a people-first, strategic, and context-driven deployment.

Technology adoption is a powerful Enabler, but without the right strategy, it can either accelerate success or create negative unintended consequences. You must carefully manage how technology is integrated into operations (low variance, efficiency-driven, and stable work) and innovation exploration (exploratory, innovative-focused growth).

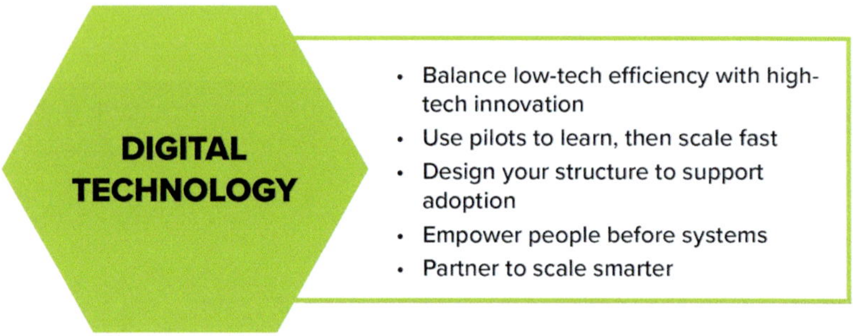

Figure 2.2 Digital Technology Enabler

How will your technology *enable* current operations and your innovation? Which ecosystem players can help? What kind of structure or structures do you need to facilitate operations and innovation?

Timing of Technology Adoption and Deployment

The timing of digital adoption significantly influences its success. Early adoption provides competitive advantages by positioning a company at the forefront of its industry, but it requires investment in workforce readiness and infrastructure. Late adoption, on the other hand, helps reduce risk by applying already successful deployment models, but may cause companies to lag behind competitors.

Workforce Readiness and Digital Capabilities: Building Skills for the Future

> You have probably heard it many times before: digital transformation is not just about technology, it's about people.

In my career, I have led and co-led several very large global digital transformations. I have seen it firsthand, and the statement above is true. Of course, it's a precondition that the software satisfies a need for the executive team (safety, efficiencies, first-mover reputation, etc.) and adds value to the end user, which is a great show of a lasting positive impact on both business (executives) and social (end users) results.

Even the best digital tools will fail if employees are not trained, empowered, or engaged in the digital transformation process. Companies must invest in reskilling employees, fostering data-driven decision-making cultures, and integrating technology as part of their decision-making process. Without workforce adaptation, digital adoption risks increasing resistance, job dissatisfaction, and ultimate failure. A successful digital strategy must ensure that employees grow alongside the technology being introduced.

Low-Level Digital Adoption: Efficiency and Stability in Operations

Technology adoption at a lower level is most effective in operations, where stability and efficiency are key. Tools like robotic process automation (RPA), AI-assisted scheduling, and process optimization software enhance productivity by handling repetitive tasks. The impact is clear: workloads decrease, errors are minimized, and processes become more reliable. Socially, this level of adoption reduces resistance, as employees experience greater job stability and a smoother transition into digital work environments. Repetitive tasks in finance, HR, or manual data entry are good examples of easy-to-automate processes that will support your employees and set them up for a more engaging workday.

High-Level Digital Adoption: Innovation and Growth

In contrast, your business may benefit from high-level digital adoption, where technology drives new capabilities, customer engagement, and industry transformation. Technologies such as AI-supported decision-making, blockchain, Internet of Things, and advanced robotics enable companies to scale faster, increase agility, and attract top talent. However, this level of adoption demands cultural adaptation, new workforce skills, and an organizational structure that supports innovation; otherwise, it risks creating friction and resistance. For example, your company wants to digitize paper-based process across your department. This will require careful change management, communication, continued training, and support for your employees.

Sequential vs. Concurrent Deployment

Deployment strategy plays a critical role in how well employees and business processes adapt to digital transformation. A sequential approach introduces new technology step by step, ensuring stability and reducing employee resistance. Meanwhile, concurrent adoption accelerates innovation but requires strong leadership, structured change management, and a culture of empowerment to prevent operational disruption. Choosing the right strategy depends on company readiness, industry demands, and workforce adaptability.

You also have to be mindful of the risks. Sequential deployment may be beneficial for some end users, but it may also cause fatigue if the deployment stretches out over a long term. You will have to be careful about training your people – if you train them too soon, they will forget, and if you train them too late, they will feel uncomfortable. For concurrent deployment of digital technology, you will need a significant amount of resources: Project teams, change champions, tech leads and support/training staff, as well as clear top-down support from the senior team.

You may need to apply a combination of both; first, a sequential deployment (or you can call it a pilot or a trial), and when your communication package, training, and technology leads are tested and proven successful, you deploy concurrently.

Practical Steps for Your Consideration

- ✓ Balance technology adoption across operations and your innovation unit: clearly define where technology will drive value. Low-tech tools (e.g., process automation) enhance efficiency and stability in operations. While high-tech solutions (e.g., AI and IoT), discovered and tested in your innovation unit, enable disruptive innovation, and enable green field projects. Ensure both approaches complement each other to avoid competing priorities.
- ✓ Use digital tools to empower employees, and be open about the impact. Automation should free employees to focus on higher-value tasks, not eliminate their contributions. Frame technology adoption as a tool to enhance roles, foster creativity, and build new capabilities within your workforce. When automating the repetitive processes, your entry-level employees will have more complex tasks from day one. Additional training may be needed and longer time to competence.
- ✓ Strategically sequence technology deployment: Deploy technology step by step in operations to maintain stability, focusing on gradual process optimization. Where needed, prioritize rapid, exploratory adoption to gain first-mover advantages while managing risks with structured pilots. Note, you can use sequential first, after you have a proven deployment model, you can do it concurrently.
- ✓ Align technology with structural design: Ensure that your organizational structure supports technology integration. For instance, does your current design allow for cross-functional collaboration? Adapt workflows, reporting lines, and team dynamics to accommodate digital transformation seamlessly.

✓ Ensure employee engagement in digital transformation: Actively involve employees early in the process. Identify your "technology hero" to support your change management efforts. Clearly communicate the vision, provide training tailored to their roles, and create spaces for feedback. When employees understand their role in the transformation and feel ownership, resistance decreases, and adoption accelerates. On several occasions, I have experienced a change from folks first not wanting the technology, then getting a pull from the end users and their leadership. All based on proper application of the above points.

Considerations for Your Digital Technology Adoption

Where should technology be applied, incrementally in operations or disruptively based on findings in your innovation? Perhaps you need to embed your technological findings based on an urgency from a client or changing market conditions?

Identify how technology can best drive value: Incremental adoption in operations focuses on stability and efficiency, while disruptive technology from your exploration units unlocks growth. Ensure alignment between these approaches to avoid silos, such as product and design teams developing new solutions without involving operations. This can lead to tools that aren't needed, used, or understood.

How does your structure support digital adoption – does it encourage collaboration or create bottlenecks? Assess whether your organizational design fosters agility or creates barriers. A streamlined structure enables smooth integration of technology, while bottlenecks can delay or undermine progress. Adapt your structure to facilitate seamless collaboration across teams. Bottlenecks can slow decision-making, or worse, a lack of decision-making due to insecurities or silent pushbacks from key players.

Are your employees empowered to embrace the next technology, or is resistance slowing transformation? Empower your workforce by involving them early on in the process, providing clear communication, and offering tailored training. Resistance often stems from uncertainty, and you'll need to equip your people with the tools and confidence to succeed in a digital-first environment.

Do you have a central location for support material? Do your impacted employees know who to contact for support? Do they have access to short how-to videos? Detailed user manuals? Live drop-in sessions? Remember to keep your support resources updated with the latest technology revisions.

Are external partnerships, i.e., ecosystem, supporting your digital strategy? Can you leverage ecosystem players such as technology providers, advisors, and industry experts to fill capability gaps, scale initiatives, and ensure faster, smoother execution? Are there strategic collaborations that can amplify your digital transformation?

TIP

Here are some good examples of hiring a third party to review your technology and/or your data flow, which has proven to be highly beneficial. If you are a small company, use folks from other parts of the business. For example, reviewing your data architecture and making it ready for a new software deployment can enable qualitative and quantitative contextual insights which you may have lost without this partnership.

Are you investing in workforce training to ensure long-term success?

Technology is only as effective as the people using it. Continuous investment in reskilling and upskilling ensures your workforce evolves alongside digital advancements, driving both immediate and sustained success.

KEY TAKEAWAYS:

- Empowerment is key – employees need clarity, autonomy, and training to embrace digital transformation.
- Technology adoption must be contextual and based on your overall vision, market needs and technology readiness.
- Low levels of technology drive process efficiency and workforce stability, while high levels create competitive advantage and growth.
- The right timing and sequencing of digital adoption is critical to success.
- Digital adoption isn't just about business growth, it influences social impact, job satisfaction, and inclusion.

By integrating digital technology with structure, empowerment, and ecosystems, leaders can ensure their organization thrives today and innovates for tomorrow.

ENABLER 6: BUSINESS TRANSFORMATION – BRIDGING OPERATIONS AND INNOVATION

This final Enabler serves as the bridge between operations and innovation. Imagine you've identified a new software technology, tested it within your innovation unit, and now need to embed it into your core operations, or even your client's. Success depends on more than just the tech – you need the right people empowered, structures that facilitate transformation, identified ecosystem partners, and a clear technology path. Here are the high-level steps:

1. **Empower the Right People**
   Assign individuals who have both the trust of the organization and the mandate to drive change across teams. Empower them, understand who forms operations and who from innovation needs to be empowered to drive the transformation.
2. **Define the Supporting Structure**
   Clarify how decisions will be made, who owns implementation, and how operational teams will be engaged. Matrix, spin-off, new department?
3. **Engage Ecosystem Partners**
   Involve relevant external collaborators early, whether for integration, scaling, or long-term support.
4. **Align on the Value of the Technology**
   Ensure all stakeholders understand what the technology does, how it benefits operations, and how success will be measured.

These steps ensure the transition from innovation to operations isn't just a handover, but a strategic integration that creates lasting value.

Now you need to understand how to transform the enablers and bring them all together, so that you transition from innovation to operations. You will need to train your teams, retrain existing people who will be impacted, and move people from innovation to operations to sustain the innovation, all of which requires distinct leadership traits and knowledge of this model. Your transformation Enabler is the one who will help you do all of this. It addresses both from an internal perspective and how you can enable innovation for other companies in the ecosystem (Figure 2.3).

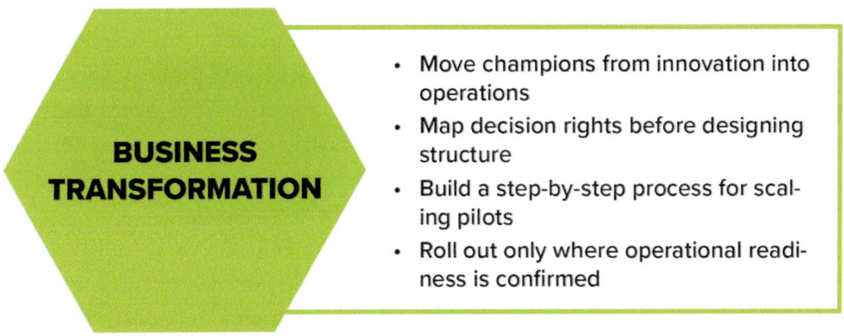

Figure 2.3 Business Transformation – Bridging your Enablers

Question and Considerations

How will you transform your business to create a lasting positive impact from your discoveries? Will technology to lead the way? Will the players in the Ecosystem help?

What kind of structure or structures do you need to facilitate operations and innovation? Or is it the empowerment of your people who will in turn *enable* the right level of decision-making?

Business Transformation: Tying It All Together

> Business transformation is not an isolated activity, it's a process that depends on the seamless integration of multiple Enablers to succeed. To effectively bridge operations and innovation, leaders must rely on three core Enablers: empowerment and transparency, structures, and ecosystem.

Owning the change through empowerment ensures employees feel equipped and trusted to contribute meaningfully to the planned transformation. Start by clearly defining how each team member's role fits into the transition from innovation to operations, creating ownership at every level. Balance autonomy with clear guidance so employees have freedom to act within a strategic framework. You'll need to provide the tools, training, and financial resources they'll need to succeed, and constantly work to foster a culture of trust and accountability.

Empowerment Strengthens Structure and Enables Collaboration with Ecosystem Partners

The transparency you create reduces uncertainty for the risk-averse and builds trust during periods of transformation. As much as this book is focused on the "how," you'll constantly be asked to answer the "why" to your wider teams.

Structures are built to guide the transformation. Start by defining clear decision-making frameworks – should innovations be integrated into existing operations, or spun off and handled by separate units? Can you ensure that your organizational design supports this strategy, with streamlined reporting lines and cross-functional collaboration?You'll need to keep *enabling* your team and assigning roles and accountability to avoid bottlenecks and confusion.

When determining your ecosystem, keep the holistic view in mind that transformation usually never happens in isolation; it always relies on a strong ecosystem. Map out your key stakeholders, including technology providers, advisors, and industry partners, and define their roles in supporting the process. The biggest job is to keep focus on long-term collaboration, building relationships that not only help with transformation but also position your organization for future growth and innovation.

Practical Steps for Enablers

- ✓ Embed findings from your exploration activities that lead to innovation. Assess whether insights from innovative initiatives should be adapted into operations.
- ✓ Decide whether to integrate or spin off – some innovations will fit within the existing structure, while others need their own projects or independent units. This decision must align with the company's structure to ensure accountability and execution.
- ✓ Establish a clear process for transitioning innovations/new technologies.
- ✓ Create a structured framework for moving ideas from concept to execution, ensuring transparency so employees understand their roles in the transformation.
- ✓ Redesign processes to support transformation and ensure workflows, decision-making structures, and incentives align with the new business direction while maintaining agility within the structure.
- ✓ Enable innovation for partners – if your company provides innovative services, develop structured approaches to help clients integrate transformation into their own operations, leveraging ecosystem partnerships to expand impact.

Considerations and Questions

Ask yourself, are we integrating innovation into operations at the right time, or are we moving too fast or too slow? Timing is everything in transformation and integrating an innovation too early can overwhelm operations, creating inefficiencies and resistance, while waiting too long can result in lost opportunities or competitive disadvantages. You need to assess readiness carefully, both in terms of the maturity of the innovation and your business ability to absorb it into day-to-day workflows.

Ask your team: do we have a structured process for assessing whether an innovation should be absorbed, spun off, or established as a separate project? (tied to structure and decision-making). You'll agree that not every innovation belongs to operations, whether it aligns with existing capabilities, requires a dedicated innovation team to evaluate, or should operate independently as a spin-off.

Develop a clear and structured decision-making framework that ensures innovations are deployed where they deliver the most value without disrupting other priorities. This decision framework must align with organizational structure to ensure accountability and execution. *Note: some parts of your business or even ecosystem partners may be willing to accept mistakes and temporary setbacks, as long as they become first-movers.*

Are the internal teams equipped and prepared for transformation, or are they resisting change? It is well documented that even the best innovation projects can fail if employees are not equipped to adopt and execute them. Resistance often stems from a lack of understanding or inadequate support and communication. Transparent communication and employee empowerment are critical components in your change management process. You must ensure that teams are not only informed about the coming transformation but also feel supported, trusted, and ready to contribute – ideally having co-ownership of the transformation.

If you enable innovation for other clients, are you providing them with the right tools and frameworks for successful deployment? When helping clients deploy, say, technology, the role of external partnerships and ecosystem strategies becomes critical. Providing clients with well-defined tools, processes, and support frameworks ensures they can adopt and scale these innovations effectively. Collaboration with ecosystem players, such as industry experts and technology providers, enhances the value and impact of the transformation.

KEY TAKEAWAYS:

- Business transformation must be structured, not reactive. Innovations must be assessed, refined, and introduced with a clear transition plan.
- Deciding when and how to integrate innovation is critical. Not every innovation belongs in operations and leaders must determine the best path forward using a structured approach.
- Process redesign is essential for sustainable transformation. Without adjusting workflows and structures, innovative efforts will struggle to scale.
- Supporting innovation in partner organizations requires clear methodologies. If your company enables transformation for others, ensure a strategic approach to help them implement change effectively.
- Transformation success depends on Structure, Transparency, and Ecosystem alignment. Leaders must ensure these enablers work together for a seamless transition.

As one leader whom we will meet later in Chapter 12, Lucy Blount, put it:[2]

> One of my greatest achievements last year wasn't the global deployment of a new technology. It was the decision, after a six-month pilot, not to scale that technology. Despite months of effort, extensive training, and significant monetary investment, I chose to say no. Listening to my end users and understanding the potential negative long-term impacts made me decide to 'fail' and search for better solutions.

Rejecting a Pilot Project Is a Tough Decision, But an Important Lesson for All Enablers!

The next chapter will show you how to scale time impact you created through the six enablers. Ending by showing how to achieve social and business results and examples of how to be specific about your success criteria with indicators for both social and business results.

NOTES

1 Enablers 4, 5, and 6 are your next essential strategic dimensions that will help you create a lasting positive impact. You just covered Enabler 1 in Chapter 1 (balancing operations and innovation), Enabler 2 (empowerment and transparency), and Enabler 3 (structures).

2 From a recorded interview with Lucy Blount, P.E., conducted by the author in April 2025 as part of the research for this book.

Chapter 3

The Enablers Part III

Scaling to Amplify Your Social and Business Results

Scaling is more than just growth, it's about expanding business success while amplifying social impact. Leaders must strategically align customers, capabilities, and capacity to ensure that scaling is sustainable, impactful, and measurable (Figure 3.1). Scaling to amplify your impact is normally a good thing. Success drives you to hire more people, establish new teams, and partners. With this comes what can be referred to as "growing pains." How will your processes need to change and who will need to be reskilled? Will you scale up in a new regions or countries and how will you cope with the time zone differences? Will you stay up late or wake up early, and how long before you'll need hire and train local people in culture, product, and find customers?

What are the core reasons for you to scale? Which ecosystem partners will you need and most importantly, are your structures fit for scaling? If you answered yes to all of the above, then which technologies will help you amplify your positive impact?

At the core of all scaling lies a necessary precondition: having a strong measurement system. Without the ability to quantify both financial and social results, you risk expanding inefficiencies rather than having an impact.

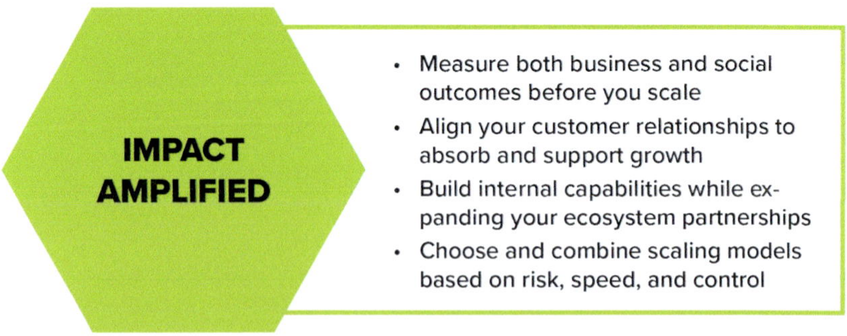

Figure 3.1 Scale and Amplify your Impact

DOI: 10.4324/9781003638551-4

BREAKING DOWN THE IMPACT AMPLIFICATION ENABLER

1. *Customers: Expanding Reach of Impact*

   Scaling begins by understanding who you serve and how their needs will evolve. Leaders must assess market demand, customer engagement, and long-term value creation. Without customer alignment, scaling becomes a costly over-expansion rather than creating a meaningful impact. Will your customer support you while you scale up? Are you aware of the impact on your customers during your scaling process; will they experience temporary setbacks? Have you clearly communicated to them what to expect?
2. *Resources: Strengthening the Foundations of Growth*

   Resources, whether human, technological, financial, leadership, or operational excellence, must grow in parallel with business expansion. Scaling without strengthening core competencies leads to inefficiencies, employee burnout, and weakened execution. Will the teams from each business take part in scaling while they continue to perform their regular assigned tasks? Do you have enough funding to pay for the necessary additional resources up front?

   What does your resources roadmap look like and are you able to present this to the board, investors, or the executive team for funding? Do you know when your budget is signed off so you can time your request for funding if needed?
3. *Build, Leverage, or Partner? Choosing the Right Path*

   Scaling can take multiple forms:

   - Build: Invest internally, develop resources in-house, and expand operations from within.
   - Leverage: Maximize existing resources, optimize current assets, and scale without major new investments.
   - Ecosystem: Use strategic alliances, acquisitions, or external expertise to amplify your impact.

   Each path has trade-offs in cost, control, and speed, and leaders must choose based on their business needs, risk tolerance, and social responsibility goals. You could combine all three, so you are building your resources in-house (such as the design and development of existing technologies), leverage by reskilling your team, and expanding your ecosystem with providers of resources to help you. This could be customer support systems and accounting services.

Practical Steps For Leaders

✓ Ensure you can measure impact before scaling. Growth should amplify financial and social results, not dilute them.

- ✓ Choose the right scaling model. Building, leveraging, or partnering each requires different investments, risks, and benefits.
- ✓ Balance speed with sustainability. Scaling too fast creates execution risk, while moving too slow may cause missed opportunities.
- ✓ Strengthen operational and leadership resources. Expanding without supporting capabilities may lead to inefficiencies and failure.
- ✓ Integrate scaling with your ecosystem. Partnerships enhance capabilities, expand market access, and accelerate innovation.

CONSIDERATIONS FOR YOU:

- Do we have the resources – financial, operational, and human – to scale effectively?
- Are we measuring impact accurately to ensure scaling creates positive business and social results?
- Or do we need to establish a measurement system for either business results or social results? Are we able to work with our customers to define a measurement system?
- Should we build, leverage, or partner, and what are the risks of each approach?
- Are our customers, capabilities, and capacity aligned for expansion?
- How do we ensure scaling amplifies both short-term success and long-term sustainability?
- During scaling, we may expect "growing pains." Do we need to set expectations with customers, investors, and our ecosystem? Will they receive the same service or could they expect a temporary drop in service, availability, or technology stability?

KEY TAKEAWAYS:

- Choosing to build, leverage, or partner impacts speed, cost, and control.
- Scaling must amplify both business success and social results.
- A measurement system is a precondition; leaders must track financial and social results.
- Successful scaling is strategic, structured, and ecosystem-driven.
- Set expectations internally and externally on what is expected, both good and bad, while you are in scaling.

Achieving Business and Social Impact: The Synergy Between Operations and Innovation

A large global digital transformation co-led by Horizon56, a company we will cover later in the book, is taking place from 2023 to 2026. Success of the transformation was measured on the following: Operational safety, operational efficiencies, end-user feedback (eNPS), level of future readiness, scalability of the software, and possibilities to integrate. If you look at this list, nowhere does it state profit, or potential for increased sales.

Why is that? Let me explain. The executive team understood that a single negative safety event could result in significant financial costs. Likewise, high eNPS scores meant lower employee turnover—reducing hiring and training costs while protecting institutional knowledge. And integration? By aligning systems and consolidating to one core provider instead of five, they improved collaboration and reduced complexity across the ecosystem. This meant managing one provider instead of five. All this translated directly into social and business results.

Let's not be naïve, it will always be paramount for profits to drive business results, but if you as a leader are able to define social impact, internally and externally, this will benefit your employees, communities, governments, and more, while having a direct positive impact on business. Therefore, the role of business is no longer solely about financial success, it's about creating both business and social value.

You as a leader and you as a next-generation leader must understand how to measure, track, and amplify impact in both areas (Figure 3.2).

- Business results include market share, profitability, customer retention, operational efficiency, and more.
- Social results cover employee well-being, safety, sustainability, economic development, accessibility of education, and more.

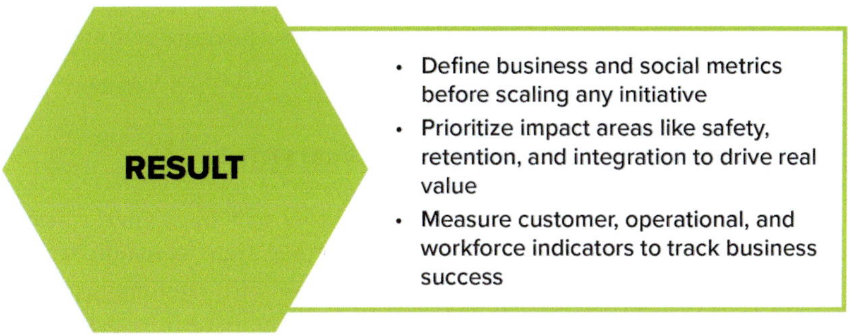

Figure 3.2 Achieving Results – Business and Social Impact

Therefore, measurement is key. What gets measured, and what gets managed? You must quantify both financial and social impact to ensure that business growth aligns with long-term social progress.

BUSINESS RESULTS: DRIVING FINANCIAL PERFORMANCE AND MARKET SUCCESS

Market Share and Competitive Advantage

Your company's market share reflects its performance in comparison to competitors. A growing market share signals that a company is successfully attracting and retaining customers, differentiating itself, and scaling its operations. Businesses that prioritize innovation, customer experience, and operational efficiency often gain a competitive edge, ensuring long-term sustainability – not only an increased market share but a benchmark for your direct competitors.

Is the overall market growing or shrinking? Are you able to keep your share in a shrinking market? By using the Enablers, are you more attractive to your clients? Are you able to make more business with existing clients?

Key Metrics to Measure Market Share

- Total Revenue Growth – Measures overall financial success in acquiring and maintaining customers.
- Customer Acquisition Rate – Tracks how effectively new customers are brought into the business.
- Competitive Benchmarking – Compares market size, pricing strategies, and brand preference against industry competitors.

How It Translates into Profit

When market share increases, businesses benefit from economies of scale, which reduce per-unit costs while increasing total revenue. A stronger market position also builds brand loyalty, enhances pricing power, and drives investor confidence. This leads to higher profitability, better risk resilience, and long-term business sustainability.

CUSTOMER SATISFACTION AND RETENTION

Customer loyalty is one of the strongest predictors of financial performance. Businesses that focus on retaining customers rather than constantly acquiring new ones reduce costs, increase revenue per customer, and improve overall profitability. Loyal customers purchase more, return frequently, and become brand advocates.

Key Metrics to Measure

- Net Promoter Score (NPS): Measures customer loyalty and willingness to recommend the company.
- Customer Retention Rate: Tracks the percentage of customers who remain engaged over time.
- Repetitive Purchase Rate: Indicates how often existing customers return to buy products or services.
- Customer Churn Rate: Measures the percentage of customers lost over a specific period. A lower churn rate signifies stronger retention and brand commitment.

How It Translates into Profit

Fact: Retaining customers is significantly cheaper than acquiring new ones.
High retention leads to:

- Lower marketing and acquisition costs since existing customers stay engaged.
- Higher customer lifetime value as loyal customers make repeat purchases and are more likely to extend contracts.
- Stronger organic growth through referrals, as satisfied customers bring in new business at no cost. Businesses that excel in customer satisfaction usually see higher revenues, improved brand equity, and long-term profitability.

Locating additional business with existing customers can also be beneficial as you already have contracts, you know their accounting systems and understand their culture of doing business.

Operational Efficiency and Cost Optimization

Efficiency in operations directly impacts profitability. Companies that streamline workflows, automate processes, and reduce waste protect their profit margins while maintaining high product and service quality. A well-optimized operation enables businesses to scale without excessive cost increases.

Key Metrics to Measure Operational Efficiency

- Cost-to-Revenue Ratio: Evaluates how much is spent to generate each dollar of revenue. A lower ratio indicates higher efficiency.
- Inventory Turnover Rate: Tracks how quickly products are sold and replaced, optimizing supply chain management.

- Process Cycle Time: Measures the time taken to complete critical business operations. Shorter cycles mean increased efficiency.
- Employee Productivity Metrics: Includes revenue per employee or output per hour worked, ensuring workforce efficiency.

How It Translates into Profit

By eliminating inefficiencies and optimizing resource allocation, businesses:

- Increase profit margins by reducing operational costs.
- Enhance customer responsiveness by delivering products and services faster.
- Achieve scalability without proportionally increasing costs.

Companies that focus on operational efficiency can reinvent themselves, reinvest savings into innovation, and maintain strong financial performance. This can be done by investing in continued improvement efforts and having process improvement initiatives working across teams and departments.

Profitability and Sustainable Growth

Financial sustainability is the foundation of a successful business. Growth is only valuable if it is profitable and repeatable. Companies that prioritize cost control, revenue diversification, and long-term reinvestment strategies position themselves for sustained expansion.

Key Metrics to Measure Profitability

- Gross and Net Profit Margins: Reflect how efficiently revenue is converted into profit.
- Return on Investment (ROI): Measures the effectiveness of capital investments in generating returns.
- Lifetime Value (LTV) of a Customer: Evaluates the total revenue a business can expect from a single customer over time.
- EBITDA (Earnings Before Interest, Taxes, Depreciation, and Amortization): Provides a clear picture of operational profitability without financial distortions.

How It Translates into Sustainable Growth

A strong profitability framework allows businesses to:

- Reinvest in innovation opportunities without relying on external funding.
- Withstand market downturns through strong cash flow and financial resilience.
- Attract investors, talent, and partnerships by demonstrating financial strength.

Companies that balance short-term profits with long-term sustainability become industry leaders, ensuring continuous growth, stability, and adaptability in evolving markets.

SOCIAL RESULTS: MEASURING AND IDENTIFYING THE RIGHT IMPACT

1. **Employee and Workplace Well-Being**

   Your workforce is by far your most valuable asset. What we concluded during Empowerment is that when employees feel supported, engaged, and motivated, they perform better, innovate more; and stay at their jobs longer because the feel valued. Investing in their well-being isn't just about morale; it directly impacts productivity, customer satisfaction, and long-term profitability. From a co-worker perspective, if there is a high turnover rate, it means that existing employees will have to onboard, train new employees each time someone is hired. HR will do interviews, and it becomes a resource-requiring cycle each time new employees join. Keeping your employees is key.

Key Metrics to Measure Workforce Well-being

- Employee Net Promoter Score (eNPS): Measures how likely employees are to recommend their workplace. A high eNPS indicates strong engagement and satisfaction.
- Turnover & Retention Rates: High turnover suggests dissatisfaction and increased hiring costs, while strong retention reflects a committed workforce.
- Absenteeism Rates: Frequent absences may indicate stress, burnout, or disengagement. A lower absenteeism rate correlates with a healthier work environment.
- Internal Promotion Rate: Measures of how often employees advance within the company, signaling opportunities for growth and development.

How It Translates into Business Impact

When employees thrive, so does the business they work for:

- Higher commitment improves customer satisfaction, driving loyalty and revenue.
- Low turnover reduces recruitment and training costs, ensuring workforce stability.
- A strong workplace culture attracts top talent, creating a competitive hiring advantage.

Are you doing exit interviews? What is the main reason people are leaving? What are the reasons they do not perform, and you have to replace them? Do you have a structured onboarding checklist and owners? Do you have a mentorship program?

Businesses that prioritize employee well-being see measurable financial returns, increased innovation, and long-term organizational strength.

2. **Community and Economic Development**

   A business does not operate in isolation, it exists within an economic and social ecosystem. Companies that contribute to their communities build stronger customer relationships, better reputations, and a more resilient operational environment. Hiring local? Is your ecosystem core based on local partners? Are there school, university, and community training programs you support?

Key Metrics to Measure Economic Impact

- Jobs Created and Local Hiring Rate: Tracks a company's role in expanding employment and economic stability. If you are not hiring local, then ask yourself, why? No talent? Do you need to expand your ecosystem with a local talent acquisition partner?
- Supplier Diversity and Local Procurement: Measures the percentage of spending directed toward small businesses and underrepresented suppliers. What are the risks of engaging with small businesses versus large businesses? Cultural fit? Expectations about processes or lack of them?
- Investment in Skills Training and Development: Assesses how much the company invests in upskilling employees and supporting workforce education. Do you invest in reskilling? Do you allocate time for you and your team to do development training? Does company policy allow your team to engage with local schools and universities to speak and join job career events?

How It Translates into Business Impact

Investing in local economic growth strengthens both society and the company's bottom line:

- Stronger communities lead to a more stable customer and employee base.
- Local partnerships create supply chain resilience and operational efficiency.
- A company with strong community ties earns higher brand trust and customer loyalty.

Businesses that invest in economic development don't just give back, they build a more secure and sustainable market for future growth. Your business may be spread out over several regions locally. Focusing on all of the above may also allow you to better lead and manage your employees, ecosystems and customers.

3. **Aligning Talent to Operations and Innovation**
   Working through the Enablers, whether in a sequence or diving into one, what we agree is that getting the right people in the right roles is key. No matter what their background is, we hire based on skills, expertise, potential, needs, and wants from the employee. Operations need steady, process-driven individuals to ensure stability, while your innovation unit demands bold thinkers to embrace uncertainty and change. But hiring isn't enough – what else can you focus on to create a positive impact?

Hiring for Operations: Stability and Excellence

Operational roles are the backbone of your business. These are the people who keep things running efficiently, deliver consistent results, and ensure systems remain reliable. Hire individuals who excel in structured environments, focus on execution, and continuously improve processes.

What to Look For: Proven problem-solvers, process optimizers, and those skilled at managing resources. Do they understand lean, process improvement frameworks or will you train them?

Hiring for Future Business: Innovation, Creativity, and Personal Resilience

Roles for your future business, or innovation unit, require explorers, people who thrive in uncertainty and can turn new ideas into tangible results. They must have the creativity to identify opportunities and the resilience to work through setbacks. They can expect a certain degree of resistance from both within and from your clients.

What to Look For: Strategic thinkers with the ability to zoom in and out, entrepreneurial minds, and individuals skilled in collaboration and experimentation. Are they aware of design thinking and change management frameworks, or will you need to train them?

Bridging Operations and Innovation

You must empower collaboration and build structures that allow innovation to flow into execution seamlessly, if that is what you decide on. Or you will spin it out or one of the other options we discussed earlier.

How to Do It

Create channels for regular communication between teams. Use cross-functional projects to encourage knowledge sharing. Set clear handover processes for transitioning ideas from innovation to operations. If you are able to, test your ideas at an early stage with people from operations. When you have your first prototype, intangible or tangible, get early feedback from operations.

Remember, it is your role as a leader to enable and develop the traits in your team – most leaders are not able to possess all required traits and must therefore enable the team.

With these Enablers, you will be able to enable your team to create a positive impact by balancing current operations with future opportunities and making decisions on how to use, scale, and amplify the innovations during your exploration efforts.

Leaders must use strategic development, reviews, and adjustment to cope with ambiguity and constantly changing demands. Use the Enablers to develop essential leadership traits, empowering teams with clarity, autonomy, and strategic thinking. Build a resilient, future-ready team by continuously refining structure, empowerment, technology, ecosystem, and impact.

These aren't abstract ideas; they're real-world tools drawn from research, interviews, and lived experience. Use them in the order that fits your situation, or jump directly to the one that matters most right now. In the coming chapters, we will dive into the Enablers one by one, using real and recent cases from established C-level leaders, leaders in the transition into C-level roles and upcoming leaders.

We've now explored each of the Enablers. You have a clear overview of how. Next, we begin a deeper dive into each, starting with empowerment and transparency.

In Chapter 4, you'll meet Claudio Caputo, an emerging leader with an adventurous mindset, shaped by life across multiple countries and cultures. He's already left a lasting positive mark, and through an interview and a real, recent business case, we will understand how he did it.

Chapter 4

Empowerment and Transparency

Claudio Caputo's Competency Matrix

In a world where businesses and organizations strive for sustained success, empowerment – or the ability to enable empowerment – stands as a crucial leadership trait. While many leaders recognize its importance, *few fully understand how to enable it.* We understand the why, but rarely the how. The good news is that the traditional top-down management model is being replaced by dynamic, agile organizations that thrive on employee autonomy. But what does empowerment truly mean, and how does it impact your business and social results? This chapter explores these questions through a case study based on a next-generation leader's efforts to enable transparency and empowerment through new tools (Figure 4.1).

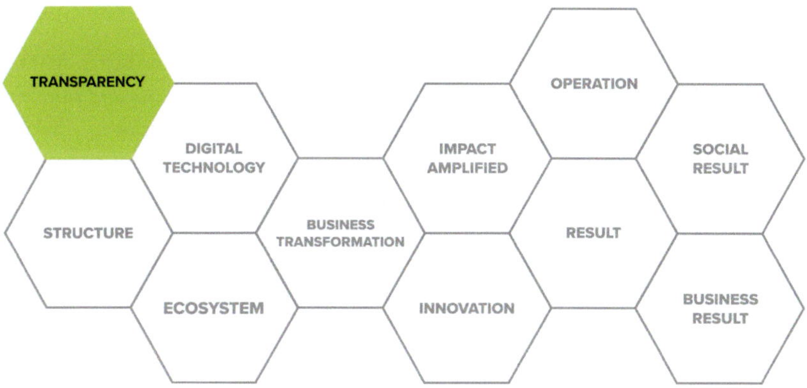

Figure 4.1 Transparency and Empowerment Enabler

DOI: 10.4324/9781003638551-5

EMPOWERMENT IN ACTION: A STEP-BY-STEP GUIDE FOR LEADERS

Empowerment is not a one-size-fits-all solution, it requires a contextual approach and intentional leadership actions tailored to your organization's culture, structure, and goals. By following these steps that I've outlined on the following page, you can begin to create an environment where empowerment thrives, enabling individual potential and collective success.

Step 1: Define Decision-Making Boundaries

Empowerment starts with clarity. Employees need to know where they have the authority to make decisions and where alignment with leadership is required. Ambiguity creates hesitation and can stifle innovation, while clear boundaries encourage confidence and autonomy. Do you know when to give autonomy? How to decentralize decision-making? How do you react if no decision is made or the "wrong" decision is made?

Leadership and Empowerment in Action: In a healthcare organization undergoing digitization, leaders empowered frontline staff to propose changes to the patient intake processes. By clearly defining which decisions required managerial approval (budget allocations) versus which could be made independently (workflow changes), the team felt both trusted and guided.

Practical Tip for Leaders: Regularly communicate decision-making boundaries through team huddles, process maps, or collaborative workshops to create clarity.

Step 2: Build Trust Through Transparency

Trust is the foundation of empowerment. Employees are more likely to take ownership when they believe leadership values their contributions and operates transparently. You can build trust by sharing the latest strategic updates, allowing them to voice their opinion, sharing data, aligning expectations, and promoting an open dialogue.

Leadership and Empowerment in Action: A logistics company implemented real-time dashboards to provide more visibility into KPIs. This transparency allowed team members to see how their efforts contributed to broader organizational goals, building trust and accountability. This led to healthy internal competition where staff felt motivated to improve their efforts, thereby amplifying the impact on the organization.

Practical Tip for Leaders: Use visual management tools like dashboards, regular updates, and open forums to provide team members with the information they need to make informed decisions.

Step 3: Enable Accountability with Shared Metrics

Empowerment doesn't mean a lack of accountability. Leaders must establish clear expectations for outcomes and align individual contributions with team or organizational goals. When accountability is shared, employees feel a greater sense of ownership and responsibility.

Leadership and Empowerment in Action: A hospital team tackling wait times developed shared metrics for success, such as reduced patient wait times and improved satisfaction scores. By tying individual tasks to these collective outcomes, leaders created a culture where everyone felt accountable for achieving results. This also led to great discussions and team huddles, handover meetings, and allowed new joiners to quickly understand where focus was.

Practical Tip for Leaders: Co-create KPIs with your team to ensure alignment, ownership, and buy-in for efficiency and quality metrics.

Step 4: Encourage Innovation and Autonomy

Empowerment thrives in an environment where individuals feel safe to take risks and propose new ideas. Leaders must create a culture that rewards experimentation and embraces learning from failure.

Leadership and Empowerment in Action: A technology firm encouraged employees to dedicate 10% of their time to passion projects unrelated to core operations. This policy led to a breakthrough product that became one of the company's most profitable innovations.

Practical Tip for Leaders: Celebrate both successes and lessons learned from failed experiments. Recognize employees who demonstrate creativity and problem-solving.

Step 5: Align Empowerment with Strategic Goals

Empowerment should not exist in a vacuum. Leaders must ensure that individual autonomy contributes to broader organizational objectives, such as growth, innovation, or social impact. This alignment helps employees understand the "why" behind their work.

Leadership and Empowerment in Action: A renewable energy company aligned employee empowerment initiatives with its mission to reduce emissions. Employees were encouraged to propose sustainability improvements, from energy-efficient workflows to community engagement programs, which reinforced the company's vision.

Practical Tip for Leaders: Regularly connect team initiatives to strategic goals in all-hands meetings or 1:1s. Use a simple question to guide alignment: "How does this idea or task move us closer to our mission?"

Doing the research for this book, and specifically this chapter, made me reflect on my own leadership experience. I used to think *empowerment* was a soft word, something leaders said in keynotes but rarely applied in practice. That changed when I saw smart, capable people stall. Not because they didn't care, but because they weren't sure if they were allowed to act. Or worse, they were not sure how to act. That was on me. I hadn't created enough clarity. I hadn't built the trust they needed. I hadn't connected their decisions to something bigger. Over time, in various industries, I began to see what real empowerment looked like. And it wasn't a motivational poster on the wall.

It's when a team redesigns a process without asking for permission. When someone junior calls out a gap and offers a fix. When people move not because they were told to, but because they understand the why and trust they're supported.

That's what the five steps in this chapter are about. They're not theory. They're field-tested lessons from places where empowerment didn't come easy. Each one – clarity, trust, shared metrics, autonomy, and alignment – takes courage to lead and consistency to sustain.

So don't treat these like a one-and-done checklist. **Think of them as lenses**, ways to assess how your team operates today and where you can lead differently tomorrow to enable your team. Use these five steps. Share them. Revisit them as your context evolves.

CASE STUDY: EMPOWERING PEOPLE THROUGH TRANSPARENCY AND STRATEGIC LEADERSHIP

Claudio Caputo, originally from Rome, spent eight years in Denmark and has worked on temporary assignments globally. He came from a working-class family in Italy, where his father had a lifelong service in the police force and his mother worked for public schools. Claudio earned his CIPD (Chartered Institute of Personnel and Development, a professional body for HR and people development) Chartered membership status based on his work and its impact on both business and people. He is currently on an assignment in the Cayman Islands while doing his MBA at Warwick Business School, where he was granted a scholarship to be recognized as a "Change Maker in society."[1]

Claudio is a visionary and transformational leader, who has already held leadership positions globally across several industries. I chose to feature his story here, because he has become a great example of a strategic leader of the next generation.

I met Claudio Caputo when he was working in Esbjerg, a small fishing town in Denmark and my hometown. Today it's often referred to as "the energy capital" due to its history of offshore oil and gas, and now its offshore wind energy creation. Claudio joined a rapidly expanding logistics company which was facing several challenges due to inefficiencies in workforce planning, gaps in employees' development plans, and its visibility. While working in Denmark, Claudio took on the task of addressing these issues by creating and implementing a Competency Matrix, a tool designed to align operational needs, employee development, and organizational goals.

The Competency Matrix categorized employee skills into "Products" and "Processes" and rated proficiency on a scale of 1–4.

This framework provides employees with clear insights into their strengths and areas for growth while offering managers a comprehensive view of team capabilities. The matrix became the foundation for creating structured development plans, improving workforce planning, and reducing operational risk. Additionally, it seamlessly integrated with the company's standard operating procedures to enhance overall operational structure and transparency (Figure 4.2).

In the illustration below you'll see an early Excel prototype of the Competency Matrix. It shows the two interfaces of the tool (left and right side). One the left side, the matrix is displaying the knowledge level (as a percentage) of each employee, with the corresponding knowledge gap for each product. On the right side, the matrix shows the knowledge level following the 1–4 scale mentioned previously and displayed visually with pie charts. While the left side is more useful for employees to acknowledge and assess their current knowledge in detail, the right side is more useful for managers to assess the overall team's capability and helps enhance workforce planning, as well as creating cross-training plans where gaps are shown. These combined features make it an agile and versatile tool.

Claudio's approach to deploying the tool was rooted in empowerment and collaboration. He worked closely with stakeholders across the organization, including the COO, business unit leaders, and subject matter experts, to ensure buy-in and alignment. *A key moment in the process was a kick-off meeting with all leaders, where Caputo outlined the measurable benefits of*

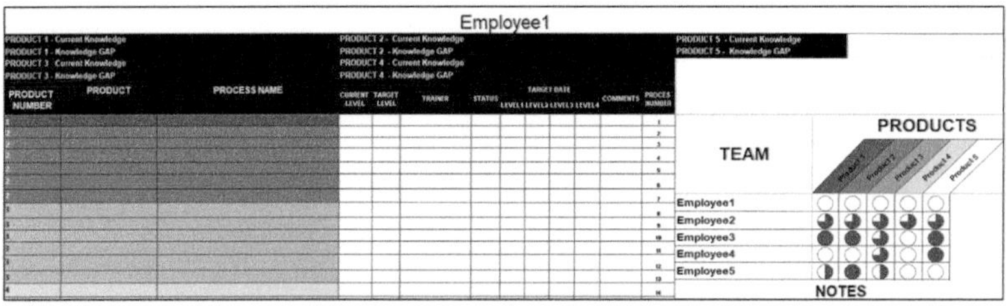

Figure 4.2 Prototype of Competency Matrix

the tool and demonstrated its potential to streamline operations and foster employee growth. Visual aids like planning boards and KPI dashboards were introduced to make the transformation tangible and accessible.

The results of this initiative were transformative. Operational efficiency improved as managers could now allocate resources more effectively and plan cross-training to cover skill gaps. Employees felt empowered by the newfound clarity in their roles and career trajectories, which led to increased engagement and job satisfaction. Turnover rates dropped significantly as employees recognized that their growth was supported by the organization. Beyond internal impacts, the Competency Matrix exceeded external audit requirements, strengthening the company's compliance with ISO standards and enhancing its reputation.

The tool's emphasis on transparency played a pivotal role in its success. Employees were able to visualize how their competencies aligned with organizational objectives, fostering a sense of ownership and accountability. Managers, in turn, gained data-driven insights that informed better decision-making and succession planning. This shared understanding bridged gaps across teams, reinforcing collaboration and the company's "one-stop-shop" concept.

Claudio's critical leadership in this transformation exemplified how empowering individuals through clear structures and transparency can drive both business success and social value. By aligning personal development with strategic goals, the company not only improved its operational performance but also cultivated a culture of growth, trust, and collaboration, setting a new standard for excellence within the organization.

I should add a disclaimer: I've worked with Claudio professionally and understand he isn't technical. Meaning, he doesn't have a technical background in the sense that he doesn't have experience in coding, data analytics, or systems engineering. Instead, his strengths lie in his passion for people, leadership and process thinking. He understood his own limitations and when he needed live dashboards, he prototyped them and got help from people in the organization with a passion for data and structure.

LEADERSHIP SHIFT: ENABLING EMPOWERMENT

Empowerment is not a one-time intervention but a foundational shift in leadership approach. In our case study example, Claudio demonstrated how rethinking the role of leadership and adopting strategies that prioritize transparency and autonomy can transform teams into promoters of change and innovation.

CREATING A SHARED VISION AND PURPOSE

Claudio understood that employees often felt disconnected from the bigger picture of the organization's goals, so used the Competency Matrix to map individual skills to the organization's operational objectives and mission. In a key leadership meeting, he shared, "You're not just part of daily operations; you're building the foundation for the future of this company." By tying personal development to organizational success, Claudio inspired employees to take ownership of their roles, reframing routine tasks as meaningful contributions to a shared purpose.

The Competency Matrix wasn't just a tool, it became an enabler for empowering employees to see their work in alignment with the company's strategic vision. This shift in perspective fostered a renewed sense of pride and responsibility, encouraging innovation and collaboration.

BUILDING TRUST THROUGH TRANSPARENCY

Transparency was a cornerstone of Claudio's leadership transformation. He recognized that a lack of visibility of goals and performance metrics would hinder engagement, so made operational data accessible to all employees. He introduced visual tools such as planning boards and dashboards that displayed KPIs and competency metrics in real time.

Claudio presented the team with clear data showing gaps in workforce skills and opportunities for cross-training. By openly discussing these challenges, he invited employees to contribute solutions rather than imposing directives. The result was a surge in engagement, with employees actively identifying opportunities to improve processes and optimize resource allocation. Trust flourished as teams realized that transparency wasn't about assigning blame but about enabling collective problem-solving and shared success.

EMPOWERING DECISION-MAKING THROUGH DIGITAL TOOLS

Claudio leveraged digital tools to decentralize decision-making, enabling employees to act confidently and autonomously. Real-time dashboards provided data on competencies, operational KPIs, and workforce planning, empowering teams to address challenges without waiting for managerial approval.

For instance, when skill gaps emerged in a critical department, managers used the Competency Matrix to identify employees who could be cross-trained to fill the void. This proactive approach reduced downtime and improved service delivery, all while fostering a sense of ownership among employees. As he reflected, "When employees have the accurate tools and data they need, they don't just perform better, they become leaders in their own right."

REDEFINING LEADERSHIP AS A SERVICE

Perhaps the most profound shift in Caputo's leadership was his redefinition of leadership itself. Moving away from a top-down and directive style, he adopted a "leadership as a service" approach. In meetings with his teams, he consistently asked, "What do you need from me to succeed?" This question became the foundation of a support-driven culture where employees felt empowered to take the initiative, knowing they had the backing of their leader.

His focus shifted to removing barriers, providing resources, and fostering an environment where employees could thrive. This cultural transformation emphasized trust and accountability, enabling the organization to operate with agility and purpose.

THE IMPACT: EMPOWERMENT IN ACTION

Claudio Caputo's leadership transformation delivered real results. By enabling transparency and empowerment, the Competency Matrix not only improved operational performance but also cultivated a culture of growth and collaboration.

- **Business Impact**: Operational efficiency soared as workforce flexibility increased, turnover rates plummeted, and compliance with ISO standards strengthened. Real-time data and autonomous decision-making reduced delays and optimized resource utilization, saving time and costs.
- **Social Impact**: Employees felt a renewed sense of purpose and satisfaction, leading to higher engagement and job retention. The culture of empowerment spilled over into the community, with employees contributing to initiatives that amplified the company's societal impact.

Below are examples of results that Claudio achieved from working methodically through the matrix on a regular basis. As you see, the impacts are real – both on people and for business results. All through use and adoption of the matrix across teams.

Below are five examples of tangible results. Note how points 1 and 5 are related to people/social impact, and 2, 3, and 4 are connected to business impact – all using the same tool:

1. Reduction in Employee Attrition: Clear career paths and skill development opportunities can enhance job satisfaction, potentially decreasing attrition by 15–25%, depending on industry benchmarks. This is also related to point 5 below, showing how the results are interconnected.
2. Increase in Productivity and Efficiency: By aligning skills with roles and optimizing training programs, organizations typically see a 10–15% increase in operational efficiency, leading to faster project completion and better resource utilization.

3. Team Interchangeability and Operational Agility: By establishing an interchangeability rate and setting a goal that was trackable with the competency matrix, the team experienced more flexibility and prevented operational deficiencies when absences or unforeseen events occurred. To achieve this goal, Claudio created a cross-training plan, displayed in the competency matrix, with regular follow-ups, and updated to reflect the interchangeability rate. The goal of training 75% of all team members in multiple processes was achieved. This meant more fulfilling work, new skill development, and also business continuity – the work no longer depended on a few key individuals, as multiple team members could now perform the work and had the necessary access to systems – and more flexibility to move people between departments.
4. Enhanced Managerial Visibility and Decision-Making: With better insights into employees' skills and gaps, managers can make more informed decisions, reducing hiring mistakes and skill mismatches by 30–40%.
5. Higher Employee Engagement and Motivation: Regular performance reviews and personalized growth plans can boost employee NPS scores by 20%, improving morale and long-term retention.

This case study illustrates a fundamental truth: empowerment is not an individual trait, but a collective outcome cultivated by intentional leadership. By enabling trust, clarity, and accountability, leaders like Caputo elevate not only their teams but also their organizations, delivering meaningful outcomes that extend far beyond the workplace.

LESSONS FOR LEADERS: THE ESSENTIALS OF EMPOWERMENT

Empowerment Begins with Accountability

Empowerment isn't just about giving away authority, it's about encouraging the responsibility to act. As one Lucy Blount said, "*We should also hold people accountable for not making decisions.*" When employees hesitate or avoid decisions, the costs to the organization are significant: missed opportunities, reduced efficiency, and frustration among proactive team members.

By fostering a culture where taking initiative is expected and inaction is addressed, then holding employees accountable for avoiding decisions is just as important as recognizing their bold, calculated risks. Instead of penalizing mistakes, leaders should actively encourage and reinforce their decision-making, even when imperfect, which is essential to growth and innovation.

LESSONS FOR EMPOWERMENT-ENABLING LEADERSHIP

1. **Clarity in Decision-Making Boundaries**

   While working in Denmark, Claudio found that employees often hesitated to act due to uncertainty about their decision-making boundaries. To address this, he introduced the Competency Matrix, which clarified each employee's strengths and areas of authority. By linking individual competencies to specific tasks and responsibilities, Caputo ensured that employees understood where they could take initiative and when consultation was necessary.

   This clarity enabled smoother daily operations, as managers and teams could allocate resources and make decisions without waiting for higher-level approval. The result was a culture where employees felt empowered to act, reducing bottlenecks and increasing efficiency. Caputo's approach reinforced the principle that clear decision-making boundaries are essential for fostering autonomy and maintaining agility.

2. **Building Trust Through a Growth Mindset**

   Psychological safety became a cornerstone of Claudio's transformation initiative. He recognized that employees needed to feel emotionally supported, also when making mistakes. During team meetings and performance reviews, he emphasized that errors were opportunities for learning, not judgment. His open discussions of operational gaps and shared solutions created an atmosphere where employees felt comfortable taking calculated risks.

   One striking example was the introduction of cross-training initiatives through the Competency Matrix. Employees initially hesitated to embrace new roles and tasks, fearing they might not perform well. However, Caputo's consistent encouragement and focus on learning transformed this mindset. Over time, employees began to see themselves as adaptable contributors, driving operational improvements and creating a stronger, more confident workforce.

3. **Enabling Decisions Through Digital Tools**

   Digital tools played a pivotal role in enabling empowerment. Claudio implemented real-time dashboards that provided employees with visibility into operational metrics, workforce planning, and performance indicators. These tools allowed teams to make data-driven decisions without waiting for managerial input.

   At the time he was doing this, there were no dedicated data nor performance roles, so Claudio found people with a passion outside of his division, and got them to support his project as a cross-functional role.

For example, when gaps in workforce skills emerged, managers used the Competency Matrix and dashboards to identify employees who could be cross-trained to fill critical roles. This not only reduced operational downtime but also gave employees the confidence to take ownership of their development. By equipping teams with the right tools, Claudio created a system where decision-making was both informed and autonomous.

THE COST OF INACTION

Claudio's leadership approach also highlighted the dangers of inaction. By enabling a culture of trust and accountability, he mitigated the paralysis that can occur when employees fear making mistakes. Teams were encouraged to embrace calculated risks, supported by data and resources provided through the matrix and dashboards.

One example involved a team faced with a critical operational gap in one department. Rather than waiting for direct instructions, managers identified skill redundancies using the Competency Matrix and quickly implemented cross-training. This proactive approach avoided potential delays and ensured continued service excellence.

LEADERSHIP ACCOUNTABILITY FOR INACTION

Claudio's work underscored that empowerment is not just about granting authority, it's about instilling the responsibility to act. He emphasized this by:

- **Creating a Culture of Trust**: Employees were supported even when decisions didn't yield perfect results, teaching a proactive mindset.
- **Establishing Clear Boundaries**: The Competency Matrix provided clarity on decision-making roles, reducing hesitation.
- **Providing Tools and Guidance**: Digital dashboards and planning boards ensured teams had the resources needed for informed choices.

By addressing both action and inaction, Claudio created an empowered workforce that drove operational success and cultivated a culture of growth and accountability.

LEADERSHIP EMPOWERMENT FRAMEWORK: *THE HOW*

The **Leadership Empowerment Scorecard** is a tool designed to help leaders assess, reflect, and take action on their empowerment strategies. Below are step-by-step guidelines on how to apply it both individually and within a team.

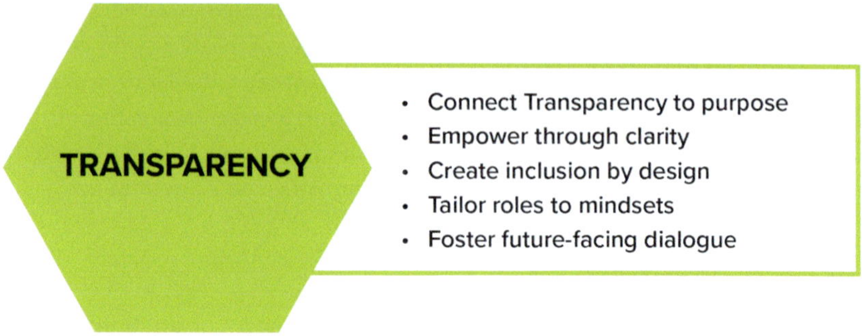

Figure 4.3 Transparency and Empowerment Enabler

To use the guide as an individual or as a team, please review the Tables 4.1 to 4.6. Your scoring key is as follows:

SCORING KEY

- 1–2: Major improvement needed – Take immediate steps to address gaps.
- 3–4: Moderate progress – Some adjustments can enhance empowerment.
- 5: Excellent – Continue reinforcing best practices!

CONCLUSION

Leaders as Enablers of Empowerment

The research, insights, and tools explored throughout this chapter, spanning case studies, frameworks, and cultural dynamics, demonstrate the multifaceted nature of empowerment. While empowerment succeeds in organizations that enable trust, clarity, and autonomy, its true power shines when sustained over time. This final section synthesizes these ideas into a cohesive strategy, emphasizing your role in embedding and sustaining empowerment as a competitive advantage.

Sustaining Empowerment: Measuring and Adapting

Empowerment is not a one-time initiative; it requires constant measurement and evolution to remain impactful. In the case study, empowerment was sustained through actionable tools such as KPIs, real-time dashboards, and continuous feedback loops. These mechanisms allowed leaders to assess progress, identify gaps, and refine strategies in real-time. Regular alignment sessions kept initiatives relevant, ensuring employees' efforts aligned with organizational objectives and priorities.

Table 4.1 Reflection Area: Leadership Style and Empowerment

Key Considerations	*Self-assessment (Rate 1–5)*	*Ease of Implementation (Rate 1–5)*	*Impact of Improvement (Rate 1–5)*	*Action Steps for Improvement*	*Sustaining High Performance*
Do I give my employees autonomy, or do I micromanage? Do I actively remove barriers for my team? Do I enable employees to act in ways that align with both organizational and societal impact goals?	[Enter Rating: 1–5]	[Enter Rating: 1–5]	[Enter Rating: 1–5]	Identify areas where I can delegate more. Hold open discussions about autonomy and its link to broader community impact. Set clear boundaries between control and guidance. For example, in our case study example, cross-training employees and implementing a competency matrix reduced dependency on top-down oversight, fostering greater autonomy and operational efficiency	Continue mentoring emerging leaders to maintain autonomy. Hold regular leadership check-ins to reinforce empowerment with a focus on societal contributions

Table 4.2 Reflection Area: Barriers to Empowerment

Key Considerations	*Self-assessment (Rate 1–5)*	*Ease of Implementation (Rate 1–5)*	*Impact of Improvement (Rate 1–5)*	*Action Steps for Improvement*	*Sustaining High Performance*
Are there cultural, structural, or personal barriers preventing employees from taking initiative? Do these barriers limit our ability to deliver positive societal outcomes?	[Enter Rating: 1–5]	[Enter Rating: 1–5]	[Enter Rating: 1–5]	Conduct an anonymous survey to identify barriers. Remove unnecessary approvals and streamline decision-making. Include social equity considerations in empowerment policies. For example, leaders at in our case study conducted workshops to address resistance to the competency matrix, ensuring alignment with employee development and organizational goals	Maintain transparency by reinforcing a feedback culture and refining policies to ensure empowerment

Table 4.3 Reflection Area: Use of Digital Tools

Key Considerations	*Self-assessment (Rate 1–5)*	*Ease of Implementation (Rate 1–5)*	*Impact of Improvement (Rate 1–5)*	*Action Steps for Improvement*	*Sustaining High Performance*
Do I use real-time feedback, transparency tools, or decision matrices to empower employees? Do digital tools enable us to measure and track progress on societal impact goals (e.g., community outreach, sustainability efforts)?	[Enter Rating: 1–5]	[Enter Rating: 1–5]	[Enter Rating: 1–5]	Implement engagement platforms or dashboards for tracking empowerment and societal outcomes. Train employees on data-driven decision-making tied to social impact metrics. For example, our case study use of dashboards for real-time skill visibility enabled teams to proactively close skill gaps, reducing overtime and improving team efficiency	Periodically review digital tool effectiveness in enabling social outcomes. Gather feedback and adjust tech usage to align with community or sustainability goals

Table 4.4 Reflection Area: Creating Purpose and Engagement

Key Considerations	*Self-assessment (Rate 1–5)*	*Ease of Implementation (Rate 1–5)*	*Impact of Improvement (Rate 1–5)*	*Action Steps for Improvement*	*Sustaining High Performance*
Do my employees feel a sense of purpose in their work? How often do I reinforce mission alignment? Do I connect their work to organizational goals that contribute to societal or environmental progress?	[Enter Rating: 1–5]	[Enter Rating: 1–5]	[Enter Rating: 1–5]	Share real stories of impact in meetings. Recognize employees who demonstrate purpose-driven work that impacts communities. For example, leaders in our case study connected daily tasks to broader organizational goals, fostering a sense of pride and ownership	Ensure continuous alignment through company-wide storytelling, recognition programs, and personalized career development opportunities tied to societal impact

Table 4.5 Reflection Area: Decision-Making Culture

Key Considerations	*Self-assessment (Rate 1–5)*	*Ease of Implementation (Rate 1–5)*	*Impact of Improvement (Rate 1–5)*	*Action Steps for Improvement*	*Sustaining High Performance*
Do I encourage risk-taking, or do my employees hesitate out of fear? Do I hold people accountable for not making decisions? Do we connect decision-making accountability to societal goals?	[Enter Rating: 1–5]	[Enter Rating: 1–5]	[Enter Rating: 1–5]	Develop a "Decision-Making Accountability" framework. Reward initiative-taking tied to organizational and societal impact goals. Create psychological safety for experimentation in areas like community engagement or sustainability. For example, the company's leadership fostered a no-blame culture, encouraging teams to suggest process changes that saved weeks of delays	Reinforce decision-making expectations in performance evaluations tied to both business and societal outcomes. Encourage peer coaching on decision autonomy within a broader societal framework

Table 4.6 Empowerment Scorecard Guide

Aspect	*Using the Scorecard as an Individual*	*Using the Scorecard as a Team*
Purpose	Self-reflection to enhance leadership empowerment skills and impact.	Encourage open discussions, align team strategies, and foster a culture of empowerment and accountability.
Step 1: Completing the Scorecard	Reflect honestly and rate each area from 1 to 5.	Each team member completes the scorecard privately before a team meeting.
Step 2: Analyzing the Scores	Identify low-scoring areas and recurring patterns.	Share overall trends without naming individuals. Collectively discuss where the team struggles most.
Step 3: Prioritizing Areas for Growth	Select 1–2 low-scoring areas to focus on for personal improvement.	Agree on 1–2 priority areas to address organizational gaps and set clear focus areas as a team.
Step 4: Developing an Action Plan	Define specific steps to improve (e.g., for "Barriers to Empowerment," remove bottlenecks in approvals).	Assign responsibilities for team-wide improvement areas. Set milestones for progress tracking.
Step 5: Implementation	Integrate strategies into daily leadership practice (e.g., delegate more, reinforce decision autonomy).	Roll out changes at an organizational level (e.g., streamline decision processes, share transparency dashboards).
Step 6: Tracking Progress	Review self-assessment results quarterly to gauge improvement and adjust strategies.	Conduct team check-ins to measure progress and refine improvement plans as needed.
Setting a Cadence	Reassess scores every 3–6 months for strategic alignment; adjust tactics more frequently if needed.	Align reviews with quarterly planning; conduct monthly check-ins for tactical adjustments.

The key lesson is clear: empowerment must be treated as a dynamic process. Leaders like Claudio Caputo embraced an iterative approach to ensure their empowerment strategies remained adaptable to evolving organizational and societal needs, keeping their teams engaged and effective.

The Competitive Advantage of Empowerment

In the case study presented in this chapter, empowered teams acted with confidence, fostering faster decision-making, operational excellence, and increased innovation. These essential qualities not only reduced inefficiencies but also substantially improved employee engagement, leading to lower turnover and higher retention rates. With this Enabler tool, you will retain and build your competences, client relationships and stay more resilient to both internal and external changes.

Empowerment also created a ripple effect beyond the workplace. Employees became advocates for the company's values, driving community-focused initiatives and amplifying societal impact. For leaders, the message is clear: embedding empowerment into operations isn't just a cultural benefit, it's a business necessity that strengthens competitive positioning and enhances social value.

What Comes Next: Structures to Enable Your Impact

Empowerment doesn't exist in a vacuum. It's shaped, and often constrained, by the very structures, systems, and cultures leaders operate within. You can have all the right intentions as a leader, but if your organization's design undermines autonomy, slows decisions, or siloes innovation, empowerment will stall.

In Chapter 5, we'll explore the structure Enabler, where you'll learn how to architect structures that make empowerment real. You'll gain critical knowledge of how leaders balance hierarchy and flexibility, how decision-making authority, communication, and funding shape momentum, and how smart organizations spin innovation out when it no longer fits inside, or needs freedom to grow.

NOTE

1 The Warwick Business School *Change Maker* scholarship recognizes individuals who demonstrate a strong drive and vision to challenge the norm in their sector. Recipients are selected based on their proven commitment to making a positive difference in business and their ability to create broader value within their organization and industry.

Chapter 5

Beyond the Org Chart

Street Cred and Mandate for Impact

Before we talk org charts, let's talk trust.

I once led a complex project where my counterpart, someone who had earned deep trust from the field, was asked to take on a leadership role in the transformation. He carried the weight. But he didn't have the mandate. One day, when I pushed to regain momentum, he told it to me like this:

"I have a lot of additional responsibility. But no mandate."

That's when it hit me. If you ask someone to lead change without real backing, they become a volunteer. And when that happens, three things follow: They burn out, the work stalls, and on top of all, they lose credibility with the people impacted by the changes.

That's why structure matters. Because it's the system through which your leadership enables impact. Structures do not matter due to reporting lines or job titles.

Leadership in structures that are not fully transparent requires you to either receive a mandate or give it. Structures can be simple with clear reporting lines from manager to employee, and with more complex structures where you have your classic organization, combined with projects that run across the organization and involve team members who may not be connected in the official structure.

Mandate is the backing behind your right to make decisions. It enables you to turn responsibility into impact. It's the backing from the company that says, "We empower you with the mandate, and we trust you to lead, and we'll support you when it gets tough." In these cases, you know you are not doing it alone. You might be on an assignment alone, at a client site which can be intimidating – but you have got the right backing, the mandate to take action, and the results of your actions are already trusted.

When you align these three – decision rights, roles, and mandate – your structure becomes more than a diagram. It becomes a leadership tool. One that earns trust, unlocks performance, and creates space for others to step up.

DOI: 10.4324/9781003638551-6

I base this chapter on my extensive experience with assignments in over 20 countries. The chapter will give you clear direction on *how* to structure for impact. With alacrity and with intent, and most importantly, with the kind of leadership that people will actually follow.

I used to think structure came later. You set the vision, you get the right people on board, and only then do you decide on reporting lines and accountability models. But over the years, I've learned something different: structure is never a neutral state. Whether you design it deliberately or not, structure, or the lack of it, is shaping behavior every day. It's telling people what matters, who decides, and where the momentum gets stuck.

I've worked in highly regulated industries, fast-scaling environments, and complex cross-border partnerships. In all of them, I've seen one truth hold up: structure either accelerates your impact, or it quietly undermines it.

Not because people don't care. But because when structure is unclear, everything else slows down. In almost all scenarios, I have seen these classic behaviors. They hesitate, they second-guess, they step back instead of stepping up. But when the structure is clear? You can literally feel it. Decisions move faster. Ownership is real, and people lead with confidence, not caution.

This chapter is about designing that kind of structure. Not with templates or default org charts, but with intention. With a leadership mindset that understands structure not as control, but as a system that protects trust, *enables* clarity, and creates space for others on your team to succeed.

The visual below sums up how I've learned to lead structure over the years, not from theory, but from hard-won experience. When structure works, it gives you direction without rigidity. It sets boundaries that free people to move, not fence them in (Figure 5.1).

Figure 5.1 Structure Enabler

Structure is one of the most powerful Enablers in this ecosystem. It's not isolated. It interacts with transparency, technology, ecosystems, and your transformation journey. And ultimately, it helps shape the results, both business and social, that you're working toward.

BEFORE WE DIVE IN: YOUR PRACTICAL TOOL FOR LEADING STRUCTURE

The Structure Enabler is a tool I've developed over years of leading teams, building systems, and navigating complexity. It's built for real-world use, when things are unclear, when responsibilities overlap, or when momentum starts to fade.

This isn't just for big reorganizations or strategy sessions. It's for the everyday leadership moments when clarity matters most. When you need to reset expectations, assign ownership, or bring direction back into the room.

You can use it to prepare for a meeting. To set up a new team. To define decision rights when roles shift. Or to make sure a change doesn't lose speed once the kickoff ends.

These seven steps are set out as practical questions that you can bring into a workshop, a one-on-one meeting, or a team of 50 or 150. They'll help you see what needs to change, and where structure can create real impact (Table 5.1).

Now that you've worked through the seven steps of the Structure Enabler, you can start to see the structure for what it really is: a series of leadership decisions. Every part of this tool is built from real-world experience, where clarity made a difference, where roles had to be reset, and where trust was built or lost through how decisions were made (Figure 5.2).

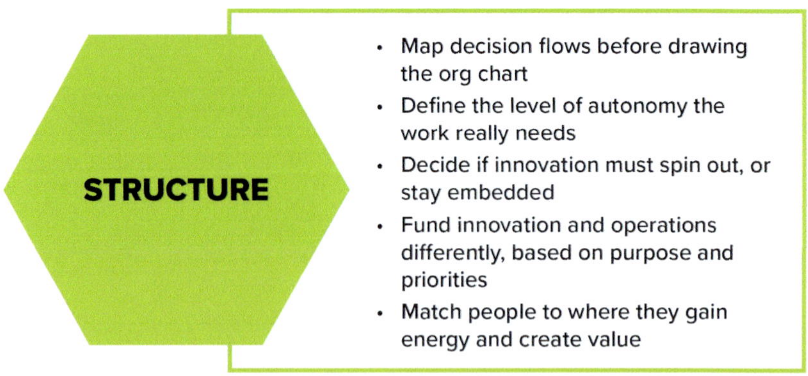

Figure 5.2 Structural Design Decisions

Table 5.1 Enabling Structures for Results: A 7-Step Guide

Step	*Key Questions*	*Decisions to Make*	*Your How*	*What Success Looks Like*
1. Understand the Context	What's changing, or not working? What's working well? Who's impacted? What does this structure need to unlock?	Clarify the purpose, urgency, and constraints. Don't jump to restructure, do your diagnostics first.	Walk the floor. Listen to how people work. Join online meetings to listen in. Spot the friction and hesitation. Map how the work actually moves.	The "why" is clear. Structure is purposeful, not reactive. Now you fully understand what needs to change and the reason for change can be explained through examples that people can relate to.
2. Decide: Integrate or Separate	Where will this work thrive? What does it need to succeed, speed, focus, credibility? Is this structure temporary or here to stay?	Embed, spin out, or run a hybrid. Set the terms: how much autonomy, how much support, and how it will reconnect back into the core when the time is right.	Look at where the work will get traction. Ask: will it move faster inside the current system, or be buried under shared steering, reporting cycles, and approval layers? If needed, give it space. But don't let it drift.	The work doesn't get stuck in the system, or sidelined outside it. You see progress. Clear accountability with the right people/skills in the right place. Both in operations and the new initiative stay focused on delivering results with synergies.
3. Map Decision Pathways	Where do decisions stall? Who decides, and is that clear to everyone?	Define decision rights, escalation paths, and handoffs. Be specific, even in small teams.	Identify five to ten key decisions. Clarify who gives input, who decides, and what to escalate. Rebuild structure around that.	Decisions match the pace of work. Accountability increases. Work stops bouncing.
4. Assign Message Carriers	Who has the street cred to deliver the message to the people? Who will people trust to explain and support the change?	Choose messengers based on credibility and reach, not just rank.	Bring in people with street cred early. Let them shape how the change is understood, not just repeat a message.	Messages land. People act without waiting. Trust in leadership grows.

(*Continued*)

Table 5.1 Continued

Step	*Key Questions*	*Decisions to Make*	*Your How*	*What Success Looks Like*
5. Appoint Credible Champions	Who can lead the change and earn followership?	Appoint respected people, not just by title, but by trust and presence.	Choose champions based on relational trust. Give them mandate, backing, and a small budget if needed. The champion will not always be the same as the "message carrier from step 4." The message carrier can be from operations and unable to allocate the needed time to champion the change on a wider scale.	People feel represented. Change has traction. Champions have energy and support. Your champion(s) have the mandate to drive the change.
6. Align to the Real World	What external constraints or system realities could break what you've just built?	Set ambition based on legal, regulatory, cultural, and operational realities. Pressure test your structure via the above-mentioned areas before you roll it out.	Bring in finance, legal, compliance, and trusted partners early. Ask where this structure could break, contractually, culturally, or politically.	Structure launches without resistance, holds up under scrutiny, and works as intended across legal, financial, and cultural boundaries. Value is delivered. You have organized to value impact.
7. Reinforce with Rhythm	What routines will make the structure stick?	Establish simple check-ins, cadences, and feedback loops.	Protect the new ways of working with real routines, weekly syncs, pairing, or shared forums that drive continuity.	Structure becomes the norm. People stay aligned and momentum continues.

Step 1: Understand the Context

Start by understanding the context, what's actually changing. Then draft your new structures.

Before you move to a single box, stop and ask yourself: What's actually shifting?

I've seen this scenario happen again and again. Leaders will make an error by jumping straight to structure, org charts, roles, and reporting lines, without taking time to understand what's really shifting. Every time a design – not an implementation – fails in the field, it always can be traced back to the same root cause: the diagnoses was skipped.

I've seen this firsthand in fast-moving deployment environments. The pace of growth can be exhilarating, but it quickly exposes the limits of legacy structures. Teams that were once aligned start to drift. Processes that worked at one scale begin to buckle under pressure. You find yourself spending more time navigating bottlenecks than delivering impact. That's when it becomes clear: the structure isn't just lagging, it's holding you back. In those moments, the most effective leaders aren't the ones who patch the old model, but those who reimagine it entirely. They build for adaptability, not just efficiency. They design for connection, not just control. Because when growth is the constant, responsiveness has to be the foundation. That's where structure starts, with clarity and always in collaboration. This is also where step 2 comes into play: do you need to spin out your innovation efforts to give them the speed and autonomy or not?

> As an example, I once took over a digital transformation where everything looked thought-out. Org chart? Check. Funding? Already in place. But the momentum was gone. When I dug in, it wasn't a talent issue, it was a mismatch. The market had evolved, demanding fresh governance, traceability, and certifications. However, the structure still rewarded speed over rigor. That startup agility allowed them to move with momentum. But now it was getting stale and in their way. Within six months, they were burning through all the trust and bleeding their best people.

I've seen the same pattern repeat in M&A settings, in tech scale-ups, in global operations. Strong teams stuck in the wrong frame. From my perspective, I realized that they weren't underperforming; they were misaligned.

In some situations, when the structure is too loose, decisions drift, and accountability is fuzzy. Other times, it's far too rigid, with multiple layers of sign-offs, too far removed from where the real work happens. And in both cases, your best people will pay the price.

This is where your job starts: not with design, but with diagnosis.

How to Make It Work

Forget the slide decks. Go to where the work lives.

Watch how decisions move. Who gets consulted. Where people stall. Then map the gaps between what's needed and what's real.

Ask yourself:

- Where is the work slowing down, and why?
- What's changed in your market, your mandate, or your maturity?
- Are decisions made where the actual work happens, or do they still travel up three levels for sign-off?
- What are your highest-value people spending their time on, and does that match their role?

Your answers won't come from theory or an MBA. They'll come from friction or conflict. When you walk the floor, sit in on the right meetings, and listen closely to who's frustrated, and why, and very quickly you'll start to see the real job your structure needs to do now.

That's precisely where the design starts. Not with ticking all the boxes, but with the truth.

Step 2: Decide, Integrate, or Separate

Place the Work Where It Can Move

Once the context is clear, the next decision is structural and practical:

Do you build this into what already exists, or do you give it its own space?

This choice shows up more often than you think. Launching a pilot. Starting a new team. Taking on a side initiative with real potential. You're not just deciding where the work goes, you're deciding how much focus, speed, and ownership it gets.

As a further example, I once led a digital initiative that needed to move fast. It couldn't wait for slow governance or shared steering groups. So we spun it out, on paper, still part of the company, but operating with its own cadence and decision rights. There was no friction, or five layers of approval, and because it still had access to core systems – HR, finance, compliance – it had just enough connection to stay legitimate. That structure gave it room to deliver real results without losing trust or momentum.

Attaining this balance is harder than it looks. Too much integration, and you suffocate it. Too much separation, and it drifts into irrelevance.

I've seen this fail when a promising idea was buried inside a slow-moving org. The people were smart and the intent was right, but they couldn't move forward because the setup wasn't built for pace.

How to Make It Work

Before you pick a structure, pressure test what you need to get the work done.

Does this need to move faster than your current setup allows?

Will integration slow it down, or give it credibility?

Who's funding it, and who can block it?

If you spin it out, how will you keep it connected, or should it be connected?

If you embed it, how will you protect its focus?

This is about removing the friction that kills momentum and ensuring you keep clarity from step 1.

When you get it right, everyone knows where the work sits, and why. Innovation runs without running off. Core operations stay focused. And your people don't waste energy figuring out where things belong.

Step 3: Map Decision Pathways

One could say this third step fits under step 1, but I think it is so essential and pragmatic that it deserves its own section. So before you draw lines or assign roles, let's clarify one essential thing: who decides what.

As a former colleague once told me:

> We held off making any org changes until we understood how decisions really moved through the business. We sat down, workstream by workstream, and asked: What are the key decisions here? Who makes them today? And where do they get stuck?

Too often, leaders start with titles and checking boxes. But structure without decision clarity creates conflicts and friction. Work bounces around, escalations pile up, and no one's sure who's actually in charge.

Instead, you should flip the process. For each critical area, you map the actual decision flow:

- What needs to be decided?
- Who provides input?
- Who makes the call?
- Who needs to know?
- Who is responsible and who will be held accountable?

Sometimes the answer was obvious. Sometimes it may be a surprise. In a few cases, the person closest to the work had been left out entirely. In other cases, people held accountable may not have known that they were, or in a worst-case scenario, they were held accountable, but did not have a mandate to make the required decisions.

Here is an example of how I was part of changing structures in a complex multiyear transformation, including some of the largest companies in the United States.

I was co-leading a multiyear digital transformation in the United States, a joint effort between three major players: two large multinationals, a smaller technology provider and a series of other partners. The team structure looked strong and had been carefully designed. We had capable people covering cybersecurity, operations, and digital systems. But due to a series of changes internally and in the market, the project wasn't moving forward.

Decisions that should have taken hours dragged on for weeks, not due to resistance, but because decision flow and rights were unclear. The original structure with responsible and accountable people had been disrupted. Changes within the major players' leadership teams and market conditions driven by a change of policy had brought uncertainty to the team, and the structure, as it stood, was not robust enough to facilitate all those changes.

So, we hit pause and remapped everything. First, we laid out the actual decision flows:

- Who makes tactical decisions day-to-day?
- Who sets strategic direction across the companies?
- Who owns funding and long-term accountability?

Then we rebuilt the structure based on that logic, included people from all involved parties and aligned on the new structure and ways of working. Finally, we called a full sponsor-level steering committee. On that call, executives made the key decisions, and, more importantly, officially empowered decision-makers at every level.

That reset gave the team forward motion. We had found clarity under this new context and understood which part of the project was integrated and which parts could be spun out. All because the structure finally supported the decisions the project needed.

Therefore, do the following before you finalize any structure, because once decision rights are clear, your org chart has something to anchor to.

Ask yourself and your team:

- What are the five to ten most important decisions in this area?
- Where do they live today, and where should they?

- Are they being made fast, well, and close to the action?
- If not, what's missing – trust, skill, authority?
- Redo this exercise once the context changes.

You'll know you're getting it right when decisions start happening at the pace of the work, not the pace of the hierarchy.

Step 4: Assign Message Carriers

Back the Shift with Street Cred

When structure changes, the first question people ask isn't *what's changing*, it's *who's behind this decision?*

They don't check the org chart. They check who's speaking. And whether they believe them.

That's why this step matters. Not because you need a comms plan. But because people move when the message comes from someone they trust. If the message falls flat, the change that is needed stalls, no matter how sharp your design is.

I've led transformations where the structure was right, the logic was sound, and roles were clear. Still, things didn't move. People hesitated, not because they disagreed, but because no one they trusted had said out loud in any meeting, "This is real."

And I've seen the opposite: a field-respected colleague explained a change with no slides, no script, just her voice. Within a day, teams were in motion. Why? Because she had street cred. People knew she wouldn't back something unless it mattered. And she stood behind it publicly.

Don't treat this like a soft step. This is the handoff that makes the structure stick.

You choose your message carrier early. You back them visibly. And you give them what they need to lead.

How to Make It Work

Start where the change hits hardest.

That's where people will ask questions, look for cues, and then decide how seriously to take what's coming.

Don't ask who's the most senior. Ask your people who they listen to when they're unsure. *Who carries trust in that space?* That's your message carrier.

Before rollout, sit with them. Walk through what's changing, what it unlocks, and how others might react. Not so they can *repeat* the message, but so they can own it. And when they speak, make it clear they speak with your support.

In a recent rollout, we did exactly that. We identified the pockets of resistance, named the people with credibility in those teams, and brought them in early. Not one of them had a formal role in change management, but every single one of them had influence. And that's what made the change actually land.

What Success Looks Like

You hear it before you see it.

Conversations are often like this: "I talked to her, she gets what's going on. She's behind it, so I'm on board."

That's when you know it's working.

Not when the slide is perfect. Not when the org chart is approved.

When someone with real trust carries the change into the room, then people will follow.

Ask yourself:

- Who has street cred where this shift matters most?
- Have you brought them in early, or are they finding out with everyone else?
- When they speak, will people move?

Choose them carefully, then equip your people fully and back them publicly.

Appoint Credible Champions

WHO PEOPLE FOLLOW, AND WHY THAT MATTERS

Once the message lands, someone has to carry it forward, not just with words, but with action. That's what a champion does. They lead from inside the new structure, making the decisions, absorbing the pressure, and building belief through what they do, not what they say.

Can the champion and message carrier be the same person? Yes, if they have both the trust of their peers and the stamina to lead through uncertainty. But often, they're different. One delivers the message. The other stays when the noise fades and things get real.

What makes a strong champion? It's not a title. And it's not just charisma. It's someone who others look to when things get messy. Someone who stays calm under pressure, knows when to escalate, and isn't afraid to step into a gray zone to protect the team.

You might have heard the saying, "it has fallen between two chairs." That is it, (the gray zone) where clarity fades, where roles blur, ownership is ambiguous, and the playbook doesn't quite fit. It's the space between "not my job" and "someone has to do it." Champions don't wait for permission there. They lean in. They make judgment calls, bridge gaps, and take responsibility when others hesitate. It's not about heroics, it's about trust. The team trusts them to act with integrity, to balance risk with reason, and to move things forward when the system stalls. In fast-paced projects, especially those with evolving structures, the gray zone isn't an exception, it's the norm. And the people who thrive there are often the ones who quietly hold everything together.

But even great champions need support. That starts with clarity. You don't just hand someone a vague mandate and hope they thrive. You walk through what success looks like, what decisions are theirs to make, and what backup they can count on. You give them air cover when stakes rise, and space to act when the moment is theirs.

A scenario I've witnessed in one of our field deployments was during the launch of a cross-functional digital tool on offshore rigs. We had the right tech and the right message, but things didn't accelerate until we asked a respected rig leader to step in, not to sponsor the change, but to live it. He owned the tool's success as if it were his own. He took feedback from users seriously. And when people saw him using it, fixing issues, and advocating for improvements, adoption followed. That's the champion.

When you ask someone to champion a structural change, you're handing them real responsibility. And with that, they need a real mandate.

You're asking someone to champion a change that sits outside their day job, so make it real. Make it visible. Say it out loud in the room. Let others hear that this person has your full backing to lead this shift.

Sometimes, that means standing beside them while they speak at the kickoff. Other times, it means having someone with street cred. Say, "I trust him or her to drive this."

> Let's talk about "street cred," because in any business, it's a powerful asset. If you've built it, you've got something many don't. And if you're working with clients, spotting who has it is your shortcut to trust.
>
> Street cred is earned by consistently showing up, solving problems without being asked, and owning both the mess and the momentum. It's the person who knows how things actually work, who others rely on when something needs to get done right. They make things easier by enabling others to do better work, not by taking over, but by clearing the path. They've built trust by being in the trenches, getting their hands dirty, and valuing action over words.

And don't forget the basics. Do they need a small budget to print materials, organize a team session, or even get t-shirts made that show people this thing matters? Give them that. Quickly.

Champions move change when the mandate is clear, the support is visible, and they have just enough fuel to keep going when it gets hard.

You don't need a formal playbook. You need to make the signal unmissable: *this person is leading, because we trust them to get us there.*

A champion without a mandate burns out and loses creditability from the people impacted. But with the right backing, they become the engine of change.

For example, in one of my own projects, I was pushing hard to get things back on track. We were behind, and I needed my counterpart, someone deeply trusted by the team, to help carry the change.

But when I brought it up, he looked at me and said,

"I have a lot of additional responsibility. But no real mandate."

That hit me. He wasn't resisting the work, he was overloaded and unsupported. We'd asked him to lead, but hadn't cleared the path. No introduction, no air cover, no room to make moves. That wasn't leadership, it was neglect.

So here's the lesson:

When you ask someone to champion a change, give them the authority to match the responsibility.

Introduce them properly, have someone with street cred or executive weight say: *"This person is leading this change. They have my full backing."*

Free up their time. Give them a small budget. Let them shape how the message is rolled out. If you're asking them to take the heat, you need to step in and block the any blow back.

Because without mandate, even your best people will stall, or burn out.

Step 6: Align to the Real World

Build for robustness through internal and external alignment.

You've already figured out why the structure needs to change. Now ask yourself: can it hold?

Too many leaders build bold structures that collapse the moment real-world friction shows up, such as compliance rules, investor requirements, union agreements, and cultural red lines. I've seen it happen in post-merger settings, in international rollouts, and in ESG programs. The design looked great. But no one asked: what will this structure run into?

At the financial institution, I remember a sustainability rollout where we had just wrapped a Northern Europe-wide pilot, ambitious targets, and clear metrics. If you wanted to do something similar in the United States, the team would push back. They wanted faster ROI, stricter accountability, and defensible metrics.

Now you can understand that the project worked out very well and now, years after, we have a great relationship and our efforts in those early project stages have created lasting relationships based on trust! What was funny was that, during a later visit to the local office, we sat down, and a woman from the first project team said, half-jokingly, "You just seemed too nice. We were all wondering, what was the catch?" We all laughed, but also remembered how no one was laughing when we first started out.

If I'd had an Enabler back then, if I'd known to scan for cultural friction, not just structural logic, I could've avoided weeks of misalignment and the risk of losing the project.

In one of our offshore projects, the structure was solid on paper. The team had clear roles, decision flows, and support from leadership. Everything went as planned – but when I asked to lead a US-based project, what once worked in Northern Europe, no longer worked.

Our core project group, mostly Scandinavian, was used to a more subtle approach. We spoke softly, avoided confrontation, and let decisions emerge through consensus. That style worked well for us. But when the same setup was introduced to teams in the United States and South America, it created confusion. What I saw as respectful and collaborative was read as insecurity in the method and a lack of confidence. People didn't know if we were serious or why we were not being assertive when decisions were required. They didn't trust that we'd push through when things got tough. It came to a point where I would no longer receive replies to emails, chats, and when we joined the project call, most did not show up. I had to change my style and align to the new context, understand the decision flows, and expected culture.

What I realized was that, more important than being assertive, when working with successful clients, were two things.

1. **Be reliable:** show up when you say you will. No matter what others do. Always be there to support the project and people who are impacted.
2. **Be predictable:** knowing that you will stick to the plan, especially during large stakeholder meetings. That you will take sensitive things offline before voicing them in larger crowds.
3. **Be useful:** make sure workflows and that the people you work with will be impacted only with tasks that add value to them. If they need to learn a new system that requires new ways of working – train them – but don't let them get caught up in IT matters or technical issues. Pave the way and the biggest compliment you can receive is, "this project seemed easy enough," when you have completed a highly complex transformation, but the impacted people did not feel all the struggles.

A year later, I visited the team at their local office. I had barely stepped foot in the office when one of their senior managers came to me and told me how much he appreciated the fact that we kept being available, kept believing in the technology and the project and that we showed so much determination to make it a success for his teams. The key thing my team and I did was the three above points – **be reliable, be predictable, and be useful.**

How to Make It Work

You don't need a playbook. You need to see the terrain. Before anything's locked in, get the right people in the room – legal, compliance, finance, HR. Not to block. To stress test.

Ask them:

- What can't we do here?
- What language won't land?
- What risks are we missing?
- Where will this hit resistance?

This isn't about lowering ambition. It's about making sure your structure won't crack under real-world pressure.

What Success Looks Like

Structure launches without resistance, holds up under scrutiny, and works as intended across legal, financial, and cultural boundaries.

Step 7: Reinforce with Rhythm

Build the routines that make the structure stick.

You can make all the right structural decisions, but if you don't embed them into how your team actually works, daily, weekly, quarterly, things will drift. Not because people don't care. But because in fast-moving environments, without rhythm, even the best structure unravels.

We'd just redesigned a multi-country team setup. Decision flows were mapped. Roles clarified. Teams were energized. But a few months in, progress stalled. Not because the design was wrong, but because the new structure hadn't been reinforced. The old habits crept back in. People defaulted to the familiar, waiting on approvals, duplicating work, and skipping alignment calls.

We set a heartbeat. Think of it is a life force or drum beat in any organization.

Same time, same four people: operations, finance, tech, and project. Thirty minutes, no slides. One shared screen. We opened the board and worked through it line by line, where's the blocker, what's the decision, who needs to move?

But here's what made it different.

Each lead came prepared. By noon Monday, everyone updated a shared prep sheet: top three issues, decisions needed, risks, and, this was key, a check on whether the team had what they needed. Not just tasks, but capacity. Did they have the right person on it? Did they know what "done" looked like? Did they have the mandate to execute?

And if not, that's what we solved in the room.

This wasn't a report-out. It was leadership in action. When the same item showed up again, it triggered a real check-in: Do we have the wrong structure, the wrong resourcing, or the wrong expectations? No blame, just clarity.

And over time, that rhythm became something more. It wasn't just a call. It was the heartbeat of the structure. It protected forward motion and made sure our setup wasn't just designed well, it was working in practice.

That's your job now. Design and implement the rhythms that make your structure real:

- A 15-minute weekly sync that prevents escalation later.
- A monthly heatmap of stuck decisions and shadow work.
- A rotation that pairs leaders from different sides of the org, tech and ops, field and HQ.
- A Q&A forum hosted by credible messengers, where people can challenge and clarify how the new setup is working.
- Revisit one or more steps in your tool on a regular basis or when things change.

Remember, **not everything needs to be a meeting**. But you need to establish a rhythm.

If you're leading post-merger integration, that rhythm might look like a joint KPI review, one deck, one story, and no "us vs. them."

If you're leading innovation inside operations, it might be a structured demo cadence, where real users test and give feedback every sprint.

If you're setting up a new team, your rhythm might be a shared check-in: "What decision did we make this week? Who did it unlock?"

What Success Looks Like

You don't need to check if the structure is working. I said it earlier, but it bears repeating: *you'll feel it.*

People know when and where decisions get made. Meetings shift from updates to decisions. Teams get ahead of blockers. They come to you with alignment, not noise.

Rhythm gives your structure staying power. Without it, even great design becomes wishful thinking. With it, you've got something stronger: a system that runs because people believe in it, and because it helps them do their best work.

Every structural decision you make, who decides, who carries the message, who champions the work, is shaping the experience your people live every day. It tells them what matters. It tells them what's safe. And it tells them whether to lean in or step back.

When you've earned trust but lack mandate, you become a volunteer.

When you assign roles without clarity, people hesitate.

When you redraw boxes without rhythm, people and teams lack clarity.

If you remember one thing from Chapter 5, let it be this: structure is how your leadership actions facilitate and enable responsibilities, decision making, and impact.

Now, structure alone won't carry you across company lines. It won't resolve power gaps in joint ventures or build trust between stakeholders with different agendas. That takes something else.

It takes ecosystem leadership, the ability to operate across boundaries, cultures, and contracts with clarity and intent. In complex offshore energy projects, success depends not just on internal alignment but on how well you navigate the broader stakeholder landscape. Investors, regulators, operators, and local teams each bring different priorities, and progress hinges on your ability to connect those dots.

This kind of leadership means knowing when to step in and when to step back. It means building trust through transparency, enabling others to act, and creating shared language around goals and risks. You're not just managing a team; you're orchestrating a network. And in that network, influence is earned through credibility, consistency, and the ability to make others feel seen and supported.

It takes knowing how to lead in the in-between, where no one person holds all the power, and progress depends on how well you align the people around you.

That is exactly where we're headed next.

In the following chapter, I'll take you inside the ecosystems, and how effective leaders build and sustain ecosystems, networks of governments, corporations, and communities, under real-world pressure. Get ready to lead when no one hands you the authority, because that's where real influence begins.

Chapter 6

Ecosystems

Build, Sustain, and Enable Impact Through Your Key Players

In this chapter, I want to move away from firm-level thinking (that I define as analyzing and making decisions with a focus on the specific needs, goals, and resources of a company, rather than through a broader lens), industry thinking, and move toward *ecosystem thinking*. You may be thinking, why? Because creating a positive impact does not happen in isolation. Both businesses and leading researchers have moved away from looking at companies, and even industries, as a unit of analysis and measure of competitive advantage – they have moved to *ecosystem thinking*.

Ecosystems are comprised of interconnected players who influence, enable, and amplify the impact. The success of an organization, both in terms of business outcomes and social value, centers on how well it engages and leverages its ecosystem(s). When you play a leadership role in shaping these ecosystems, the job is not about mastering every trait or role individually. Instead, the leader's primary responsibility is to enable the team and stakeholders to work collaboratively toward shared goals.

I've seen companies run transformation programs with flawless plans and strong budgets, only to stall because a single supplier, regulator, or community group wasn't aligned. That's what happens when you think at the company level. Now compare that to leaders who work the ecosystem: they map who matters, create trust across boundaries, and move everyone toward the same outcome. The difference is night and day.

Using the visual in Figure 6.1, I'll parachute you straight into the how. Think of it as your ecosystem toolbox – whether you're starting from scratch or need help with a specific challenge, you can follow the steps sequentially or dive directly into the one that fits your current need.

Remember that mapping and managing your ecosystem is more than listing relationships; it is a strategic endeavor that requires insight, foresight, and active engagement. Ecosystems are enablers of positive impact, providing a framework for innovation, growth, and resilience in a rapidly changing world.

DOI: 10.4324/9781003638551-7

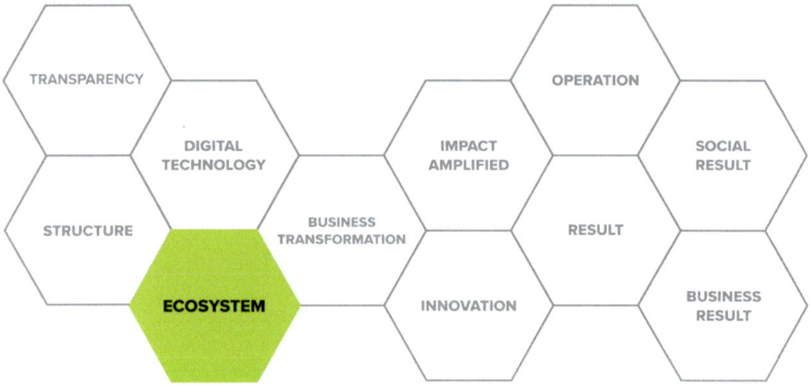

Figure 6.1 Ecosystem Enabler

THE HOW: AN ECOSYSTEM DECISION TOOL FOR LEADERS

The Ecosystem Decision Tool (see the five steps below) provides a structured approach to evaluate and enhance an ecosystem's effectiveness. By addressing stakeholder mapping, alignment, cultural dimensions, tactical priorities, and leadership implications, it enables leaders to make informed decisions that foster sustainable collaboration and long-term impact.

Participants: Involve internal leaders, stakeholder representatives, and external experts (e.g., cultural or risk specialists) in each step.

Processes: Use structured tools like stakeholder mapping, alignment dashboards, risk assessments, and phased scaling frameworks to guide execution.

Application: Treat this framework as a working tool – revisit mapping, alignment, and execution as ecosystem dynamics evolve.

STEP 1: MAP YOUR ECOSYSTEM

Focus	*Questions for Leaders*	*Next Steps and Considerations*
Identify Stakeholders	Have you identified all key stakeholders who need to be part of your ecosystem (e.g., clients, vendors, NGO, government, private sector, investors, regulators, and advisors)?	If gaps exist, for example, missing a vendor, key decision maker who needs to be involved, a cyber security representative, local community voices, frontline operators, or contract owners, add them to your ecosystem map before moving forward.

Focus	*Questions for Leaders*	*Next Steps and Considerations*
Assess Influence	Do you understand the influence and priorities of each stakeholder?	Rank stakeholders by two things: their power to stop you and their interest in seeing you succeed. Prioritize your engagement with those who have both.
Explore Synergies and Tensions	Are stakeholders aligned toward shared goals?	If misalignment exists, revisit your ecosystem players, the selection you made and ensure clear value propositions, and facilitate realignment meetings/workshops.

STEP 2: ALIGN STAKEHOLDER OBJECTIVES

Focus	*Questions for Leaders*	*Next Steps and Considerations*
Shared Goals	Have you aligned stakeholder objectives with your organization's goals?	If objectives differ, re-engage stakeholders to develop a shared vision.
Shared KPIs	Are there KPIs that reflect progress and accountability for all stakeholders?	Establish measurable KPIs that align business success with societal impact.
Value Proposition	Does every stakeholder see their mutual benefit in the ecosystem?	If not, reassess and communicate the value of participation to all involved.

STEP 3: ADDRESS CULTURAL DIMENSIONS

Focus	*Questions for Leaders*	*Next Steps and Considerations*
Cultural Norms	Have you accounted for national and organizational cultural factors in decision-making?	Adapt stakeholder engagement approaches to respect diverse cultural contexts.
Regional and Company Cultures	Are regional and company-specific cultural considerations integrated into collaboration styles?	Engage with cultural experts to align ecosystem strategies with regional expectations.
Leadership Adaptation	Is your leadership approach adaptable to different cultural dynamics?	Modify leadership strategies based on stakeholder needs and engagement styles.

STEP 4: ADDRESS TACTICAL PRIORITIES

Focus	*Questions for Leaders*	*Next Steps and Considerations*
Resource Allocation	Are resources (time, funding, and talent) distributed effectively among high-impact stakeholders?	Optimize resource allocation to ensure strategic partnerships receive necessary support.
Balance Operations and Innovation	Are you balancing current operational needs with future innovation?	Implement a structured approach that weighs efficiency against long-term exploration.
Communication Mechanisms	Do stakeholders have reliable communication channels?	Introduce tools like shared dashboards and quarterly check-ins for sustained engagement.

STEP 5: MEASURE AND SUSTAIN ECOSYSTEM SUCCESS

Focus	*Questions for Leaders*	*Next Steps and Considerations*
Define Outcomes	Have you established measurable success metrics for the ecosystem?	Develop KPIs that reflect both operational and societal outcomes.
Track Tangible and Intangible Outcomes	Are financial and relational outcomes (e.g., trust and collaboration) being measured?	Introduce surveys and collaborative tracking mechanisms to capture qualitative and quantitative impact.
Ensure Long-Term Value	Is there a structured way to track the long-term impact of the ecosystem?	Implement a legacy framework to measure sustained influence beyond short-term KPIs.

Now that you have worked through the five steps, you can read deeper into the details of how organizations can effectively map, build, and sustain their ecosystems, emphasizing the leader's role as a key enabler of collaboration.

MAP YOUR ECOSYSTEM

Let me explain how my team and I are successfully doing this.

Starting a new major global project, engaging with a new client, or a change in folks we are interfacing with, the first thing we do is to create our internal ecosystem map – mapping people and their responsibilities. During our first call with the client, or vendor, we will present them our side of the ecosystem in a visual mapping. When we have presented how our ecosystem is put together, we will illustrate who we need as immediate additions to our ecosystem for success. This way, we map internally with roles and responsibilities as value drivers as well as requesting the same from our clients and all who are needed to enable success.

As you see in Figure 6.2, we divide the mapping into two stages: first being project and change management stage and second being how to sustain the positive impact enabled by the project team.

- **Phase 1 Upper left**: our own core team, the people directly responsible for delivery, escalation, and support.
- **Phase 1 Upper right**: the key people we request from the client to be part of the ecosystem right from the start, so they know what we need for success.
- **Phase 2 Lower left**: the team inside our company who will take over when the project moves into operations, ensuring continuity.
- **Phase 2 Lower right**: the client roles we need in place for the transition into business-as-usual.

By showing both sides up front, our roles and the roles we need from them, the conversation becomes transparent. Everyone sees the responsibilities, the handovers, and the value each role brings. This mapping exercise sets the tone: the ecosystem is not abstract, it's people with names, faces, and accountabilities.

We added this visual initial mapping as most leaders, especially early in their careers, or those new to a project or operation, don't see the full picture. They

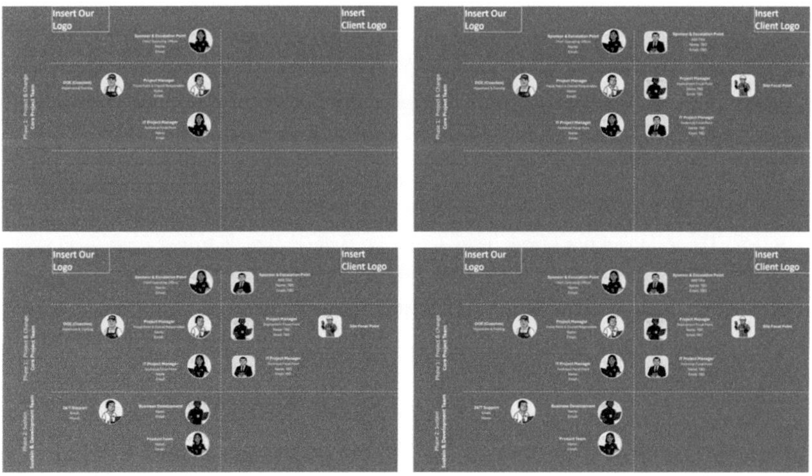

Figure 6.2 Ecosystem Mapping

know their boss, their immediate client, maybe the vendors they deal with every day. But the real ecosystem is wider than that and what are they responsible for in this specific context? It includes everyone who can speed you up, slow you down, or quietly shape whether you succeed. Yet, they rarely know who and why they need to interface with a wider group of players.

I start simple. I take a piece of paper or a whiteboard and draw a circle in the middle with my team or project written inside. Then I start writing down the people and groups connected to it. Clients, vendors, colleagues, decision-makers, users, communities, potential blockers. It doesn't need to be tidy. The point is to get the names out of your head and onto the page. By the time I'm done, the circle is surrounded by the people who can make or break momentum. This is what they polish and present to the client during our first call.

As you understand, a list of names isn't a map. You have to understand *why each one matters*. That means looking at their leverage. A client matters because they can renew or cancel your contract, escalation points, and budget approvers. A vendor matters because if their shipment slips, your deadline slips. A colleague matters because they're the only one who knows how to pull the data that your whole analysis depends on.

Once I've worked out why they matter, I go and talk to them, spend time at their office to have face-to-face contact which still works better than pure online meetings. Let me tell you this, the good relationships especially matter when things go wrong – which they will at some point. If you have strong relationships, met face to face in the office, had lunch and dinner together, you will have an easier time solving complex problems than if you do not have these relationships. Mapping helps you clearly understand who you should invest your time in.

With a client, I'll ask: *Besides the official project KPIs, what does success look like for you here?* Then I'll follow up: *What would make you hesitate about signing this off?* With a vendor: *What do you need from us to deliver on time? Where do things usually go wrong for you?* With a teammate: *What do you need to deliver your part without burning out?* At first, the answers are surface-level. But if you leave space and keep pressing, the real concerns start to come out. That's the information you need.

The map becomes powerful when you write those answers down. Next to each name, I note what their priority is, where their red line sits, and what I can give them in return. This last point is critical. Ecosystems don't run on one-way demands. If a client needs certainty, I can give them transparency. If a vendor needs early forecasts, I can commit to sharing them sooner. If a colleague needs recognition, I can make sure their work is visible. These exchanges are the currency of ecosystems.

And here's the part that I do not want you to miss: every person you map brings their own ecosystem. A vendor has suppliers, a client has end-customers, and a colleague has their own networks across the business. When you build trust, you don't just work with that person, you gain access to their ecosystem too. That's where opportunities multiply. A strong relationship with one partner can suddenly open doors to an entire supply chain you never had access to.

When the exercise is done, I have a working visual document: a set of names, what drives them, what they need, what I can give, and what other networks they connect me to. I keep it visible, I update it as things change, and I use it to decide where to spend my time. That is an ecosystem map in practice, not a concept, but a tool you can use every day to stop guessing and start leading with clarity.

ALIGN STAKEHOLDER OBJECTIVES

Once the map has been completed, the next opportunity (or some may say challenge) is alignment. You'll quickly see that every player you've listed has different priorities. That's normal. A client might care about delivery speed. A vendor might care about steady orders and clear forecasts. A colleague might care about recognition and workload balance. At first glance, these interests don't always line up and if you leave them separate, they will eventually collide.

The key to alignment is understanding how you connect the priorities and objectives of each ecosystem player. Whether it is a person, team, or company, it means finding the overlaps that tie their priorities together. The only way to do that is by holding up the bigger objective so everyone can see it.

I saw this play out clearly when we implemented a new SaaS solution. From the very start, the map from Step 1 showed me just how different the priorities were. Cybersecurity was on edge, deeply worried about exposing sensitive information and granting the wrong people access. Operations came in hard, making it clear that safety and efficiency were non-negotiable, and that they would block anything that even hinted at compromise. Digital, on the other hand, was determined to prove that digitizing paper processes was the future, even for a conservative and highly regulated industry.

On paper, these priorities looked like a deadlock. But having the ecosystem mapped meant I could sit down with each of them, listen to their red lines, and then bring them into the same conversation with the bigger objective visible to all: safer, faster, and more transparent operations. Cyber could see that strong controls were part of building trust in the system. Operations could see that efficiency gains would never come at the cost of safety. Digital could prove the case by showing how compliance and performance data were stronger when paper disappeared.

It was intense, and at times confrontational, but the map gave me the clarity to connect their opposing priorities. Instead of pulling apart, they started to see how their concerns overlapped, and that overlap is what created alignment.

Do you know where we found common ground: End User Experience.

At the end, all looked at it from the end-user perspective. The one impacted by the new digital tool. Did it make their day better? Safer? Yes! And it actually enhanced cybersecurity while the digital tool became a success after careful alignment.

In practice, this often happens around a table where frustration is thick in the air. I've been there: a vendor pushing hard for commitments you can't make, a client demanding guarantees you can't yet give, and your own team looking tired of the back and forth. The turning point comes when you shift the conversation from positions to connections. You show how each group's success depends on the others.

Here's how I do it. I'll take the client's priority, say, getting their product delivered on time. Then I'll show them how that outcome depends on the vendor getting early forecasts. And I'll show the vendor that their stability depends on the client's continued trust and orders. Suddenly, it's not two separate demands. It's a chain, and each link matters.

It takes repetition. People forget. Pressure builds, and they slip back into protecting their own corner. So, alignment is not a one-off workshop; it's an ongoing part of leadership. Every delay, every budget cut, every change in scope, those moments threaten alignment. The leader's role is to keep pulling people back to the shared outcome: *We only get there if we move together.*

The ecosystem map you built in Step 1 gives you the material to do this well. You already know each stakeholder's non-negotiables, their red lines, and what you can offer in return. Alignment means using that knowledge to stitch the system together. You make the invisible connections visible, over and over again, until people stop thinking in terms of "my piece" and start seeing how their piece holds up the whole.

When alignment takes hold, the tone shifts. Meetings stop being defensive. Conversations become more open. Instead of trying to win at each other's expense, people start looking for the points where their priorities overlap. That's when an ecosystem begins to move as one.

ADDRESS CULTURAL DIMENSIONS

I just came back from Tokyo after spending time with a major Japanese conglomerate. The culture in that room was nothing like what I'm used to in Denmark or the United States. In Denmark, we get straight to the point. In the United States, people expect directness and speed. In Japan, the pace was deliberate. Respect was shown in silence. Decisions weren't made in the meeting itself but later, after consensus had been carefully built internally.

Let me give you another example, exchanging business cards. I have had cultural classes during my bachelor's and master's. I can promise you this, no class can prepare you for what you will experience in real life. The attention to details, the efforts made when receiving the business card, the efforts made when commenting on it and acknowledging the achievements listed. The sequence of exchanging them is not random, and you need to feel the room, use your emotional intelligence to find your way in this exchange which takes place as the very first part of the meeting. Once received, you place it on the table in front of you, give it respect and after the meeting, you put it in your card holder and into your jacket pocket and do not simply stuff it in your pants.

If I had walked in with my usual style, I would have lost them immediately. Instead, I reminded myself: in this context, I am the guest. My job was to adapt. I listened more than I spoke. I gave space for silence instead of filling it. I showed patience. That shift mattered. It signaled that I was willing to work on their terms, not just mine.

This is how you become cultural aware. Every ecosystem has its own culture. Regulators may value detailed reports and formal processes. Contractors may prefer quick, no-nonsense updates. Teams in Tokyo wanted patience, respect for hierarchy, and time to build trust before making commitments. If you use the same style everywhere, you will eventually break the ecosystem.

Leading across cultures means preparing enough to know what matters in their world and then framing your message in that language. It's not about faking or playing a role. It's about respect. And when you get it right, the ecosystem responds. Doors that would have stayed closed begin to open.

ADDRESS TACTICAL PRIORITIES

Big visions and alignment are important, but ecosystems live or die on the practical details. By mapping your ecosystem, you already know what is important for each party. This is different, as the tactical items will be easier to hold people responsible for delivering, or not delivering. Once people are around the table, the question becomes: how do we actually move forward? That means getting very clear on resources, on balancing today's operations with tomorrow's opportunities, and on how everyone will stay connected day to day.

In Barcelona, the ecosystem was under strain. Operations could not keep the employees and experiences 3 digit attrition rates, and new hires took 16 weeks to become competent. The client wanted faster service and better outcomes. Employees wanted leadership that supported them instead of punishing mistakes. On paper, we had aligned on the bigger goal in Step 3: stability, speed, and improved experience. But alignment would have collapsed without tactical outline of tasks – these tactical steps kept our ecosystem moving forward and the progress kept trust among the players.

That is where Step 4 came in. We made three specific changes:

1. **Training redesign:** We broke a 16-week program into shorter modules, each with a practical check. New hires could handle real tasks within weeks, not months. That gave the client faster service and gave employees an early sense of achievement.
2. **Daily routines for leaders:** We built standard start-of-day and end-of-day check-ins, visual boards, and short huddles. Team leaders had a structure to guide their teams instead of improvising, and operations could finally trust that the work was consistent.
3. **Recognition system:** We introduced simple scorecards and public acknowledgment of good performance. Employees saw their effort counted for something, which helped reduce attrition.

These steps did more than fix problems in the moment as they gave each stakeholder proof that their priorities were being acted on. That reinforcement kept the alignment from Step 3 alive and pushed the ecosystem forward together.

As you can understand by now, balancing operations with innovation is critical also for your ecosystem. The teams on the ground often want proven routines, because that's how they stay safe and efficient. Leadership, however, has to carve out space for trial, error, and learning if the system is going to evolve. I've handled this by running dual tracks: one for current delivery, another for pilot projects, testing new ideas, and tools. The message to the teams was clear: we won't risk today's results, but we will carve out resources to explore tomorrow's. Both matter. Both have to run in parallel.

And none of this works without strong communication channels. Ecosystems unravel fast if people are left in the dark. In my experience, it's better to set up simple, reliable routines and I book them as frequent, reoccurring check-ins.

Until we have the right traction on the tactical bi and we continue to be aligned, I may consider changing the frequency of our check-ins. You can always create fancy dashboards, just be sure that people know how to use them and make decisions based on the data you present. One, or more, short weekly call with key stakeholders, a visible tracker everyone can access, quarterly check-ins where issues are put on the table. These touchpoints keep the ecosystem connected, stop small issues from festering, and build the rhythm needed for trust.

Tactical priorities may not sound glamorous, but this is where ecosystems either hold together or fall apart. When resources are clear, operations and innovation are balanced, and communication flows, the big vision suddenly feels achievable. Without it, even the best alignment will collapse under day-to-day pressure.

MEASURE AND SUSTAIN ECOSYSTEM SUCCESS

I suggest you revisit Figure 6.2 Ecosystem mapping on p.79, where I have added a "Phase 2" to ensure that the positive impact is sustained. Now it is time to activate these ecosystem players.

Success looks different to every player in the ecosystem. The only way to keep them engaged is to define and track what matters to them.

- For a client: on-time delivery, error rates, and satisfaction scores.
- For a vendor: forecast accuracy, stable order volumes, and payment on time.
- For a community: number of hires, retention rates, and training delivered.
- For your team: safety incidents, turnover, and engagement pulse results.

In Barcelona, we made this real by tracking time-to-competence. Training used to take 16 weeks, and most new hires quit before they were ready. We redesigned the program and cut that to six weeks. The client saw faster results, employees felt progress sooner, and operations finally had stability. That single measure became the proof point that alignment from Step 3 was holding.

Don't tell, show. Regulators want documented compliance, not promises. Vendors want early forecasts in their inbox, not vague reassurances. Communities want to see names on hiring lists, not a press release. Teams want recognition in front of peers, not a quiet thank you. Proof creates trust.

How to Measure

- Data you already have: delivery dates, quality checks, uptime, safety logs, and attrition.
- Surveys: quick pulse surveys for employees and partners, one or two questions, answered in minutes. ("Do you have what you need to succeed this week?" "Do you trust the project is on track?")

- Structured feedback: stakeholder check-ins every quarter. Ask: *What's working? What's frustrating? What one thing would build your confidence?* Record answers and track themes over time.

Weekly updates for operations, monthly reviews for performance, quarterly sessions for strategy. Not long meetings, just short and consistent touchpoints. Predictability builds confidence. Silence creates doubt.

Ensure continues improvement and for example, every few months, ask: is this still working for everyone? Who no longer fits? Who is missing? Reset expectations and adjust priorities before cracks appear.

The real test is simple. If the system only works when you are in the room, it won't last. Shared KPIs, joint reviews, and routines people own themselves are what keep ecosystems alive when you step out.

That is how you measure and sustain success: define proof that matters, collect it, make it visible, and keep a rhythm that builds trust.

LEADERSHIP IMPLICATIONS

This Enabler is the ecosystem. And ecosystems don't move forward on their own. They only work when you, the leader, enable them.

Enabling means working the five steps with discipline: mapping who matters, aligning objectives, adapting to culture, setting tactical priorities, and measuring and sustaining progress. Each step gives you leverage, but together they create momentum.

Your role is to enable and connect the ecosystem, keep people aligned, and hold the shared goal steady under pressure. Leaders who enable ecosystems make it possible to achieve outcomes that no single team or company could deliver alone. Those who don't will see the system stall and break apart (Figure 6.3).

Figure 6.3 Ecosystems for Lasting Partnerships Enabler

THE ROLE OF TECHNOLOGY IN ECOSYSTEM LEADERSHIP

When I first started leading across ecosystems, technology was treated like an add-on, something the IT team would handle once the "real work" was done. But I've seen how wrong that thinking is. Technology, when used well, becomes one of the strongest enablers of ecosystems. It doesn't replace leadership, but it makes the work of leadership possible at scale.

Think back to Step 1: Mapping your ecosystem. When you have multiple players, clients, vendors, partners, regulators, technology gives you the ability to make the invisible visible. A shared platform, even a simple collaborative dashboard, lays out who's involved, what they're responsible for, and how dependencies flow. Without that visibility, you're guessing.

Or Step 2: Aligning objectives. Alignment often comes down to trust in the facts. I've sat in meetings where two sides argued for hours over who caused a delay. The moment we pulled up a digital log with time stamps, the debate stopped. The focus shifted from blame to solutions. That's tech as an alignment tool.

Culture matters too (Step 3). In Tokyo, what worked wasn't flashy apps but quiet, reliable systems that showed respect for process and hierarchy. In the United States, the same partners expected quick, visible updates. Tech can flex to those differences; one group reads reports, another checks live feeds, but the ecosystem stays connected.

When it comes to Step 5: Sustaining success, tech is the rhythm keeper. Instead of me chasing updates, the system itself shows progress and flags issues. Everyone sees the same picture, which keeps momentum alive.

Think of technology as the infrastructure that keeps your ecosystem alive. When you are working across cultures, companies, and time zones, people will change, and organizations will shift. What holds everything together is the way information is shared and how rules of engagement are set.

Use open platforms so partners can connect without being locked in. Use shared data spaces so everyone works from the same facts. Use verifiable records, so trust doesn't disappear when faces change. Do this, and your ecosystem won't collapse when conditions shift. It will adapt and keep moving because the foundations are already in place.

And remember what I told you about personal relationships and why they matter. Technology enables all of this, but whenever you can, get face-to-face. Trust deepens faster when people meet in person.

CONCLUSION AND TAKEAWAYS: LEADERSHIP DRIVES ECOSYSTEM SUCCESS

An ecosystem, when led well, becomes more than a network of partners, it becomes a platform for progress. Sometimes you'll move through them one by one. Other times, you'll pick the one that matters most in the moment, like addressing cultural dimensions when everything else is stuck.

The point is simple: ecosystems don't succeed because the right players are in the room. They succeed because those players are engaged, enabled, and aligned to a shared purpose. That's the leader's job.

And here's the shift to make as a next-gen leader: the real amplifier of ecosystems today is technology. Not as a gimmick or a bolt-on, but as a way to create transparency, strengthen trust, and carry collaboration further than you can alone.

TURNING TO TECHNOLOGY

We've seen how ecosystems expand your reach, but they only hold together if leaders enable them with trust, clarity, and rhythm. That's human work. But here's the truth: in today's world, no ecosystem can thrive on human effort alone. The load is too big, the pace too fast, the complexity too high.

This is where technology steps in. Not as the star of the show, but as the amplifier. Used well, digital tools can spark collaboration, carry trust across boundaries, and give ecosystems resilience they could never build on their own. Used badly, they create noise, resistance, and wasted effort.

In the next chapter, we dive into technology as its own enabler of leadership. We'll explore what happens when bold ideas meet real-world complexity, like Dr. Nis Alstrup's push for virtual consultations long before the rest of the world was ready, or his use of augmented reality to give patients clarity and confidence. And we'll break down a five-step framework for adopting advanced tools, from AR to generative AI, in ways that build trust, scale with purpose, and stick.

Because it's never the tool that transforms an organization. It's how you lead people into it.

Chapter 7

Mastering the Art of Technology

This chapter is really a practical how-to. I sincerely hope that by the end, you'll understand how the five steps apply in a real-world case, so you can confidently lead your own digital journey.

Before we leap ahead, I'd like to briefly recap what we've covered regarding the general themes of digital transformation. Some critical thoughts to consider:

- It's almost like running a political campaign; you have to get out on the trail, meet the people where they are, listen to their concerns, and explain how you're going to address them.
- It requires a marathon level of empathy and humility that most struggle to sustain until the end.

This is what my good colleague and client, Lucy Blount, stated when we were 18 months deep into a complex global digital transformation at one of the world's largest companies.

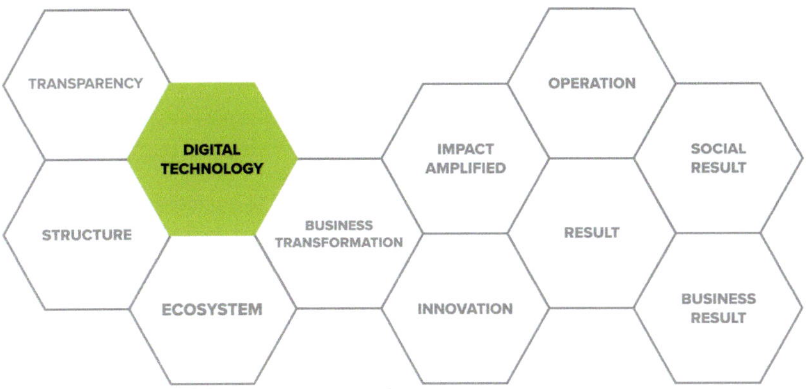

Figure 7.1 Technology as the Enabler

DOI: 10.4324/9781003638551-8

Deploying digital technology is rarely just about systems – it changes workflows, behaviors, and skill requirements. If you're leading a transformation, you'll need to shape your change approach: who to involve, how to communicate, what skills are needed to train, and how to keep people engaged throughout.

This is common knowledge; *digital tools are essential for modern leadership.* Chapter 7 goes beyond the obvious. You'll find practical insights, real examples, and a clear five-step framework that you can use to drive both business results and positive impact.

Unlike earlier chapters, it doesn't center on a single case study. Instead, it draws from multiple sectors to show you how timing, technology level, and your other Enablers influence success.

THE 5-STEP FRAMEWORK FOR LEADING DIGITAL ADOPTION: THE HOW

I have created a simple framework that will help you make the right decision based on a series of steps and considerations. First, I will present a guide on how to use the framework, either by yourself and then later to enable others, or as a team event.

The 5-Step Framework for Leading Digital Adoption is a practical tool designed to help you make clear, informed decisions about adopting and implementing digital technologies.

Whether introducing low-level automation or scaling advanced systems like AI, this framework provides step-by-step guidance to balance operational stability with innovation, empowering teams and driving impactful transformation. In this framework, you will rate each step from 1 to 5, where 1 is not ready and 5 is fully ready. Then apply the suggested strategies or find your own based on your score.

GUIDE TO USING THE 5-STEP FRAMEWORK FOR LEADING DIGITAL ADOPTION

Step	*What to Do (Individual and Team)*	*When to Review*
1. Assess Readiness	Score digital capacity and culture; run a team workshop.	Quarterly.
2. Select Adoption Level	Decide where to start (low/high); align on strategic fit.	During tech planning cycles.
3. Choose Approach	Match adoption speed (sequential/concurrent) to readiness.	At the start of each rollout.

Step	*What to Do (Individual and Team)*	*When to Review*
4. Align Operations and Innovations	Map key risks and opportunities to business goals.	Quarterly. During annual strategy planning and investor meetings.
5. Monitor and Sustain	Track progress, reinforce habits, and adjust as needed.	Monthly.

Step 1. Assess Readiness with Yes/No Questions: Are You Ready, or Do You Need to Slow Down and Build Trust?

Factor	*Key Question*	*If Score ≤3*	*If Score ≥4*
Workforce Readiness	Are employees ready to use new tools?	Start with low-tech + training.	Move to advanced adoption.
Infrastructure	Do IT systems support digital adoption? Legacy systems, APIs, other.	Upgrade before scaling.	Deploy high-tech tools.
Cultural Readiness	Is there openness to change?	Use intense change management; go on a campaign to share the vision and create urgency. A phased rollout is recommended, if you have the time and resources.	Consider faster adoption.
Leadership Alignment	Are executives aligned on digital priorities?	Clarify vision & ownership. What is your digital roadmap? Are leaders ready for digital? Upskilling of management?	Accelerate transformation.
Market Speed	Do we need to adopt quickly to stay competitive?	Focus on stability, quality, and take time to understand how to amplify your impact.	Create urgency, use concurrent adoption if possible, set a strong deployment team to understand how to prioritize speed.

Step 2. Select the Adoption Level: Start Small or Scale Big, What's Your Digital Maturity Telling You? Use the Table Below to Decide between Low-Level and High-Level Technology Adoption Based on Your Goals

Factor	*Key Question*	*If Score ≤3 → Actions for Low-Level Adoption*	*If Score ≥4 → Actions for High-Level Adoption*
Workforce Readiness	Do employees have digital fluency and confidence?	• Start with RPA, templates, or workflow automation in known processes. • Offer onboarding for digital tools (e.g., dashboards, task tracking, MS Power Automate, and Notion).	• Roll out advanced tools (e.g., AI assistants and predictive analytics) in high-capacity teams. • Build peer-led tech champion programs to support usage.
Use Case Complexity	Are current problems/data sets complex enough to benefit from advanced tech?	• Target repetitive/manual tasks (e.g., invoicing, scheduling, and data entry). • Focus on stability, error reduction, and time-saving automation.	• Apply AI/ML to forecasting, personalization, or quality control. • Use tools like digital twins, intelligent document processing, or real-time insights.
Digital Maturity	Do we already use basic digital tools effectively?	• Audit current tool usage (who uses what, and how). • Standardize low-level tools (RPA, dashboards, and shared platforms) across teams.	• Build on mature systems with new layers (e.g., AI on top of ERP/CRM). • Introduce integrated toolchains across business units.
Cross-Functional Readiness	Are we able to work across silos to implement and scale tech?	• Assign tech liaisons in each function to coordinate early efforts. • Use small pilots in single departments before scaling.	• Create joint innovation squads across business, IT, and ops. • Roll out scalable platforms with shared governance.

Factor	*Key Question*	*If Score ≤3 → Actions for Low-Level Adoption*	*If Score ≥4 → Actions for High-Level Adoption*
Change Momentum	Do we have recent success stories to build on?	• Share internal case studies of small wins to build confidence. • Celebrate improvements in efficiency or service.	• Use existing momentum to accelerate broader rollout. • Set bold transformation goals with visible exec sponsorship.

Step 3. Choose an Adoption Approach: Phased or All-in? Match Your Rollout to Your Organization's Capacity. This Step Helps You Decide Whether to Use a Sequential (Phased) or Concurrent (Broad) Rollout

Factor	*Key Question*	*If Score ≤3 → Actions for Sequential Rollout*	*If Score ≥4 → Actions for Concurrent Rollout*
Workforce Capacity	Can the workforce absorb multiple new tools or changes at once?	• Start with one tool or department. • Use Kaizen or sprint workshops to co-design adoption with teams. • Share early wins to build momentum.	• Prepare teams in advance with cross-training. • Assign digital champions to support adoption. • Launch multiple tools with shared onboarding and peer support.
Infrastructure Readiness	Can systems and data layers support integrated tech rollout?	• Upgrade legacy systems in stages. • Pilot tools where infrastructure is strongest.	• Ensure platform integration and data pipelines are stable. • Deploy enterprise-wide tools with API/ connectivity readiness checked.

(*Continued*)

Factor	*Key Question*	*If Score ≤3 → Actions for Sequential Rollout*	*If Score ≥4 → Actions for Concurrent Rollout*
Cross-Functional Alignment	Are departments ready to coordinate under shared timelines?	• Appoint adoption leads per function. • Hold joint planning but stagger implementation.	• Set up cross-functional working groups. • Run synchronized rollouts with clear governance and shared metrics.
Risk Tolerance	Can the organization handle disruption or failure during rollout?	• Limit initial scope to low-risk areas. • Prepare fallback plans and support channels.	• Accept short-term turbulence to gain long-term advantage. • Communicate clearly that speed is strategic, not reckless.
Leadership Commitment	Are leaders prepared to guide, resource, and course-correct in real time?	• Leaders should be highly visible in early phases. • Reinforce alignment through regular updates, storytelling, and celebrating wins.	• Leadership sets bold tone, aligns departments under one vision. • Weekly leadership pulse checks to respond to blockers quickly.

Step 4. How to Align Operations and Innovation: Balance Today's Efficiency with Tomorrow's Breakthroughs

Factor	*Key Question*	*If Score ≤3 → Focus on Core Operations (Efficiency)*	*If Score ≥4 → Focus on Exploratory Innovation*
Process Stability	Do current operations need more consistency, compliance, or risk reduction?	• Prioritize automation for routine tasks (e.g., RPA and dashboards). • Use structured SOPs and governance to reduce variation.	• Introduce flexibility for process experimentation. • Redesign workflows to support iterative testing and learning.

Factor	*Key Question*	*If Score ≤3 → Focus on Core Operations (Efficiency)*	*If Score ≥4 → Focus on Exploratory Innovation*
Innovation Readiness	Are there structures that allow for safe testing and risk-taking?	• Define "protected zones" for testing small changes without disruption. • Build early business cases in non-critical areas.	• Launch pilot teams for emerging tech (e.g., AI, digital twins). • Use dedicated innovation squads with isolated success metrics.
Cultural Orientation	Do employees feel safe experimenting and learning from failure?	• Build trust through transparent change messaging. • Reward compliance and stability during operational shifts.	• Promote "fail-fast" learning loops. • Publicly recognize experimentation and cross-functional contributions.
Leadership Priorities	Are leaders actively supporting both operational discipline and exploration?	• Align incentives around KPIs like cost, quality, and process adherence. • Communicate stability and control as success factors.	• Dedicate leadership bandwidth to exploration (e.g., 20% time and innovation councils). • Set stretch goals tied to future growth metrics.
Resource Allocation	Are budgets and talent aligned to enable both efficiency and innovation?	• Invest in productivity-enhancing tools and training. • Measure ROI on operational improvements before scaling.	• Allocate seed funding for high-risk and high-reward experiments. • Create budget space for cross-functional and exploratory initiatives.

Step 5. Monitor and Sustain the Transformation: Make Change Stick, Don't Let Adoption Fade Over Time

Factor	*Key Question*	*If Score ≤3 → Foundation Building (Control Plan and Stability)*	*If Score ≥4 → Sustained Adoption and Optimization*
Process Ownership	Are roles, responsibilities, and handovers clearly defined?	• Create a control plan: document ownership, actions, escalation paths. • Assign digital process owners by team/function.	• Build cross-functional accountability models. • Empower process owners to iterate and scale improvements.
Monitoring & Control	Is performance tracked to catch deviation early?	• Set clear KPIs tied to adoption (usage and value delivered). • Use simple tools like scorecards or checklists. • Set up alerts for drift or gaps.	• Implement real-time dashboards and alerts. • Use control charts or trend analysis to monitor performance over time.
Cultural Reinforcement	Is the team motivated to sustain digital habits and improvements?	• Celebrate small wins. • Reinforce change stories and role models. • Embed digital goals into team routines.	• Shift from compliance to ownership mindset. • Create rituals (e.g., innovation days and peer demos) to embed continuous improvement.
Training & Upskilling	Are we continuously growing capability as tools evolve?	• Schedule refresh training every 6–12 months. • Provide toolkits and just-in-time guides.	• Build internal learning communities. • Offer career paths linked to digital capability (e.g., automation expert and data translator).

Factor	*Key Question*	*If Score ≤3 → Foundation Building (Control Plan and Stability)*	*If Score ≥4 → Sustained Adoption and Optimization*
Governance & Adjustments	Do we regularly review outcomes and adapt where needed?	• Review KPIs quarterly. • Include digital adoption metrics in management reviews. • Create a cadence for reviewing and revising digital practices.	• Conduct digital audits to identify friction. • Refresh goals and measures as strategy and tools evolve.

TOO DIGITAL? THE FIGHT FOR DIGITAL HEALTHCARE

Dr. Nis Alstrup, MD,[1] was ready to revolutionize Danish healthcare. As a CEO and former surgeon, he saw the potential of online consultations – a decade before others did – a way for patients to meet their doctors remotely, cutting wait times and increasing access.

But when he pitched the idea to the authorities, their response stunned him:

"This is a bit too electronic for healthcare."

Too electronic? Isn't the world going digital? Nis was baffled. Telemedicine was already proving successful in other countries, yet in Denmark, bureaucracy clung to outdated methods.

Rather than backing down, Nis and his team pushed forward. They refined their approach, gathered data, educated decision-makers, and won over skeptics one step at a time. It wasn't easy, given the pace of regulatory change, but over time, the undeniable benefits of digital consultations became clear.[2]

AUGMENTED REALITY AND THE UNEXPECTED PR WIN

However, one of Nis' boldest moves, one that combined augmented reality with patient education, unexpectedly turned into a national debate.

Nis' team developed a plastic surgery augmentation app, allowing patients to visualize potential surgery outcomes using augmented reality. Users could take a photo of themselves, make adjustments, and see a realistic preview of what they might look like post-surgery. But it wasn't just a gimmick, as the app also provided serious medical information about the procedure, risks, and recovery process.

When Nis and his team launched an augmented reality app to help visualize breast surgery outcomes, the backlash came fast. Within days, critics labeled the app "grotesque," accusing the hospital of exploiting insecurity and glamorizing cosmetic surgery.

But the team's goal wasn't to push procedures; it was to provide younger women with accessible, visual tools to understand their options and risks. As Alstrup explained:

> The app was intended as a gimmick and part of our broader campaign focused on quality consultation and care around breast enlargement surgery. The initiative targeted younger women, who are difficult to reach through traditional channels.

The lesson? Innovation that challenges norms may spark criticism, but when guided by values like education, access, and transparency, it can also move the conversation forward. Leaders must be ready to listen, adjust, and stand by their intent when introducing bold technology to sensitive ecosystems.

Within days, the app shot to the top of the App Store, gaining 20,000 downloads on the first day. Then came the backlash. Politicians and media pundits criticized it as unethical, questioning whether a healthcare provider should promote cosmetic surgery in such an accessible way. Under mounting pressure, Nis decided to shut it down, and announced he was going to.

The result? Another 20,000 downloads overnight.

By the time the app was pulled, the hospital had received unprecedented publicity, far beyond what any traditional marketing campaign could have achieved.[3]

THE 2024 US PORT WORKERS' STRIKE – A MAJOR CRISIS AVERTED

In October 2024, the United States faced a massive port strike across 36 East and Gulf Coast ports. At its core was a breakdown in trust between leadership and the workforce. Port workers feared that automation would lead to widespread job losses, and leadership failed to address these fears convincingly. This fear, compounded by stalled wage negotiations, brought supply chains to a halt, costing the US economy billions of dollars weekly.

The result? The dockworkers didn't lose jobs; they gained better ones. Instead of processing transactions, they provided real advisory support. Instead of chasing data, they made decisions.

This crisis wasn't just about technology, it was about how leadership handled its introduction. The strike was a result of neglecting the essential *human* dimension of digital transformation: empathy, inclusion, and communication.

Once given responsibility for tactical automation at a financial institution, *I learned first-hand that automation wasn't about cutting jobs, it was about freeing people to do more inspiring work.* What I also learned was that for automation to succeed, our employees and frontline staff had to be part of the process, not just passive recipients of change.

We started with Kaizen events,[4] where teams mapped their daily workflows, pinpointing the most frustrating, repetitive tasks. Once mapped, we handed the improvement opportunity to our local automation expert, who would realize the savings.

One major benefit of training local automation experts who could code simple automations was that instead of waiting for a central robotic team to build solutions, employees on the ground learned how to automate their own tasks. They built unattended bots that ran processes independently, 24/7, cutting wait times and reducing process errors.

One team automated a complex process that previously spanned several departments and regions. By combining several independent digital capabilities, we eliminated dependency on legacy systems – no more expensive maintenance, no more manual workarounds.

And the products we need made it to your shelves.

LEADERSHIP LESSONS: WHY AUTOMATION FAILS OR SUCCEEDS

> It's almost like running a campaign, you have to get out on the trail, meet people where they are, listen to their concerns, and explain how you're going to address them. It requires a marathon level of empathy and humility that most struggle to sustain until the end.

This quote from my colleague Lucy captures exactly what was missing in the 2024 US port workers' strike. The crisis wasn't caused by automation itself, but by a failure of leadership, a failure to engage workers, communicate transparently, and create a structure where employees felt empowered, not threatened.

MAKE AUTOMATION A HUMAN-CENTRIC JOURNEY

Automation isn't about replacing workers; it's about eliminating repetitive, exhausting tasks so they can focus on more valuable work. When leaders fail to frame automation in this way, fear spreads.

In the case of the financial institution, we made automation about opportunity, and not loss. Employees weren't just informed about change, they were leading it, identifying the tasks they wanted to automate and training to take on more strategic roles. By contrast, the dockworkers at the port strike saw that they had no clear future and leadership never positioned automation as a path to better jobs. As a result, workers resisted and voted to strike. When automation is seen as a threat, resistance is inevitable.

COMMUNICATE EARLY AND KEEP THE DIALOGUE GOING

Silence breeds fear, and automation announcements without sustained communication cause panic. Dock company leadership should have engaged workers from the start, explaining the why, how, and what's next in a way that build trust.

Nis Alstrup faced this challenge when he introduced online consultations to the Danish healthcare system. The government rejected the idea, calling it "too digital," not because the technology was flawed, but because there was no clear understanding of how it fit into the existing system. His timing was also too early, as decision-makers lacked understanding of how a digital future could look. He eventually won stakeholders over through education and dialogue. The lesson is clear: if leaders and innovators don't communicate automation's purpose consistently, they leave a vacuum where fear and misinformation take over.

SHOW THE VALUE OF TECHNOLOGY

This is always true: *People trust what they can see.* Automation can't be a theoretical improvement; it must be demonstrated with real, tangible benefits.

Nis Alstrup's augmented reality app was a perfect example of this. It gave patients a tool to visualize surgery outcomes in a way that made sense to them. It was wildly successful, topping the App Store with tens of thousands of downloads. But when politicians and regulators misunderstood its purpose, it was shut down. Leaders should have built a stronger ecosystem of support to reinforce its value. In the port strike, leaders failed to prove how automation would improve safety and efficiency. Without proof, the workers assume the worst.

***

ADVANCED GUIDANCE FOR LEADERS TO APPLY TECHNOLOGY AT SCALE[5]

You've now worked through the core framework. What follows is more advanced. We'll explore how to manage technology across layers of your organization, what integration looks like over time, and how to lead through complexity without a clear roadmap. It ends with a real-world case that applies the full framework in a high-stakes setting.

Putting these ideas into practice takes time. It may take months or even years to align systems, teams, and technology.

If you've worked through the steps and built that foundation, the next section is for you.

We will look at how different levels of technology adoption affect your business and your people. Topics include adoption rates, cultural impact, and how to decide between sequential and concurrent rollouts. This section is for leaders who have built confident teams, are preparing for large technology shifts, or want to see what comes next.

LEVELS OF DIGITAL TECHNOLOGY ADOPTION

Digital technology adoption impacts not just processes but the people who drive them, from foundational tools that simplify tasks to advanced systems that unlock innovation. I argue that the role of strategic leaders is to ensure that technology empowers employees and enhances collaboration. The results? It creates growth, as well as being an attractive player in the market for both clients and employees. Each level of adoption provides opportunities to improve how people work, connect, and contribute to the organization's success.

LOWER LEVELS OF DIGITAL TECHNOLOGY

Lower levels of digital technology may seem like a steppingstone toward broader transformation, but they are, in fact, the foundation on which organizations build their digital capabilities. These tools, such as robotic process automation (RPA), basic analytics, and communication platforms, streamline operations, free up employee capacity, and set the stage for cultural change. Strategic leadership is vital at this stage to ensure that these technologies are deployed purposefully, aligning them with the organization's operational needs and people-focused goals.

Strategic leaders and Enablers play a pivotal role in ensuring that even simple digital technologies are adopted effectively, laying the foundation for long-term transformation. This begins with careful preparation, creating an environment where technology serves as a tool for empowerment rather than disruption. Leaders must identify the areas where these tools can have an immediate impact, such as automating repetitive tasks or streamlining processes.

However, successful implementation requires more than just identifying use cases; it demands clear communication about the purpose behind these changes. Leaders must set the tone by framing digital adoption as part of a broader strategy aimed at reducing workloads, improving accuracy, and ultimately delivering better outcomes for both employees and customers.

Infrastructure readiness is another critical consideration. Even seemingly straightforward technologies require alignment with existing systems and processes to function seamlessly. Leaders must ensure that their organization's digital and operational ecosystems are primed to integrate tools like automation software or communication platforms, preventing disruptions that might hinder adoption or create frustration. During my banking role, we trained local automation experts to own and maintain these processes, which meant we didn't have to wait for centralized IT support, allowing for smoother integration and faster adoption.

Lower-level digital technologies often have a direct impact on employees' daily workflows, which makes thoughtful engagement essential. Demonstrating the value of these tools through early, tangible results is key. For instance, when a regional logistics firm automated shipment tracking, it not only reduced errors but also allowed staff to focus on building customer relationships, outcomes that were widely celebrated across the organization. *Similarly, in our banking automation initiative, employees moved from transaction processing to client advisory, proving that automation wasn't a job killer, it was a career accelerator.*

At the same time, leaders must address the underlying concerns that automation often triggers, such as fear of job loss that can undermine adoption efforts, even at the lower levels of technology implementation. Transparent communication about how these tools enhance, rather than replace, employees' roles is essential to alleviating these anxieties. As an example, during Nis Alstrup's fight for digital healthcare, his biggest hurdle wasn't the technology; it was resistance from regulators who feared change. His approach, proving the benefits step by step, mirrors what leaders must do internally when introducing automation.

This is where proactive training programs become invaluable. By equipping employees with the skills to use collaborative platforms or basic analytics tools, leaders can ensure that workers feel empowered rather than threatened.

Empowerment extends beyond training. Leaders can involve employees in the implementation process itself, inviting their input on how new technologies are integrated into workflows. This not only increases engagement but also creates a sense of ownership, ensuring smoother transitions and higher levels of acceptance.

For leaders, aligning digital tools with measurable business goals is paramount. Lower-level technologies should be directly tied to addressing inefficiencies or enhancing productivity. Automating processes like payroll or inventory tracking often yields immediate cost savings while improving operational outcomes. For example, a customer service outsourcer reduced manual work related to invoicing by 20% through unattended automation of invoices. This directly reduced the invoice-to-cash cycle which then improved cash flows and at the same time eliminated late payments.

Equally important is that these technologies must be seen as building blocks for future advancements. Lower-level tools should be scalable and adaptable, creating a foundation for more sophisticated digital capabilities as the organization matures. This structural thinking, how small changes lay the groundwork for major transformation, is what enabled the automation journey to scale from simple bots to machine learning-powered decision-making. Similarly, Nis' augmented reality app didn't just create engagement; it exposed the broader potential of digital healthcare, showing how ecosystems evolve when digital capabilities are introduced at the right time.

Lower-level digital adoption is not just about immediate gains; it is about setting the stage for sustained growth and transformation. By thoughtfully preparing the organization, engaging employees, and aligning these technologies with strategic goals, leaders can create a foundation of trust and efficiency that paves the way for higher-level digital initiatives. In this way, even the simplest technologies become catalysts for meaningful change.

HIGHER LEVELS OF DIGITAL TECHNOLOGY

Higher levels of digital technology adoption are transformative, enabling organizations to unlock substantial business results while innovating at the forefront of their industries. These technologies are characterized by their complexity, capacity to disrupt markets, and ability to drive efficiency and innovation at scale. However, their implementation requires thoughtful leadership, careful integration, and a recognition of their differing impacts on business and social outcomes.

UNLOCKING BUSINESS RESULTS THROUGH ADVANCED TECHNOLOGIES

Strategic leaders must understand that higher levels of digital adoption primarily amplify business outcomes. By leveraging tools like advanced analytics, AI, and blockchain, organizations can enhance productivity, increase competitiveness, and open new revenue streams.

For example, higher levels of adoption include advanced analytics for predictive modeling, which allow businesses to anticipate market trends and make informed decisions. AI-powered systems, when integrated thoughtfully, optimize operations by identifying inefficiencies, forecasting demand, and tailoring customer experiences. According to research, companies that implemented predictive analytics in their supply chains experienced a 20–50% reduction in inventory holding costs – resulting in leaner operations, improved cash flow, and stronger cost efficiency.[6]

Blockchain, another high-level technology, adds transparency to supply chains, bolstering customer trust and driving higher brand loyalty. A seafood exporter implemented blockchain to trace their supply chain end-to-end, a move that enabled premium pricing due to heightened trust and alignment with sustainability-focused buyers.

Similarly, in Nis Alstrup's augmented reality project, digital technology was used not just to optimize operations, but to enhance customer engagement. The AR app allowed patients to visualize surgery outcomes, merging advanced technology with consumer trust and empower potential patients with a better foundation for decision-making. However, without ecosystem alignment, including regulators and public perception, the technology faced backlash. This demonstrates that even high-level digital solutions require careful integration with broader business and societal structures to succeed.

INNOVATION IN EXPLORATION UNITS

The experimental use of high-level digital technologies thrives in innovation units where organizations focus on future opportunities rather than current operational efficiencies. Unlike operational units, which rely on technology for stability and optimization, innovation units allow for experimentation with complex systems that might feel disruptive in established settings.

For instance, digital twins, a virtual replication of physical products and processes, enable organizations to test performance scenarios before manufacturing begins. This approach, particularly used in high-stakes industries like engineering, reduces errors and accelerates innovation cycles.

In the example I gave from my work as a process management lead, automation was initially introduced at a smaller scale before expanding. Instead of forcing immediate adoption across all departments, we trained local automation experts who gradually built adoption from within. This created a structured approach that prevented disruption while proving the value of automation.

BALANCING IMPACTS ON SOCIAL AND BUSINESS OUTCOMES

You should be aware that while higher levels of digital technology adoption drive substantial business outcomes, they may not yield equivalent social benefits in the short term. Employee apprehension around job security, particularly from AI and automation, can create internal friction. In industries like healthcare, digital adoption has increased efficiency in patient record management but introduced concerns about depersonalization of care.

To mitigate these challenges, leaders should focus on gradual, sequential adoption of high-level technologies. Fast, concurrent implementation can overwhelm employees, leading to resistance and a potential loss of organizational trust. As discussed above, the US port workers' strike illustrated this failure – automation was perceived as a sudden, imposed change, fueling resistance. Had leadership introduced automation in phases, framed around job evolution rather than elimination, workers may have embraced rather than fought the transformation.

By contrast, in our financial automation case, employees were given ownership of automation initiatives. Rather than feeling displaced, they were upskilled and empowered, proving that when technology adoption is transparent and structured, it enhances both business and social outcomes.

LEADERSHIP FOR HIGH-LEVEL ADOPTION

Implementing advanced digital technologies is not just a matter of technical upgrades or financial investment; it requires a profound shift in how organizations operate and innovate. At the heart of this transformation lies strategic leadership. Leaders must balance the technical, cultural, and organizational demands of high-level digital adoption, ensuring it becomes a source of sustainable growth rather than disruption or resistance.

High-level digital adoption thrives in an environment that values adaptability, experimentation, and learning. Strategic leaders must actively cultivate a culture that supports these traits.

FOSTERING INNOVATION IN EXPLORATORY UNITS

Exploratory units are ideal for testing advanced technologies like AI, IoT, or blockchain without jeopardizing core operations. Leaders can position these units as innovation hubs, allowing teams to experiment, fail, and iterate in a low-risk environment. For instance, a major engineering firm introduced a digital twin platform within its exploratory division, enabling rapid prototyping and reducing product development cycles by 25%.

Nis' push for online consultations was ahead of its time. While the government initially resisted, his team treated it as an exploratory initiative, iterating and proving its effectiveness until it became the new standard. Exploratory approaches allow organizations to test innovation without the immediate constraints of legacy systems and traditional resistance.

EMBEDDING ADAPTABILITY ACROSS THE ORGANIZATION

Beyond exploratory units, adaptability must permeate the organization. Leaders can promote cross-functional collaboration by breaking down silos and encouraging shared learning. For example, pairing IT teams with product development units can drive more effective digital integration.

In my case, the success of automation wasn't just in the technology, it was in the structure we created around it. Local automation experts weren't just trained to use new tools; they became part of a decentralized structure that allowed automation to scale organically. This approach built adaptability directly into the organization's fabric, preventing the rigidity that often kills digital transformation.

DEPLOYING TECHNOLOGY: SEQUENTIAL VS. CONCURRENT ADOPTION

How technology is deployed determines how people react. This is a critical strategic decision, with significant dependencies in communication, training, and infrastructure readiness.

SEQUENTIAL APPROACH: BUILDING STABILITY AND TRUST

The sequential approach involves implementing digital technologies in phases, starting with simpler tools and progressing to more advanced systems over time. This method allows employees to adjust incrementally, reducing resistance and minimizing disruptions.

Research shows[7] *that sequential adoption is particularly effective for fostering social outcomes, as employees are given time to adapt and build trust in new tools.*

We started with basic automation in routine processes, proving small wins before expanding into machine learning-powered decision-making. This step-by-step approach prevented resistance and allowed employees to see how automation enhanced their work rather than threatened it.

For Nis and his plans for digital healthcare, a sequential model was used, first proving online consultations, then advocating for their expansion across the system. His biggest challenge? Overcoming initial skepticism from regulators who resisted change without seeing early-stage proof points.

CONCURRENT APPROACH: ACCELERATING TRANSFORMATION

The concurrent approach involves implementing multiple technologies simultaneously across the organization. This method is often used when rapid transformation is necessary to remain competitive or meet urgent business objectives.

Concurrent adoption tends to drive significant business results, particularly in exploration units where the focus is on innovation and future growth.

If we revisit the financial automation case, concurrent adoption was possible because employees were already trained in automation, and the infrastructure supported rapid scaling. By contrast, the port strike highlighted the dangers of uncoordinated, large-scale automation – without the right groundwork, resistance became inevitable.

For concurrent adoption to succeed, leaders must prepare for the complexities of large-scale implementation, including potential resistance from employees and challenges in aligning different technologies. This approach is most effective in digitally mature organizations where employees are comfortable working with advanced tools and where infrastructure supports seamless integration.

CHOOSING THE RIGHT APPROACH

The choice between sequential and concurrent adoption depends on several factors:

- **Organizational Readiness**: Sequential adoption suits organizations with low digital maturity or significant employee apprehension. Concurrent adoption is better for organizations with a culture of adaptability and robust digital infrastructure.
- **Desired Outcomes**: Sequential adoption aligns well with improving social outcomes, such as employee satisfaction and trust. Concurrent adoption is ideal for achieving rapid business impact and innovation.
- **Technological Complexity**: More complex technologies often benefit from a sequential approach, while simpler tools may be implemented concurrently without overwhelming employees.

  Strategic leaders must assess their organization's unique context and tailor their approach accordingly. Whether implementing technology step-by-step or all at once, the focus should remain on aligning these tools with both operational goals and employee well-being.

By striking this balance, leaders can ensure a smoother adoption process and maximize the impact of digital transformation.

LEADERSHIP AS THE ENABLER OF DIGITAL ADOPTION

Digital transformation isn't only about technology, it's about leadership. Tools alone don't drive change; how leaders introduce, communicate, and integrate them determines success or failure.

The US port workers' strike proved what happens when automation is framed as a cost-cutting measure instead of an opportunity. Workers resisted because leadership failed to show them a future. In contrast, we successfully introduced automation by involving employees directly in the process, training them proactively for new roles, and integrating automation specialists within teams to foster ownership and smooth adoption.

VISION BEFORE EXECUTION

Technology must serve a clear business and workforce goal. Without alignment, resistance grows. Nis' push for online consultations was blocked not because of the technology, but because leadership failed to secure early buy-in from regulators. Visionary leaders connect technology to strategy and communicate its benefits before opposition forms.

MANAGING FEAR AND RESISTANCE

Employees fear job loss, not automation itself. Leaders must engage them early, listen, and ensure technology enhances roles instead of eliminating them. In my experience leading automation initiatives, it is possible to avoid backlash by letting employees identify automation opportunities through process improvement events and training local automation experts to manage bots themselves.

The port strike was just the opposite – workers were left out of the process, leading to conflict, an eventual strike vote, and ports shut down. Had leadership introduced automation gradually and tied it to upskilling, this coast-to-coast resistance might have been avoided.

When you actively use digital tools, you signal that change is collective, not imposed. Nis' augmented reality app was a spectacular breakthrough, one that sparked national attention. While external resistance ultimately blocked its continuation, the initiative showed what's possible when visionary leadership meets real-world complexity.

EMPOWER, DON'T REPLACE

I'll write that again for emphasis: **Empower, don't replace.** The port strike happened because leadership failed to reassure workers about their future. In contrast, digital leaders protect jobs during transitions, provide upskilling, and ensure employees have a role in automation. What I took from the banking sector was that automation didn't cut jobs, it moved employees into higher-value roles, proving that digital transformation can be an opportunity, not a threat.

APPLYING OUR FRAMEWORK

Now let's examine how the five steps apply to an early-stage digital adoption example, Nis Alstrup's initiative with augmented reality and digital healthcare consultations. This case illustrates how complex digital transformations can encounter unforeseen obstacles, highlighting why applying a structured adoption framework early is essential, even when precise outcomes seem unpredictable (Figure 7.2).

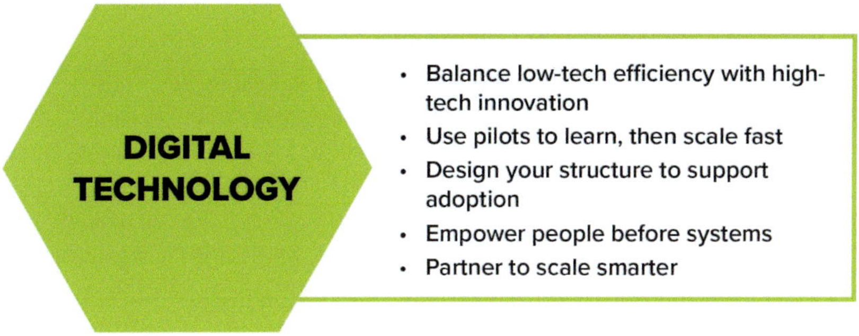

Figure 7.2 Digital Technology Enabler

Nis Alstrup pioneered digital healthcare in Denmark, advocating early for online consultations to improve patient access. Initial resistance from regulators, who saw digital healthcare as "too digital," slowed adoption despite proven international successes. Later, Nis launched an augmented reality app enabling patients to visualize cosmetic surgery outcomes, achieving immediate popularity but triggering ethical debates. Under political and media pressure, Nis withdrew the app, unintentionally amplifying public attention.

Let's walk through the framework to see how Nis' initiative might have unfolded differently.

STEP 1: ASSESS READINESS

Factor	*Score (1–5)*	*Insight for Executives*
Workforce Readiness	2	Healthcare teams were hesitant, not because they lacked skills, but because digital tools were unfamiliar. Early dialogue and training were planned to reduce uncertainty and upskill the workforce.
Infrastructure Readiness	4	Denmark had robust digital infrastructure ready to go. Nis was right to trust the tech foundation, his challenge lay elsewhere.
Cultural Readiness	2	Regulators weren't ready, labeling Nis's vision "too digital." Understanding cultural barriers upfront could have shifted Nis's strategy from persuasion to collaboration sooner.

(*Continued*)

Factor	*Score (1–5)*	*Insight for Executives*
Leadership Alignment	3	Leaders supported digitization, but underestimated how deep skepticism ran. Stronger alignment through early pilots and internal advocacy might have eased concerns.
Market Speed	3	Telemedicine was advancing globally, creating moderate pressure. Nis had timing on his side, but not patience; taking slower initial steps might have avoided backlash.

What Can You Learn from Nis' Experience?

As a leader, it's critical to assess your organization's readiness honestly. Nis was visionary but underestimating cultural and workforce readiness meant setbacks. By proactively evaluating these factors, you'll not only anticipate challenges, but you'll also inspire your team by making them integral to the transformation journey.

STEP 2: SELECT THE ADOPTION LEVEL

Factor	*Score (1–5)*	*Insight for Executives*
Workforce Readiness	2	Medical teams were highly skilled clinically, but digital tools required gradual introduction. Nis' vision was pioneering, and he aimed high, highlighting the importance of progressive digital fluency.
Use Case Complexity	4	Nis selected complex, transformative technology (augmented reality) that offered clear patient value and education; bold, yet inherently challenging to regulators and practitioners unfamiliar with digital innovation.
Digital Maturity	3	Denmark's healthcare system had basic digital maturity, enough to support Nis' ideas technically, yet cultural integration was still emerging. Leveraging existing telemedicine foundations might have meant smoother adoption.
Cross-Functional Readiness	2	Nis navigated silos between healthcare providers, tech teams, and regulators. His relentless advocacy broke barriers but revealed how early-stage cross-functional alignment dramatically influences success.

(*Continued*)

Factor	*Score (1–5)*	*Insight for Executives*
Change Momentum	3	Nis generated significant public momentum and enthusiasm around digital health innovations, yet internally, the cultural shift was just beginning. Celebrating small early wins could have further accelerated buy-in.

What Can You Learn from Nis' Bold Move?

Nis courageously aimed for a groundbreaking transformation, selecting advanced digital tools to revolutionize healthcare, a truly visionary move. As a leader, your role is to balance ambitious innovation with careful alignment of your organization's capability and readiness. Nis' remarkable initiative underscores the value of introducing digital tools progressively, matching complexity with confidence to ensure lasting success.

STEP 3: CHOOSE AN ADOPTION APPROACH

Factor	*Score (1–5)*	*Insight for Executives*
Workforce Capacity	2	Medical professionals were new to this type of digital engagement. A carefully scoped pilot, focused on one use case like virtual consultations, could have served as a bridge between ambition and adoption while being an example for regulators.
Infrastructure Readiness	4	The systems were ready, what needed more attention was helping people feel confident using them.
Cross-Functional Alignment	2	Medical, regulatory, and IT teams weren't moving together. Structured pilots would have created early alignment and raised potential conflicts before scale.
Risk Tolerance	2	Nis operated in a high-accountability environment where skepticism was natural. A phased rollout would have helped regulators see the benefits early, minimizing perceived risk.
Leadership Commitment	4	Nis showed extraordinary commitment. The key challenge was translating that vision into shared momentum by including hesitant stakeholders in shaping the path forward.

What Can You Learn from Nis' Digital Path?

Choosing the right approach is not about slowing down vision, it's about sequencing ambition so others can follow. Nis' efforts remind us that even with strong leadership and technical readiness, the adoption journey depends on people feeling involved and safe. As a leader, your task is to design trust-building moments, pilots, early involvement, visible learning, that make big ideas feel approachable. That's how bold innovation becomes real progress.

STEP 4: ALIGN OPERATIONS WITH FUTURE INNOVATION

Factor	*Score (1–5)*	*Insight for Executives*
Process Stability	4	Core healthcare operations were stable. Digital innovations needed to complement, not disrupt, existing workflows.
Innovation Readiness	2	Structures for testing and scaling innovation were limited. Formal pilot mechanisms would have supported faster learning.
Cultural Orientation	2	There was openness from some, but strong skepticism from others, especially regulators. Structured engagement was needed to build psychological safety.
Leadership Priorities	4	Innovation was a clear priority. Greater integration of stakeholder concerns could have strengthened execution.
Resource Allocation	3	Resources were invested in technology, but more could have supported engagement, education, and proof-of-concept pilots.

What Can You Learn from Nis' Strategic Balance?

Nis pushed the boundaries of what was possible, balancing vision with operational realities. His experience shows that bold innovation can coexist with stability, when pilots are used to test, build trust, and gradually embed change. As a leader, your job is to connect today's workflows with tomorrow's ideas without creating disruption. When innovation aligns with daily operations, transformation sticks.

Had Nis' digital initiatives received full regulatory support, the next challenge would have been sustaining momentum across the healthcare system. Sustaining innovation isn't just about keeping the technology running, it's about embedding it into the way people work, learn, and lead. For initiatives like AR and digital consultations to stick, leaders must prepare the ground early: define ownership, measure what matters, build internal champions, and create space for continuous learning. Here's what that could have looked like.

STEP 5: MONITOR AND SUSTAIN

Factor	*Score (1–5)*	*Examples of What Great Looks Like*
Process Ownership	4	Assign ownership early, appoint digital leads within clinical teams to maintain, adapt, and champion the tools post-launch.
Monitoring and Control	5	Build real-time dashboards that track adoption, user experience, clinical outcomes, and feedback. Include KPIs like consultation completion rates, patient satisfaction, and engagement trends.
Cultural Reinforcement	4	Celebrate early adopters, share internal success stories, and spotlight staff who evolve their practice with digital tools. Make digital wins visible.
Training and Upskilling	4	Roll out digital literacy training across all roles – clinicians, support staff, and administrators. Pair training with practical, scenario-based learning.
Governance and Adjustments	5	Establish a cross-sector digital health panel with regulators, patient groups, and tech partners. Conduct quarterly reviews to iterate and align with evolving expectations.

What Can You Learn from This?

Today, the efforts from Nis have been implemented by the government. The hospital are using their app for various purposes. His impact and work paid off years later, and it was his leadership and vision that created the foundation, not luck. Strong KPIs, clear ownership, regular check-ins, and ongoing learning have turned a breakthrough into the new normal.

LOOK AROUND YOU!

Look around now, digital consultations are everywhere. AR is becoming standard in surgical planning and patient education. Nis was ready. The system and regulators weren't.

When he introduced virtual consultations, people said it was "too digital." When he launched an AR app to help patients make informed decisions, it went viral and then got shut down. It worked and potential patients wanted it. It just didn't fit the time.

That's what this chapter was really about.

Not dashboards or adoption plans, but technology as an enabler for making a positive impact. The quiet, exhausting work of pushing something new into a system that isn't ready. Nis saw the future, and he moved before it was popular. And he left behind a roadmap for the rest of us.

If you're leading with technology, you're not managing a rollout, you're changing how people think, decide, and act. That's where real work begins.

In the following chapter we leave behind friction and start to move. This is where the Enablers align. The right people step up. Pilots become systems. Leadership turns momentum into transformation. You've seen how to start, now I will show you how to make it last.

NOTES

1 Nis Alstrup, a medical doctor specializing in healthcare innovation and digital transformation. Nis co-founded and scaled a private hospital chain in Denmark and successfully sold it. Nis currently serves on numerous boards and engages in consulting work.
2 Nis Alstrup, expert interview conducted by Kristian Schlosser in 2025. Provided key insights on leadership strategies for integrating technological advancements in medical practice, highlighting practical approaches to balancing patient care with operational efficiency.
3 Interview with Dr. Nis Alstrup, conducted by Kristian Schlosser in 2025 for this book project. The conversation explored the development, public response, and eventual shutdown of the augmented reality app designed for patient education in plastic surgery.
4 A kaizen event, also known as a kaizen blitz or kaizen activity, is a process improvement exercise performed by a team of cross functional employees in a limited timeframe, usually one to five days.
5 The research and analysis for this topic was done together with two of my advisors, Prof. Tatjana Volkova and Prof. Aivars Spilbergs. The section is based on years of research and analysis and you can find more information on docschlosser.com
6 Konstantin Babenko, "30% Less Overstock and Stockouts? How Predictive Analytics Helps Optimize Inventory for SMBs and Enterprises," LinkedIn Articles, September 30, 2024. Summary includes findings from a 2022 McKinsey report on inventory cost reduction.
7 Empirical evidence from my doctoral research highlights that sequential adoption of digital technologies, from simpler tools to advanced systems, significantly enhances social outcomes, as phased implementation allows employees adequate time to adapt and build trust in new tools.

Chapter 8

Transforming Your Enablers

Getting It Right

In this chapter, I'll show you exactly how my team and I, working on a digital transformation project in the offshore energy sector – navigated a network of complex stakeholders in a highly regulated environment to achieve real, measurable results. And how you can, too. This digital transformation didn't happen by luck; it happened through thoughtful teamwork across time zones and cultures. It demonstrates how the use of the Enablers we've explored throughout this book is creating impact.

The Transformation Enabler will answer the question: How will you transform your business to create lasting positive impact from your discoveries? Not to take part, but to lead the transformation! This Enabler serves as the bridge between operations and future business exploration (Figure 8.1).

Get it wrong, and even brilliant innovations collapse under complexity, resistance, or misalignment. Get it right, and you'll turn ideas into real-world impact, not just within your company, but across your entire ecosystem.

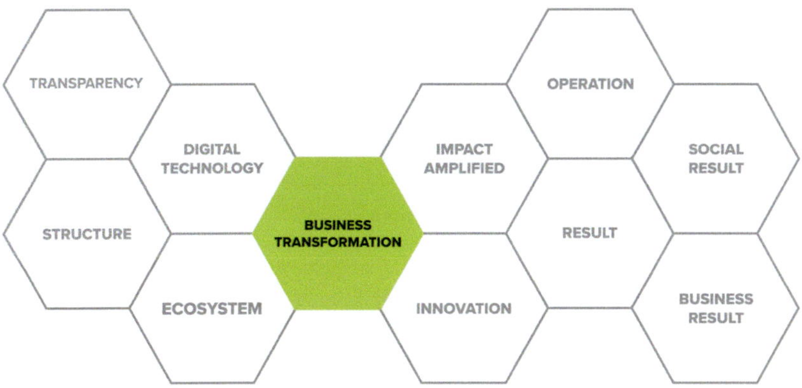

Figure 8.1 Our Business Transformation

DOI: 10.4324/9781003638551-9

I'll also introduce the Transformation Success Framework, a practical, research-backed tool developed through first-hand experience. You'll discover how to make critical decisions when moving from exploration to operations: knowing when to integrate, when to spin out, and when to pause. You'll also learn how to drive business outcomes while making a genuine social impact and how to avoid seven common pitfalls that sabotage even the best-planned transformations.

To ground this framework in reality, I'll share two transformations, one digital and one-non-digital, I've personally led. I have selected these two as they demonstrate that this works even in completely different sectors, one with a large budget, and one with no budget, and in a different cultural setting with vastly different metrics:

- A digital operations transformation in Guyana, radically enhancing offshore efficiency. Context: High-risk, high-cost oil and gas environment complex, manual processes and a desire to improve performance while maintaining the highest safety standards, all within a conservative sector! Resistance was even higher in Guyana due to previous failed digital rollouts.
- A global customer service turnaround, rescuing a critical client relationship from the brink. Context: Low-margin, high-pressure outsourcing environment with skyrocketing attrition, collapsing KPIs, and a major client threatening to walk. No transformation budget, limited time, and a burned-out workforce with zero trust in existing leadership to make the needed changes.

After exploring these real-world stories, we'll zoom in and analyze one case step-by-step, applying the framework in detail. This practical exercise will clearly show you how the framework components come together in the real world, and how you can adapt them to your own challenges.

Let's begin with the framework itself.

SUCCESS FACTOR 1: CLARITY OF PURPOSE

How to Do It	• Write one sentence clearly stating the business outcome your transformation must achieve. • Write one sentence clearly stating the social impact outcome your transformation must achieve. • Test clarity: Ask three frontline employees separately to explain the transformation's purpose. If answers differ, rewrite and communicate again.
What Success Looks Like	• Every leadership team member consistently states both outcomes. • Frontline employees clearly articulate the transformation's purpose.

Example	As you will learn through the Guyana digitalization project: Outcomes were clear: • Business: digitize workflows for offshore efficiency. • Social: enhance offshore safety and allow engineers and supervisors to focus on their actual job rather than doing repetitive tasks. All teams consistently stated these outcomes.

SUCCESS FACTOR 2: EMPOWERED AND ENGAGED PEOPLE

How to Do It	• Directly involve employees: gather input from frontline teams on what they need to succeed. • Immediately provide training and tools addressing these identified needs. • Establish feedback channels to regularly capture and act on employee insights during the transformation.
What Success Looks Like	• Employees proactively suggest improvements without prompting. • Frontline teams consistently demonstrate confidence using new systems or processes.
Example	GlobalCX Transformation: Frontline employees were actively included via interviews and focus groups and through this they shaped their own training. The "Lagoon" program[1] increased morale, productivity, and reduced staff turnover.

SUCCESS FACTOR 3: EFFECTIVE GOVERNANCE AND DECISION-MAKING

How to Do It	• Clearly define and communicate roles: Who decides, who leads, and who's accountable for each decision. • Create a simple decision-making framework (RACI or similar) and distribute widely. • Regularly review and refine decisions based on frontline feedback and results.
What Success Looks Like	• Decisions occur swiftly without repeated escalations. • Employees have the mandate to make decisions and understand the consequences of not making a decision. • Establish qualitative and quantitative indicators.

(*Continued*)

Example	Guyana digitalization project: Roles clearly defined through a RACI matrix. Success criteria were established for (1) early success and (2) sustained success. Early success criteria included, but were not limited to: 1. Reduced admin hours on the critical path. 2. Management of Change improved speed. 3. End user satisfaction measured via NPS. "Early success" was evaluated during a "Stage gate review," where project leads and project sponsors evaluated if the project had satisfied all success criteria. Once agreed, the gate was open and the project team continued to deploy the system.

SUCCESS FACTOR 4: CULTURAL AND STRUCTURAL ALIGNMENT

How to Do It	Culture: • Clearly define three essential behaviors critical to achieving your transformation (e.g., openly sharing knowledge, proactively collaborating between teams, rapidly testing, and adapting). • Explicitly communicate and repeatedly reinforce these behaviors through daily management meetings, employee onboarding, and leadership communication. Structure: • Immediately adjust organizational structures (such as team compositions, reporting lines, and incentive programs) to explicitly reward and enable these behaviors. • Identify and remove structural barriers (e.g., performance metrics rewarding individual effort over team results and departmental silos blocking information flow) that undermine desired behaviors.
What Success Looks Like	• Employees consistently practice and visibly demonstrate the defined behaviors in daily work (e.g., proactively sharing lessons without prompting and solving problems across team boundaries). • New hires quickly adopt these behaviors as "the norm" because onboarding and leadership consistently reinforce them. • Teams independently suggest and implement adjustments to structures or processes that further support these behaviors.
Example	GlobalCX Transformation: Clearly established behaviors like peer-to-peer mentoring, daily frontline feedback loops, and cross-team collaboration. Immediately redesigned team structures, reporting lines and incentives to directly reward and reinforce these behaviors, creating rapid, and lasting cultural change.

SUCCESS FACTOR 5: TECHNOLOGY AND TOOLS AS ENABLERS

How to Do It	• Clearly define the specific business problem the technology solves (e.g., eliminate manual paperwork, reduce downtime, and improve customer response times). • Use the Digital Technology Decision Framework: decide if the technology will be adopted widely at once (concurrent deployment) or gradually, team by team (sequential deployment). • Provide immediate hands-on training directly linked to employees' daily tasks, with real examples, not generic demos.
What Success Looks Like	• Employees confidently and routinely use new tools to simplify or enhance their work (e.g., reduced manual paperwork and faster issue resolution). • Clear, measurable improvement in daily tasks and results (e.g., increased efficiency and reduced downtime). • Employees actively suggest new ways to expand or enhance technology use, demonstrating ownership.
Example *(full case study on the following page)*	Guyana digitalization project: Deployed RigFlow™ sequentially with tailored, hands-on training for drillers and engineers. Teams quickly adopted the system, significantly reducing manual processes and improving real-time communication. The sequential approach allowed the project team to adjust the approach, and after deploying on the first unit, the project team received requests from other units that they wanted to be next – a remarkable achievement and application of the Enablers and the four previous success factors.

SUCCESS FACTOR 6: SUSTAINABILITY

How to Do It	• Provide immediate and ongoing post-deployment support by assigning dedicated operational and technical experts to proactively assist end users with daily workflow issues. • Officially embed new processes into your organization's Standard Operating Procedures (SOPs) to ensure long-term adoption.
What Success Looks Like	• Employees confidently and consistently use new processes or systems long after initial rollout. • End users independently access support when issues arise, swiftly resolving problems and preventing reversion to old ways. • Teams proactively suggest improvements and expansions, signaling deep-rooted adoption.
Example *(full case on the following page)*	GlobalCX Transformation: Immediate availability of operational and technical experts helped frontline employees permanently adopt new processes. SOPs formally reinforced these processes, ensuring sustained, measurable success.

THE GUYANA DIGITALIZATION PROJECT: A TRANSFORMATIONAL SUCCESS STORY

The Challenge: Moving from Manual to Digital

Off the coast of Guyana, home to some of the world's largest untapped oil reserves, a groundbreaking digital transformation unfolded. In this high-stakes environment, drilling operations require absolute precision, efficiency, and adaptability. Yet offshore teams initially relied heavily on paper-based manual processes including various email chains to run offshore operations.

At the center of this initiative were RigFlow™ and RigBridge™, innovative digital tools designed to revolutionize how offshore and onshore teams collaborate, planning phases, and operational execution. The journey began with the deployment of these systems on the first offshore drillship – one of five in Guyana – where teams worked tirelessly to replace traditional workflows with an integrated, digital-first approach. These tools provided a centralized platform for managing operations, giving teams real-time access to live procedures, updates, and collaboration spaces. This was no ordinary rollout; it was a systemic transformation that redefined how people worked and interacted.

A major challenge, and a critical factor in the project's success, was the transition from manual, paper-based workflows to fully digital processes. Before RigFlow™, offshore teams relied heavily on paper forms, ring binders, and email chains to document and communicate procedures. These methods were time-consuming, manual, and it would take time to print, distribute, and review paper-based instructions. The software improved these process steps by providing a centralized, digital hub for all procedural information. As one driller described, "It's so much easier to thumb through digital workflows than flipping through binders to find the next step or follow the procedure." This shift not only streamlined day-to-day operations but also significantly reduced the administrative burden on drillers and engineers, freeing them to focus on planning and execution.

However, the transition to these digital tools wasn't just about technology; it was about people. To sustain the transformation, the engineering company invested heavily in onshore and offshore training. Digital coaches worked directly with teams onboard the first drillship for eight weeks, offering hands-on support to ensure that every member of the crew understood and could effectively use the new tools. This coaching extended beyond initial training, emphasizing cross-training to build long-term capability and ensure knowledge transfer among new staff. The training wasn't limited to technical skills either; it also fostered a mindset shift. Teams were encouraged to embrace the new digital workflows, recognizing the long-term benefits of increased efficiency, transparency, and collaboration.

As the project progressed, sustaining the transformation became a priority. Transitioning from exploration to core operations required a deliberate effort to capture lessons learned and institutionalize best practices. Engineers and offshore teams were empowered to provide direct feedback, which was immediately integrated into updated procedures. This iterative approach ensured that the tools evolved alongside the organization's needs, creating a cycle of continuous improvement. As one engineer put it, "The direct and instantaneous feedback from the teams offshore, and the ability to implement that feedback into procedures, makes the digital way of working a perfect solution."

Another key to sustaining the transformation was the cultural adoption of the tools. By democratizing access to procedural information and encouraging collaboration across rigs, the system fostered a sense of ownership and accountability among team members. This cultural shift was transformative in its own right. For the first time, teams on different rigs could easily compare procedures, identify discrepancies, and harmonize processes. This cross-rig collaboration not only improved consistency but also created a shared commitment to finding the "one best way" of doing things.

Leadership also played a vital role in transitioning the initiative into core operations. The decision to deploy the digital system on multiple rigs demonstrated a commitment to scaling the innovation across the organization. Leaders ensured that resources were allocated to support the transformation, while actively communicating the strategic importance of the tools.

The results of the Guyana digitalization project were nothing short of extraordinary. The system not only streamlined communication and planning but also created new capabilities for scaling innovation. Teams no longer had to rely on fragmented, paper-based processes. Instead, they operated with a centralized system that provided real-time visibility and feedback. This transformation not only improved operational efficiency but also positioned the organization to disrupt the market with a more agile and collaborative approach.

As the project transitioned fully into core operations, its success became a blueprint for future transformations. By investing in training, prioritizing cultural adoption, and fostering continuous improvement, the partners demonstrated how exploration findings could be effectively scaled into sustainable, revenue-generating capabilities. The Guyana Digitalization Project stands as a testament to the power of leadership, innovation, and teamwork in driving meaningful change, an inspiring example for any leader looking to transform their organization.

KEY TAKEAWAYS:

1. **Transformation Requires Strong Leadership and Innovative Vision**
   - Leaders must clearly articulate the purpose and benefits of the transformation while maintaining a consistent vision. In the

Guyana project, leadership actively communicated the value of the system, securing buy-in from all levels of the organization.
- Leaders who embrace a collaborative and inclusive approach, as demonstrated here, enable smoother adoption of transformative initiatives.

2. **Invest in People, Not Just Technology**
    - Training is as critical as the technology itself. The hands-on coaching provided to teams on board the first drillship ensured that employees were equipped to embrace new workflows confidently and sustainably.
    - Cross-training and knowledge sharing among staff ensured continuity and resilience, enabling long-term success.
3. **Empower Teams to Own the Transformation**
    - By democratizing access to tools and information, the new digital workflows fostered accountability and engagement across offshore and onshore teams. Empowering employees to give feedback and actively contribute to procedural improvements created a sense of ownership.
    - The transformation shifted organizational culture toward continuous improvement, setting a foundation for future innovation.
4. **Sustainability Hinges on Feedback Loops and Iteration**
    - The iterative process of gathering feedback from offshore teams and immediately integrating it into procedures ensured continuous improvement. This approach allowed the tools to evolve alongside the organization's operational needs.
    - Leaders must establish mechanisms to capture lessons learned and ensure those insights are applied to sustain and scale innovation.
5. **Transitioning Exploration to Operations is a Deliberate Process**
    - The success of the system was not an accident, it was the result of deliberate planning, resource allocation, and phased implementation. Leaders must carefully evaluate whether innovations are ready to integrate, spin out, or remain in development.
    - Transitioning from exploration to core operations requires not only technical readiness but also cultural alignment and strategic prioritization.

6. **Collaboration is the Catalyst for Success**
   - The cultural shift toward cross-rig collaboration in the Guyana project demonstrates how transformation can break down silos and foster a unified approach to problem-solving. Leaders should actively encourage collaboration within their teams and with external partners to amplify results.
7. **Using Digitalization for a Strategic Advantage**
   - While RigFlow™ streamlined processes and reduced inefficiencies, its greatest value was enabling real-time decision-making and visibility across operations. Leaders should view digital tools as enablers of strategic agility, not just operational upgrades.
   - The project also positioned the partners to set new industry benchmarks, highlighting how successful transformations can disrupt markets and secure competitive advantage.
8. **Celebrate Wins and Build Momentum**
   - Positive feedback, such as that from the company president, demonstrated the importance of acknowledging success and celebrating progress. Recognizing and rewarding team efforts creates momentum and fosters a culture of transformation readiness.

FROM CRISIS TO GLOBAL EXCELLENCE: THE TRANSFORMATIONAL JOURNEY OF GLOBALCX

In the bustling, high-pressure world of global customer service, success hinges on precision, efficiency, and seamless coordination. For GlobalCX, a leader in marketing communications and customer experience outsourcing, the stakes had never been higher. Their most prominent client, KParkStay, a groundbreaking platform reshaping the hospitality industry, was on the verge of terminating its contract. With over 1,000 agents dedicated to KParkStay's customer experience and KPIs spiraling downward, GlobalCX faced not just a financial crisis but an existential threat. Employee turnover skyrocketed to an alarming 140%, with over 500 employees leaving in a single year, while customer satisfaction plummeted. The situation demanded urgent and radical change.

By 2018, after two years of failed solutions, GlobalCX's senior management made a bold decision: they hired a consultant as the new "Head of Transformation." This role was not merely symbolic; it signaled a shift in how the organization would tackle its challenges. With a mandate to rebuild the company's relationship with KParkStay, reduce attrition, and create a sustainable future, the transformation journey began.

TRANSFORMATION ROOTED IN PEOPLE: A PEOPLE-CENTRIC TOOLBOX

The crisis at GlobalCX was not simply about metrics; it was about people. Behind every low KPI and missed target was an employee struggling with confidence, unclear expectations, or insufficient support. While GlobalCX had mountains of data and dashboards, the transformation team chose a different path. They placed the focus on the individuals driving the operation. Success would come not from managing numbers but empowering people.

This philosophy shaped every phase of the transformation. From the start, the head of transformation emphasized that the true key to solving GlobalCX's challenges lay in creating an environment where employees were trained, confident, and supported. If employees felt valued and empowered, performance metrics would naturally follow.

LISTENING TO EMPLOYEES: INTERNAL NPS AND GEMBA WALKS

One of the first breakthroughs came during the measure phase. Traditional metrics like external net promoter score (NPS) and solved cases per day (SPD) highlighted gaps in customer satisfaction and efficiency, but they didn't tell the full story. To uncover the root causes of attrition, dissatisfaction, and underperformance, the transformation team introduced an internal NPS system to give employees a voice. The results revealed a painful truth: many agents felt unsupported, undervalued, and burned out.

To complement the internal NPS, the team conducted Gemba walks, or Gembutsu walks,[2] direct observations of agents in action. These walks revealed just how disconnected leadership had become from the day-to-day realities of employees. Agents were overwhelmed by the complexity of their tasks, and training programs left them unprepared for the demands of the job. Team leaders were also struggling, many lacking the tools and training needed to effectively coach and inspire their teams. These insights laid the foundation for the transformation strategy.

BUILDING CONFIDENCE THROUGH TRAINING AND TALENT PIPELINES

Armed with these insights, the transformation team launched "Project Lagoon," a two-week immersive program that redefined how agents were trained and supported. Lagoon was not just another training initiative; it was a cultural reset. Combining role-playing, shadowing of top performers, and one-on-one coaching, Lagoon focused on building both technical expertise and soft skills like communication, empathy, and problem-solving. It gave agents the confidence to excel in complex customer interactions.

For team leaders, Lagoon provided a parallel track of development. Rather than relying on outdated micromanagement tactics, leaders were trained to coach and inspire their teams. They learned to create psychologically safe environments where employees felt supported and motivated. The results were transformative. Agents who completed Lagoon didn't just meet expectations, they exceeded them. Time-to-competency plummeted from 16 weeks to just 5. External NPS soared from 42 to 55, and efficiency climbed from 8 solved cases per day to 14. Attrition rates, once a crippling challenge, began to fall dramatically.

SUSTAINING SUCCESS THROUGH SUPPORT STRUCTURES

The transformation didn't end with Lagoon. To ensure long-term success, the team built robust support structures around Lagoon graduates. A mentorship program paired new agents with experienced mentors, creating a pipeline of talent and reinforcing best practices across the organization. Graduates of Lagoon became mentors themselves, embedding the program's principles at every level.

The daily management system (DMS) became another cornerstone of sustainability. It provided team leaders with clear guidelines, accountability frameworks, and tools to manage their teams effectively. Standard operating procedures (SOPs), real-time performance dashboards, and a *Responsible, Accountable, Consulted, Informed* (RACI) matrix helped ensure alignment and consistency across operations.

Feedback loops were critical to maintaining momentum. The internal NPS system continued to monitor employee satisfaction, while focus groups and one-on-one sessions allowed leadership to stay connected to the frontline experience. When challenges arose, like a temporary drop in performance during Lagoon's early rollout, these feedback mechanisms helped identify and address root causes quickly, ensuring continuous improvement.

OVERCOMING RESISTANCE AND SCALING THE TRANSFORMATION

As with any major transformation, resistance emerged. Senior managers accustomed to the old way of working pushed back against the new culture. But the transformation team was prepared. They applied Kotter's 8-step change model[3], building a guiding coalition and relentlessly communicating the program's successes. Lagoon's results became undeniable, gradually winning over skeptics.

The success of Lagoon inspired two spin-off programs tailored to Tier 1 and Tier 3 agents, creating a seamless talent pipeline across the organization. The transformation unit, once a small operation, grew into a central department with decentralized squads supporting every corner of GlobalCX's operations. What began as a response to a crisis evolved into a long-term strategy for excellence.

A GOLD STANDARD FOR CUSTOMER EXPERIENCE

At the annual strategy review with KParkStay, a senior leader summarized the impact of the transformation: "This isn't just a transformation of metrics. It's a transformation of people. GlobalCX has set the gold standard for how to care for your employees and, in turn, your customers."

By prioritizing people over numbers, GlobalCX achieved results that far exceeded its expectations. Over 700 agents completed Lagoon, with more in the pipeline. NPS scores continued to climb, and GlobalCX transformed from KParkStay's worst-performing partner to its most valuable one. The initiative didn't just save the contract, it elevated GlobalCX to become a global benchmark for customer service excellence.

LESSONS FOR LEADERS

The GlobalCX case offers powerful insights for leaders navigating transformation:

- **Start with People:** Technology and processes matter, but empowered, confident employees are the true drivers of success. Focus on training, mentoring, and creating a supportive culture.
- **Listen and Act:** Internal employee NPS (through online surveys) and Gemba walks revealed issues that traditional KPIs couldn't. Listening to employees and acting on their feedback is key to building trust and driving improvement.
- **Sustain the Change:** Transformation isn't complete until it becomes the new normal. Programs like Lagoon and structures like the DMS ensured long-term sustainability.
- **Communicate Results Relentlessly:** Overcoming resistance requires persistence. Highlighting wins and celebrating progress can turn skeptics into allies.

CONNECTING THE CASES TO OUR ENABLERS

Both of the above examples were highly successful transformations – and they did not happen by chance! In the case of CX, there had been attempts to solve this issue for two years before my team came in. When we started working on it, we kept getting told "we've already tried this" or "you have no experience with CX, so you will not solve it." Other comments I will leave out of this book. Nonetheless, my team and I did it.

Table 8.1 is an overview of how you can relate the case studies to what you have read so far in this book.

Table 8.1 Why Transformation Efforts Succeed

Key Finding/ Enabler	*Why It Drives Success*	*Guyana Digitalization Case*	*GlobalCX Transformation Case*
Empowering Employees	Empowering teams with skills, autonomy, and feedback builds confidence and ensures long-term engagement.	RigFlow™ training and cross-training empowered employees to take ownership of operations.	Lagoon program boosted agent confidence and emphasized coaching over micromanagement.
Leadership Commitment	Visible and engaged leadership drives buy-in and inspires employees to embrace transformation.	Leadership prioritized digital adoption and supported teams through visible commitment.	Leadership actively addressed resistance and celebrated Lagoon's successes to inspire trust.
Clear Organizational Structures	Well-defined roles, frameworks, and processes reduce complexity and align teams around shared goals.	Structured decision-making (e.g., spin out, integrate, or establish projects) provided clarity.	The DMS and SOPs gave team leaders clear tools to manage effectively and scale results.
Scalable Support Systems	Systems like mentorship programs and dashboards ensure transformation can be sustained and scaled.	Lessons learned from digital workflows were operationalized and transferred across rigs.	Mentorship pipelines and the RACI matrix scaled Lagoon's impact organization-wide.
Adapting Technology to Needs	Technology succeeds when it aligns with operational goals and simplifies workflows for teams.	The technology reduced paper-based workflows, improving efficiency and real-time collaboration.	Lagoon introduced feedback mechanisms and real-time dashboards tailored to employees.
Cultural Alignment	Embedding transformation into the culture ensures adoption and long-term success.	Digital workflows fostered cross-rig collaboration and cultural consistency.	Internal NPS and feedback mechanisms reinforced cultural adoption of best practices.

(*Continued*)

Table 8.1 (Continued)

Key Finding/ Enabler	*Why It Drives Success*	*Guyana Digitalization Case*	*GlobalCX Transformation Case*
Feedback Loops for Adaptation	Continuous feedback allows teams to adapt quickly and improve results over time.	Offshore and onshore teams provided real-time feedback to refine operations.	Internal NPS and Gemba walks revealed employee concerns and led to actionable improvements.
Stakeholder Collaboration	Engaging stakeholders fosters shared accountability and amplifies innovation outcomes.	The engineers co-created high-quality workflows, improving collaboration.	KParkStay alignment helped secure trust and ensure transformation outcomes.
Training as a Catalyst	High-quality training reduces time-to-competency and builds future-ready teams.	Horizon56 coaching reduced the time to adoption and built skills transferable across rigs.	Lagoon program accelerated onboarding, reduced attrition, and developed talent pipelines.
Sustainability Structures	Embedding processes, tools, and support systems ensures long-term success beyond initial implementation.	Horizon56 coaches and shared lessons created scalable, transferable knowledge across rigs.	DMS, SOPs, and mentorship structures reinforced performance improvements and cultural shifts.
Technology-Driven Agility	Technology creates transparency, reduces complexity, and enables faster decision-making.	The technology provided real-time operational visibility, simplifying offshore-onshore workflows.	Performance dashboards and digital feedback tools created clarity and operational agility.
Celebrate Success	Recognizing achievements builds momentum, motivates teams, and fosters long-term commitment.	Company leadership praised team efforts and shared project successes, reinforcing morale.	Lagoon's early wins were celebrated widely, turning skeptics into supporters.

THE LEADER AS AN ENABLER OF TRANSFORMATION: BRIDGING BUSINESS AND SOCIAL IMPACT

Great transformation leaders never work in isolation. They build bridges, connecting innovation and strategy, and linking internal ambitions with broader social impacts. When leaders embrace the role of enabler, transformation transcends operational improvements and amplifies positive change for teams, partners, and entire communities.

Both the Guyana Digitalization Project and the GlobalCX transformation exemplify how enabling others, employees, partners, or collaborators, can create ripple effects far beyond immediate business outcomes. These initiatives demonstrated that a leader's role extends to empowering ecosystems, ensuring that transformation outcomes address not just profitability but also societal progress.

In Guyana, the transformation efforts went beyond simply adopting a new technology. The project actively transferred knowledge and skills to local teams, equipping them to work more efficiently and safely in a highly complex offshore environment. This empowerment created value at multiple levels: for the teams involved, who gained confidence and expertise in operating cutting-edge systems, and for the local economy, which benefited from the development of high-quality talent in a critical industry. By focusing on shared learning and collaboration, the Guyana project fostered innovation that will ripple across the region for years to come. The project not only met the operators' business objectives but also elevated the capacity of its partners and workforce, creating a model for sustainable and inclusive progress.

Similarly, the GlobalCX transformation focused heavily on improving employee well-being and development, generating a powerful social impact alongside business success. By prioritizing training, mentorship, and employee satisfaction, GlobalCX turned its workforce from a struggling, overburdened group into a thriving, confident community. The introduction of the Lagoon program wasn't just about achieving KPIs, it was about creating career pathways and a culture of empowerment for over 1,000 employees. Attrition rates dropped, employees expressed greater satisfaction through internal NPS scores, and the organization became an example of how investing in people leads to both operational excellence and long-term societal value.

These cases illustrate four critical ingredients for transformation success.

SHARED OBJECTIVES

Transformation succeeds when business goals and social impact objectives align clearly. In Guyana, digitizing workflows boosted offshore efficiency and simultaneously empowered local workers with valuable new skills, strengthening regional economic resilience. For GlobalCX, improving customer satisfaction went hand-in-hand with dramatically enhancing employee well-being, creating clear pathways for professional growth. By blending financial goals with community aspirations, leaders can ensure meaningful and lasting engagement.

ACTIVE KNOWLEDGE TRANSFER

Real transformation happens when knowledge and capabilities spread beyond immediate users. In Guyana, collaboratively developed digital workflows enabled local teams to confidently manage complex offshore operations independently. At GlobalCX, structured mentoring and feedback loops empowered employees, creating sustainable talent pipelines and positioning the organization for future growth. Knowledge transfer doesn't merely solve today's challenges – it equips teams for tomorrow.

COLLABORATIVE STRUCTURES

Co-creation unlocks the true potential of transformation. In Guyana, structured collaboration between engineers, offshore teams, and partners ensured that new systems were practical, inclusive, and effective. Similarly, GlobalCX's leadership engaged closely with frontline teams, embedding continuous feedback and improvement into their daily operations. Collaborative structures create ownership, ensuring solutions resonate deeply and drive sustained impact.

EMBEDDING SUSTAINABILITY

Long-term success requires embedding transformation into organizational culture and systems. Guyana's legacy of shared knowledge and skill-building laid a foundation for future innovation and resilience. At GlobalCX, sustainability meant integrating mentorship, daily management systems, and structured support into everyday work, reinforcing empowerment and collaboration long after the initial transformation effort concluded. Embedding transformation ensures lasting positive outcomes, both for the business and its broader community.

Together, these case studies illustrate how transformation can achieve more than business success – it can drive societal progress. By empowering employees, enabling partners, and creating scalable frameworks for shared success, transformation becomes a force for positive change. Leaders who embrace this dual focus of business and social impact are not just enablers of transformation, but also catalysts for building stronger, more sustainable communities. When leaders facilitate innovation-driven change, they create lasting value for their organizations, their partners, and the society they serve.

Transformation, at its best, becomes the bridge between innovation and a better future for all.

NOTES

1 The project is based on the author's documented case study of a multi-month transformation project using Six Sigma DMAIC methodology to improve dropping quality and efficiency metrics. The project had a people-first approach, addressed poor morale and high employee turnover, assuming that improving how people felt at work would translate into improved business results (NPS and efficiency improvements). Ultimately the project led to significant improvements in NPS, staff retention, and operational efficiency.

2 Gemba walks, or Gembutsu walks, are a lean management practice where you visit the actual place where work is done (the Gemba) to observe processes, interact with employees, and identify improvement opportunities. The author did this at the outset of his assignment. At this point no one knew him and this allowed him to observe, interact and identify root causes without the employees noticing or knowing the intent.

3 Kotter's 8-step change model is a well-established framework for driving organizational transformation. The steps include building urgency, forming a guiding coalition, creating and communicating a vision, empowering action, generating short-term wins, and anchoring change in culture. For applied insights and tools, visit www.docschlosser.com. See also: Kotter, J.P. (1996). *Leading Change*. Harvard Business Press.

Chapter 9

Transforming Your Enablers

How to Lead Successful Change

We just covered a lot. If the last chapter felt like drinking from a firehose, don't worry, that's by design.

That was the core of the book, packed with the "how" you don't usually find in leadership theory.

But before we dive into the next big topic, change management, let's take a breath. This next chapter gets practical fast.

It's about what actually happens when people (and organizations) try to *do* all the good stuff we just covered.

A PRACTICAL FRAMEWORK FOR CHANGE MANAGEMENT: WINNING HEARTS AND MINDS

I would like to take you deeper into two areas. One being change management – that is, how to support people and win over hearts and minds. Second, being the link between the Enablers, the transformation they cause and how they impact both social and business results.

This chapter gives you a practical, battle-tested playbook for driving change that sticks, by aligning timing, communication, and human behavior. As you'll read in the previous chapter, the GlobalCX and Guyana cases didn't succeed by chance. They succeeded because change was designed around people.

Effective change management focuses on aligning people, communication, and timing to ensure the transformation is embraced and sustained. Leaders must balance operational needs with human-centered strategies, ensuring the transition is as seamless as possible.

IDENTIFYING TRANSFORMATION HEROES

Transformation heroes are employees who lead by example, influence their peers, and embody the values of the change desired. These individuals act as champions,

DOI: 10.4324/9781003638551-10

translating a vision into relatable and actionable steps. Leaders should identify these heroes early, looking for those with natural influence and a proven ability to adapt to change. Once selected, transformation heroes can serve as communicators, trainers, and motivators throughout the process, bridging leadership's vision with the realities of daily operations.

Who They Are: Employees who are respected by their peers and embody the values and goals of the transformation. They act as champions, influencers, and motivators. As an example, a large digital transformation took place for one of the world's largest land drillers, and the organization had no doubt, "the heroes of our transformation will be our frontline staff, those risking it every day, being away from their families and those who will use the technology, enabling an ocean of new opportunities based on data."

Why They Matter: Heroes inspire others to embrace change, translating the transformation vision into practical, relatable actions.

How to Identify Them: Look for natural influences in different departments and levels of the organization. Select individuals who have demonstrated adaptability and a positive attitude toward prior changes.

ALIGNING TRAINING WITH A TRANSFORMATION ROLLOUT

Training plays a pivotal role in preparing employees for change, but its timing is just as critical as its content.

Pre-Deployment: Provide foundational training to introduce concepts and prepare employees.

Deployment Go-Live: Deliver hands-on, role-specific training. At this point, you should already be thinking about how end users will sustain the change once you leave.

Post-Deployment Coaching: Offer continuous support, such as one-on-one coaching or team workshops, and remote support to embed knowledge and address gaps.

Foundational training should occur early enough to provide an understanding of the transformation, but practical, role-specific training must be delivered closer to deployment. Hands-on coaching or team workshops can be scheduled post-deployment to reinforce knowledge and address any remaining challenges. By phasing training strategically, leaders ensure employees feel equipped and confident without overwhelming them.

STRUCTURING COMMUNICATION TO BUILD MOMENTUM

Clear, consistent communication keeps the transformation moving forward. Leaders must continuously reinforce the "why" behind the change, tying it back to business goals and social impact. Regular updates on progress and milestones help maintain excitement and trust, while two-way communication channels allow employees to voice concerns, ask questions, and share feedback. A detailed communication plan ensures that updates are delivered at the right moments and with the right tone, creating alignment across all levels of the organization.

TIMING IS EVERYTHING

Training or communication that is poorly timed can derail even the most well-intentioned transformation. If training comes too early, employees may forget what they've learned. If it's delivered too late, it can cause unnecessary stress. Leaders should map training and communication activities to key project milestones. Early stakeholder involvement builds alignment, while mid-way reviews allow for course corrections. Celebrating successes post-deployment reinforces the transformation's positive impact and keeps morale high.

CONNECTING TRANSFORMATION TO SOCIAL IMPACT

The success of transformation isn't just measured in profitability or operational efficiency; it's also reflected in its positive impact on employees, partners, and society. Explicitly linking transformation outcomes to social impact builds a deeper sense of purpose and commitment among stakeholders.

Guyana Digitalization Project

For the Guyana project, digitizing workflows significantly improved safety and operational efficiency. Offshore teams benefited directly from enhanced safety measures, as manual processes were replaced with precision digital tools. The eight weeks of hypercare[1] following deployment ensured these changes became embedded into daily operations. Beyond the immediate benefits for workers, the project created a ripple effect across the offshore ecosystem, providing a scalable model for sustainable innovation.

This transformation highlighted how social impact could drive commitment. Employees took pride in working within a safer, more efficient environment, while the partners leveraged these successes to enhance their collaborative operations. Leaders can learn from this by framing the social benefits of transformation as central to its purpose, inspiring employees and external stakeholders alike.

GlobalCX Transformation

In the GlobalCX initiative, the transformation prioritized employee empowerment alongside customer satisfaction. Employees were actively involved in redesigning workflows, and their contributions were reinforced through training and feedback loops. This not only prepared them for the changes but also enhanced their long-term career prospects. As job satisfaction increased, so did service quality, creating a positive cycle that benefited both employees and customers.

The transformation also reinforced how customer experience can be a societal value. By improving service, the organization built greater trust and loyalty, while empowering employees to find fulfillment in their roles. This dual impact, enhancing customer relationships and employee morale, showcases how transformation can achieve both business and social outcomes simultaneously.

KEY INSIGHTS FOR YOUR SOCIAL IMPACT

When you will be driving transformation, you must focus on human-centered change strategies while tying outcomes to meaningful societal benefits. Identifying transformation heroes, structuring well-timed training, and maintaining consistent communication are critical for minimizing resistance and fostering engagement. At the same time, you should frame transformation outcomes in terms of their broader social impact, ensuring all stakeholders see the value of the change beyond the bottom line. By balancing these elements, transformation efforts can achieve sustainable, long-term success.

I don't want to come across as naïve – it is also about business results. What you have read above drove significant business improvement results and impacted the whole organization.[2]

FROM THEORY TO MONDAY MORNING ACTION: THE GLOBALCX STORY

At this mid-point in the book, we've traveled through the highs and lows of transformation, exploring both powerful concepts and vivid, real-world stories. Now, it's your turn to step into the shoes of a transformational leader. Imagine it's Monday morning, and your company is facing a crisis similar to the one GlobalCX overcame. How exactly would you put the six success factors into action? How do you translate ideas into impact? Let's roll up our sleeves and get practical, using the GlobalCX case as our living playbook. Here's precisely how you'll lead your own transformation story, step-by-step, starting right now.

SUCCESS FACTOR 1: CLARITY OF PURPOSE

What You Do Monday Morning	*How GlobalCX Did It*
1. Gather leadership and define: – One business outcome (critical KPI, e.g., save a key client). – One social outcome (employee satisfaction and reduced attrition).	***GlobalCX set clear goals from day one:*** – **Business outcome:** Retain StayProvider by dramatically improving customer satisfaction, as it was responsible for 70% of their income. NPS needed to improve to 60s and efficiency metrics had to improve with NPS. – **Social outcome:** Increase employee satisfaction, confidence, and reduce high attrition (140% annual turnover). Create a safe environment where employees feel empowered to work in this high-paced environment.
2. Clearly communicate these goals company-wide before noon, emphasizing their combined importance.	GlobalCX repeatedly communicated both goals in every team meeting and training session, creating a shared sense of urgency. All monitors in the office were displaying the goals and the Lagoon teams. Each floor in the office got equipped with whiteboards where goals and vision for the project were listed. They were everywhere!

SUCCESS FACTOR 2: EMPOWERED AND ENGAGED PEOPLE

What You Do Monday Morning	*How GlobalCX Did It*
1. Run a quick, anonymous survey to ask frontline staff and focus groups: "What one thing would help you do your job better immediately?"	GlobalCX immediately implemented an internal NPS survey to uncover employee frustrations, discovering they felt unsupported and overwhelmed. We ran several focus groups. I matched top performers with underperformers to see what the top performer had which the underperformer did not. I then clearly understood that about 80% of all agents underperformed, and with this, I focused on the 20% that did perform. I wanted to structure a support and training model that would reflect what the 20% had and put the 80% through that training model – this was very powerful.

(*Continued*)

What You Do Monday Morning	*How GlobalCX Did It*
2. Schedule Gemba walks to directly observe and openly discuss frontline struggles.	GlobalCX conducted Gemba walks, directly observing daily operations, confirming the employees' lack of preparation and support. By doing this, it became evident that team managers were too far from their teams, a lack of visual management, and no clear objectives for the agents working. Note, performance management is a social activity, and visual management is a key driver here!
3. By Friday, design targeted training explicitly addressing survey and Gemba insights.	Launched "**Project Lagoon**," a two-week immersive training program to directly address identified employee needs (role-playing, shadowing, coaching). We brought in top performers who would rotate as mentors within Lagoon. Sharing their knowledge, giving confidence to the agents, and deep diving into tough cases as a team. Visuals, office decorations, social events, and awards were also introduced!

SUCCESS FACTOR 3: EFFECTIVE GOVERNANCE AND DECISION-MAKING

What You Do Monday Morning	*How GlobalCX Did It*
1. Clearly define accountability for transformation decisions (who decides and who consults).	GlobalCX established a dedicated "**Transformation Unit**" with clear roles and responsibilities, using a RACI matrix. My request was that this Unit was at the heart of the business, with decision-making power, and a direct line to the director. We needed fast decision-making to realize our bold vision.
2. Immediately create a rule: "Transformation decisions must always include frontline input before approval."	GlobalCX consistently used frontline feedback (from NPS and Gemba) to shape decisions on training, processes, and tools. We held daily interviews, focus groups, and Gemba walks to ensure we always captured frontline input. We now understood that if the frontline workers felt safe and empowered, NPS, efficiencies, and employ turnover metrics would all improve as a consequence. **That is, we focused on people/social as our primary objective – business results came as a consequence.**

(*Continued*)

What You Do Monday Morning	*How GlobalCX Did It*
3. Communicate these decision rules clearly by the end of the day.	Rules and accountability were transparently shared, ensuring clarity, and quick decision-making at all organizational levels.

SUCCESS FACTOR 4: CULTURAL AND STRUCTURAL ALIGNMENT

What You Do Monday Morning	*How GlobalCX Did It*
1. Clearly define two or three behaviors critical for transformation (e.g., transparent communication and peer-to-peer coaching).	GlobalCX explicitly defined critical behaviors: peer-coaching, open feedback, and proactive problem-solving. Agents started speaking up, not afraid to fail, and we created a culture of coaching, sharing, and top performers by creating a culture based on the above behaviors.
2. Adjust existing processes or incentives by the end of the day to clearly reward these behaviors.	GlobalCX updated team leader roles from micromanagement to coaching, explicitly rewarding collaborative and supportive behaviors. We created process maps, mapped "the perfect week," and gave guidance to team leads and support roles on visual management.
3. Publicly announce these changes on Tuesday morning, linking explicitly to desired behaviors.	Team leaders and agents were formally briefed on changes, explicitly connecting new behaviors (coaching and collaboration) with revised performance metrics. Not only that, the staff was put forward to communicate the changes, making them owners, and true drivers of transformation.

SUCCESS FACTOR 5: TECHNOLOGY AND TOOLS AS ENABLERS

What You Do Monday Morning	*How GlobalCX Did It*
1. Ask frontline employees directly: "*Which current tool or process slows you down?*"	GlobalCX employees indicated through NPS that current dashboards and KPIs were overwhelming and unclear.

(*Continued*)

2. By Wednesday, select a simpler digital tool or process improvement that directly solves the identified issue.	GlobalCX developed simpler real-time dashboards and internal NPS surveys, providing clear, actionable insights for employees.
3. Clearly communicate your chosen tool and rollout strategy by Friday.	GlobalCX incrementally rolled out new dashboards alongside "**Project Lagoon**," aligning technology deployment with employee readiness.

SUCCESS FACTOR 6: SUSTAINABILITY

What You Do Monday Morning	*How GlobalCX Did It*
1. Assign operational and technical experts to continuously support frontline teams after deployment.	GlobalCX built structured post-training support: operational coaches and technical support staff available immediately post-Lagoon. We teamed up with the Quality department, and we got resources who would come and train the Lagoon teams, train the mentors, and support with monitoring of performance remotely.
2. Formally embed new processes into standard operating procedures (SOPs) immediately.	GlobalCX integrated Lagoon principles and new dashboards into daily management systems (DMS) and SOPs. This was also clearly communicated to the client. What was changed, how we did it, and how we transformed and scaled!
3. Establish a weekly 30-minute frontline "check-in" meeting starting this Friday for continuous improvement.	GlobalCX maintained continuous feedback loops (weekly check-ins, internal NPS, and focus groups), quickly adapting, and sustaining improvements.

SEVEN PITFALLS TO AVOID IN YOUR TRANSFORMATION JOURNEY

Even with the best intentions and a clear action plan, transformations can stumble if leaders overlook common pitfalls. After planning your Monday morning actions, take a moment to ensure you steer clear of traps that have derailed other promising transformations. Keep this list close – regularly reflecting on these pitfalls can save you time, resources, and morale, helping you deliver real, sustainable impact for your employees.

1. **Rushing the Process**

   Transformation is a journey, not a sprint. Leaders often face pressure to show quick results, which can lead to skipping critical steps like assessing readiness or aligning teams. Rushing can result in poorly executed initiatives that fail to take root in the organization.

   Why It Happens: Pressure from stakeholders, lack of patience for long-term investments, or a focus on immediate gains.

   How to Avoid It: Emphasize the importance of building a solid foundation with clear purpose, readiness assessments, and incremental wins.

2. **Ignoring Frontline Feedback**

   The frontline employees who implement and experience the transformation daily will have valuable insights. Ignoring their feedback can lead to disengagement, resistance, and blind spots in the strategy.

   Why It Happens: Leaders may assume they know the full picture or prioritize top-down directives over inclusive engagement.

   How to Avoid It: Create mechanisms for two-way feedback and involve employees in shaping the transformation through co-design workshops, surveys, or focus groups.

3. **Overloading Teams**

   Introducing too many changes at once can overwhelm employees, dilute focus, and create resistance. Teams need time and resources to adapt, especially when balancing day-to-day responsibilities alongside transformation efforts.

   Why It Happens: Leaders may feel the need to address multiple priorities simultaneously or fail to account for team capacity.

   How to Avoid It: Sequence transformation efforts to match the organization's capacity and readiness. Prioritize quality over speed, allowing employees to adapt to change incrementally.

4. **Misaligned Communication**

   Inconsistent or unclear communication about the transformation's purpose, progress, and impact can lead to confusion and skepticism. If employees and stakeholders don't understand "why" the change is happening, they are less likely to support it.

   Why It Happens: Lack of a coordinated communication plan or failure to address diverse stakeholder needs.

   How to Avoid It: Develop a detailed communication strategy that reinforces the purpose, celebrates milestones, and addresses concerns. Ensure the messaging resonates across all levels of the organization.

5. **Neglecting Post-Implementation Support**

   Transformation doesn't end with deployment. Without post-implementation support, such as coaching, mentorship, or ongoing training, employees may revert to old habits or fail to fully adopt new systems.

Why It Happens: Leaders may assume that once the transformation is launched, their job is done.

How to Avoid It: Build post-implementation phases into the plan, including long-term coaching, feedback loops, and refresher training to sustain adoption.

6. **Overlooking Culture**

   Cultural resistance is one of the biggest obstacles to transformation. Misaligned cultural values or failing to prepare employees for shifts in behavior and mindset can derail even the best strategies.

   Why It Happens: Leaders may focus on systems and processes without addressing cultural readiness or underlying resistance.

   How to Avoid It: Embed cultural alignment into the transformation process, ensuring employees understand and embrace new values, behaviors, and expectations.

7. **Focusing Only on Technology**

   While technology can enable transformation, it's not the driver. Overemphasizing tools and systems without addressing the people side of change often leads to poor adoption and disengagement.

   Why It Happens: A belief that technology alone will solve problems or create efficiencies.

   How to Avoid It: Balance technology rollout with training, empowerment, and communication to ensure employees can use the tools effectively.

HOW YOU CAN USE THIS

You should use this list of pitfalls as a reflective exercise throughout the transformation process. Periodically ask:

- *"Am I rushing this to get quick results?"*
- *"Have I included and listened to frontline employees?"*
- *"Are my teams overwhelmed with too much change at once?"*
- *"Have I ensured long-term support for sustainability?"*

Transformation is only the beginning. The real impact comes from scaling success and amplifying its reach, both within your organization and across your ecosystem. Scaling isn't just about replicating change; it's about building momentum and driving lasting value.

In the following chapter, we'll explore how to take transformation further, ensuring your efforts deliver meaningful and sustained impact for both business and society.

NOTES

1 Hypercare at Horizon56 is led by the Project and Deployment team. Hypercare means that a digital coach will go offshore on the rig to train the end-users. The digital coaches comes with a lifetime of experience in offshore operations. They are Horizon56 frontline change makers!

2 In the CX example, due to improvements in NPS and other metrics, the client decided not to cut the contract, meaning several hundred people kept their jobs, and GlobalCX kept their biggest client and continued to improve revenue. For Guyana, the project led to operational efficiency improvements, enhanced safety, and a digital tool that facilitates quality and continues improvement across the fleet. In addition, the project led to establishing a reputation of trust, quality, and a partner for future operations which again has resulted in additional projects globally.

Chapter 10

Scaling and Amplifying Impact

Chapter 10 will help you understand how to scale in order to amplify the positive impact you have created through balancing the Enablers.

As with the other chapters, you will be presented with a practical framework that will guide you and your teams. I will also present two case studies that you already are familiar with from Chapter 4, Claudio Caputo's Competency Matrix and Chapter 8, where we met the project team driving technology adoption in Guyana. With this contextual background, I'll give you the tools that you can use to construct your own scaling and amplifying framework.

If you've built something that works, then you've aligned your teams, clarified decisions, connected strategy to operations, and embedded the right Enablers: empowerment, structure, ecosystems, technology, and transformation.

Now comes the question that will define whether your effort stays local or becomes something bigger: *How do we grow this without losing what made it work? Or, will what got you here be what will take you to the next level?*

Figure 10.1 Scaling and Amplifying your Impact

DOI: 10.4324/9781003638551-11

THE AMPLIFIED IMPACT FRAMEWORK: THE HOW

The framework below can be applied both individually and collaboratively with your team to ensure effective scaling and amplified impact. As a leader, your focus should be on creating alignment, providing clarity, and enabling adaptability throughout the process. I've mapped this out as a five-step framework. You'll note that I've separated the context for individuals and teams.

For Individual Leaders: You can use the framework to assess your team's, department's, and organization's readiness. It will help you identify the gaps, skills, systems, or missing clarity needed. Prioritize what matters most: workforce preparedness, operational agility, and ecosystem alignment.

As you move forward, you'll need to create feedback loops. During pilots or early rollouts, use real-time data and team insights to refine your approach. Model transparency and share how you're using metrics to build trust and momentum.

For Teams: Start by aligning the framework's pillars: Develop, Leverage, and Ecosystem Engagement. Clarify team goals and assign ownership for key areas, such as training, tech adoption, and stakeholder collaboration.

Set measurable targets, track progress, and create space for honest feedback. Celebrate wins and reflect on what you're learning together. Scaling is a team sport, so keep it open, iterative, and purpose-driven.

STEP 1: DEVELOP READINESS FOR SCALING

Key Actions	*Example Insight*	*Practical Leadership Moves*
Define what success looks like before scaling.	Without clear outcome metrics, early teams struggled to identify which processes were truly ready to scale.	Establish criteria to evaluate what's worth scaling (speed, quality, engagement, cost, etc.). Build a simple scorecard or dashboard. This sets the foundation for real-time adjustments later (Step 5).
Run small-scale pilots to test readiness.	Early pilots found gaps in team coordination and workflows, which were addressed before wider rollout.	Consider different forms of testing: phased launches, simulations, or regional rollouts. Use your measurement criteria to decide what's scalable and what isn't. Involve team leads early to test assumptions.
Evaluate operational strength.	Targeted training helped close skill and process gaps before scaling.	Use training completion rates, task simulations, or process reviews to assess readiness. Link this step to the empowerment Enabler – are people confident, skilled, and decision-ready?

(*Continued*)

Key Actions	*Example Insight*	*Practical Leadership Moves*
Align on clear scaling goals.	Shared goals helped reduce friction and improve onboarding speed.	Facilitate cross-functional alignment sessions. Use visual tools (e.g., OKRs and impact maps) to define what success looks like *on a scale*. Connect to your structure Enabler: who owns delivery, and how are teams supported?
Set up real-time feedback loops.	Feedback from early stages led to process improvements.	Build mechanisms like daily huddles, lightweight retros, or in-app feedback tools. Reinforce the transparency Enabler to create a safe space for learning and adjustment.

STEP 2: DESIGN AND LEVERAGE TECHNOLOGY FOR SCALE

Key Actions	*Example Insight*	*Practical Leadership Moves*
Build flexible systems to meet diverse needs.	A modular platform allowed workflows to be adapted across teams and geographies. Build or integrate with APIs. Ensure you have the right flexibility to satisfy a need now, and in the future.	Prioritize systems that are configurable across regions *or user groups*. Involve end users in defining what should be standardized vs. adapted. Make sure your structure supports this, e.g., who owns platform decisions across units or functions?
Automate repeatable tasks without losing trust.	Digitizing manual workflows reduced errors and freed time, but required active engagement to ensure adoption.	Start with tasks that frustrate or slow down users. Co-design automation with those closest to the work. Communicate clearly and involve teams in rollout decisions. Tech change should support, not displace, people.
Design for ecosystem integration from day one.	An SaaS model enabled partners and contractors to onboard quickly and collaborate at scale.	Select tools that allow external access, permission layers, and real-time data sharing. Design with partners in mind from the beginning, not as an afterthought. This builds stronger, more scalable ecosystems.
Future-proof for long-term scalability.	The platform became a foundation for future transformations, beyond initial scaling goals.	Avoid point solutions. Map your future needs, integrations, analytics, or AI, and choose systems that can evolve. Where needed, run tech pilots in low-risk zones to test future capabilities before full rollout.

STEP 3: EMBED AND RESOURCE FOR SCALING

Key Actions	*Example Insight*	*Practical Leadership Moves*
Translate innovation into operational models.	Pilots succeeded in controlled settings but failed to transfer without adapting to operational realities.	Document what worked, and why. Turn pilot insights into clear processes, toolkits, or playbooks that delivery teams can adopt. Don't aim for perfect replication; support thoughtful adaptation.
Resource the scale, intentionally.	Teams underestimated staffing, onboarding, and budget needs as scale accelerated.	Map out what it will actually take to scale: people, time, tech, and funding. Model these costs across phases. Ask: *Do we have the capacity, not just the desire, to scale this?* Plan for what needs to grow and what needs to shift.
Design the organization to support scaled delivery.	New roles emerged as the solution scaled, such as support teams, onboarding leads, and data monitors.	Revisit org design and structure. What functions must evolve? What roles need to be created or redefined? Don't just plan a handoff, plan a transition, with clear ownership and support structures.
Clarify what's core vs. adaptable.	Local teams sometimes altered key features, weakening impact.	Define non-negotiables (values, outcomes, and standards) and what can flex (methods, tools, and language). Make this distinction clear so teams scale with consistency *and* ownership.

STEP 4: ALIGN ECOSYSTEM PARTNERS FOR AMPLIFIED IMPACT

Key Actions	*Example Insight*	*Practical Leadership Moves*
Map the ecosystem and align early.	Partners were essential from the pilot phase through rollout.	Identify who can accelerate, or block, scaling. Involve them early. Don't wait for alignment, create it by discussing shared goals, risks, and value. Scaling is coalition-building.
Build trust through consistency and transparency.	Partner engagement grew through open dialogue, training, and long-term support.	Be visible when things get hard. Set expectations. Share data, decisions, and tradeoffs. Trust is earned through humility and follow-through.

(*Continued*)

Key Actions	*Example Insight*	*Practical Leadership Moves*
Design partnerships for mutual performance.	When partners saw productivity gains, their commitment to adoption increased.	Co-define success metrics and invest in joint capability building. Share credit and celebrate partner contributions as part of your impact narrative.
Put the right agreements in place.	NDAs, data-sharing protocols, and service-level expectations helped avoid delays and legal risk.	Work with legal and procurement teams to develop lightweight, flexible contracts that protect data, clarify roles, and reduce onboarding friction. Consider MOUs, NDAs, pilot agreements, or phased commitments based on trust level.

STEP 5: MEASURE SUCCESS TO REFINE AND SUSTAIN

Key Actions	*Example Insight*	*Practical Leadership Moves*
Establish clear ownership and roles post-scale.	After initial success, some regions experienced drop-off due to unclear responsibilities and support gaps.	Define ongoing ownership across functions: operations, training, governance, improvement. Update org charts and decision rights. Make sustainability someone's job, not everyone's assumption.
Embed routines to protect quality and relevance.	High-performing teams used consistent rhythms, monthly check-ins, feedback loops, and process audits, to keep performance high.	Introduce scalable operating routines: retrospectives, quality reviews, service-level tracking. Use metrics like *cycle time, defect rates*, or *take time* to monitor performance.
Secure long-term resources and support infrastructure.	Some initiatives lost momentum when funding and staffing didn't match post-rollout needs.	Plan and secure resources for ongoing support, people, tools, and time. Embed these into workforce planning, budgeting, and onboarding. Ask: *What does it take to run this every day at scale?*
Keep learning loops active, even after scale.	Teams that continued to reflect and iterate uncovered new use cases and avoided stagnation.	Build in learning mechanisms like quarterly partner reviews, cross-functional learning sessions, or anonymous user surveys. Don't treat launch as an endpoint, treat it as a checkpoint.

(*Continued*)

Key Actions	*Example Insight*	*Practical Leadership Moves*
Track long-term impact, not just activity.	Output metrics remained flat, but impact continued through system-level outcomes and stories of change.	Revisit goals from Step 1. Use indicators like net promoter score (NPS), incident reduction, employee or partner satisfaction, or cost per outcome. Stay focused on whether you're still achieving the positive impact you set out to scale.

WHY SCALING AND AMPLIFYING MATTER

Scaling and amplifying impact are the ultimate steps in turning ideas and innovative initiatives into sound business. For executives and investors, it is important that you scale. After progressing through the previous Enablers – empowerment, structures, ecosystems, technology, and transformation – you are now equipped to extend the reach of their efforts.

At this stage, the challenge becomes clear: *how do we ensure that what has been built and tested can grow sustainably and deliver exponential impact?* Scaling is about growth, while amplifying focuses on enhancing the reach and depth of impact through collaboration and innovation. These efforts are only possible with a solid measurement system in place to track progress and outcomes, a precondition that cannot be overstated.

In the upcoming sections, we will explore the three pillars of scaling and amplifying: develop, leverage, and ecosystem engagement. These pillars offer a structured approach for leaders to grow their impact while maintaining alignment with organizational values and ecosystems.

CASE STUDIES, FRAMEWORKS, AND BUILDING ACTION

Step 1: Develop Readiness for Scaling

Key Question: Have We Built the Trust, Systems, and Capabilities Required for Sustainable Scaling?

Scaling only works when the foundation holds.

In both Claudio Caputo's and the Guyana cases, early success created momentum. But momentum isn't the only indicator that you're ready for scaling. As an example, in the oil and gas industry, scaling that may work in one location with a small team of people, on one drilling rig, requires more than enthusiasm. It requires structure, clarity, and confidence in the system's ability to stretch. Before moving forward, both Claudio's team and the Guyana project team stepped back to test whether their systems could stand on their own. Here is how.

This step, that is focused on the word **develop**, is about validating that foundation. It includes five leadership actions: defining what success looks like, piloting in real conditions, assessing operational capability, aligning expectations across functions, and embedding feedback from the start.

Define What Success Looks Like Before Scaling

Claudio Caputo's team resisted vague definitions of success. Instead, they identified three clear indicators that had to be in place before any new team could go live with the matrix:

1. Supervisors consistently using it in development conversations.
2. Teams referencing it during staffing discussions.
3. Clarity ratings from new hires exceeding baseline thresholds.

In Guyana, the scaling team used onboarding time, error rates, and daily usage of RigFlow™ by offshore supervisors as success markers. Rigs that hit those markers moved forward. Others paused for additional coaching.

Insight: Success wasn't assumed. It was operationalized.

Action: Build a simple readiness scorecard to ensure you're scaling real outcomes, not pockets of goodwill.

RUN SMALL-SCALE PILOTS TO TEST READINESS

Both organizations ran targeted pilots in varied contexts. Claudio's team tested the matrix in both high-performing and lower-capacity teams to see if outcomes were repeatable. In Guyana, the leadership team ran the software on one rig with full support, then on a second with minimal involvement from central IT.

The results were telling. In both cases, usage held. Friction surfaced. And fixes were made before full deployment.

Insight: Pilots were used for learning, early success, and to capture lessons learned.

Action: Don't just test performance. Test autonomy. Can teams operate the system without hand-holding?

EVALUATE OPERATIONAL STRENGTH

Claudio Caputo's team assessed whether frontline supervisors could lead capability conversations confidently. If they couldn't, they delayed rollout. In Guyana, rigs that required frequent intervention from the platform team were flagged as not yet ready to scale.

Rather than press ahead, both organizations invested in training, clarified ownership, and retested before expanding.

Insight: Readiness isn't about interest. It's about consistent, independent use.

Action: Observe behavior in the field. Don't rely on intent. Rely on execution.

ALIGN ON CLEAR SCALING GOALS

Both cases avoided isolated decision-making. Claudio's leadership aligned with HR, operations, and site managers to set shared expectations for what scaling would require, across onboarding, capability building, and team readiness.

In Guyana, project members from the digital rollout team worked with engineering, ops, and the offshore leadership to define the success metrics and implementation sequence.

Insight: Scaling isn't just a technical rollout, it's a cross-functional contract.

Action: Align early. Define what success looks like from multiple vantage points, before rollout, not after.

SET UP REAL-TIME FEEDBACK LOOPS

Claudio's teams used short weekly retrospectives[1] to flag confusion, misuse, or friction. These uncovered small but critical issues, like inconsistent application of capability levels. In Guyana, offshore teams logged tool feedback directly into a shared Slack channel, enabling fast response and continuous learning.

Insight: Feedback loops were part of the rollout infrastructure.

Action: Embed lightweight, real-time feedback channels from the beginning. Don't wait for post-mortems. Set regular after-action reviews (AAR).

In both cases, readiness wasn't announced. It was earned, through clarity, behavior, and performance under pressure. Only once that foundation was tested, and trusted, did either leader move to scale.

Framework for Step 1: Develop Readiness for Scaling

Key Action	*Case Insight*	*What to Do as a Leader*
Define what success looks like before scaling.	Claudio tracked: (1) % supervisors using the matrix in check-ins, (2) onboarding clarity score, (3) internal mobility rates, (4) retention rate. Guyana tracked: (1) reduction in time spend on procedural compliance, (2) number of insights/lessons learned from offshore embedded in future plans, (3) NPS from field engineers.	Choose three practical indicators: e.g., supervisor adoption (target: >80%), onboarding time (target: <30 days), field NPS (>+30). Make them visible. Scale only if all three are met.

(*Continued*)

Key Action	*Case Insight*	*What to Do as a Leader*
Run small-scale pilots in varied settings.	Claudio tested the matrix in a top performer site, a stretched team, and one with high turnover. Guyana tested RigFlow™ on two rigs: one with where a large number of service partners were involved and going live during a more complex operation. Secondly a rig with fewer service partners involved and a more familiar operation for go live.	Run at least three pilots: high readiness, average, and low. Observe adoption *without* HQ support. Document what works across all. Don't move forward if only the "easy" pilot succeeds.
Assess operational independence.	In Claudio, supervisors led without escalation. In Guyana, offshore leads updated and used the tool with the minimal support from the start. The need for support declined while adoption, based on defined success criteria, increased.	Ask: Can frontline teams use the system without daily support? Measure by # of escalations, % accurate usage, and time to resolve issues locally. Require >80% independence. Revisit your success criteria to understand if they are fulfilled by the end users post kick-off.
Align on rollout expectations.	Claudio aligned HR, ops, and training on support responsibilities. In Guyana, digital teams, project, product, and operations defined rollout rhythm together.	Hold one cross-functional alignment meeting. Define and document: who owns what, rollout sequence, resource roles. Publish a shared visual roadmap to avoid conflict later.
Embed real-time feedback from day one.	Claudio held weekly 10-min retros. Guyana used live AARs and direct system feedback via already established channels.	Set up one feedback loop per site/team OR in a way so you can make a distinction between the data you are receiving – which pilot end users is this coming from? A Slack/Teams channel, weekly retro, AARs or comment board. Assign one local owner to triage and escalate top issues. Use input to improve and adjust within an agreed timeframe – for pilots this is usually within hours or days.

Step 2: Design and Leverage Technology for Scale

Key Question: What Needs to Be Built, or Rebuilt, for Scalable Delivery?

Scaling what works means shifting from pilots to systems. Both Claudio and the Guyana teams learned early that what succeeded in one location wouldn't hold under broader use without thoughtful redesign. Their systems, whether a capability matrix or a real-time rig operations digital ecosystem, had to evolve to support more users, more complexity, and more variability.

This phase required intentional infrastructure: tools, templates, roles, and technology that could support growth without breaking.

In the section below, I've mapped out how both teams navigated scaling, using four key actions from the framework.

Build Flexible Systems to Meet Diverse Needs

Claudio's matrix began as a shared spreadsheet, customized by teams, and interpreted in slightly different ways. But as it spread, inconsistencies emerged. Capability levels were applied differently, coaching styles varied, and data became harder to track. Rather than clamp down, the team defined a minimum viable structure:

- What had to stay fixed (language, levels, and update cycle).
- What could flex (visual design and additional role categories).

In Guyana, the software started as a custom setup for one offshore team. As new rigs came online, it became clear that different teams, contractors, and site conditions needed some adaptability, without losing the core workflow. In response, they built configurable templates, structured permission layers, custom integrations to service partners, and a user experience that allowed teams to access only what they needed, when they needed it.

Insight: Flexibility is not the opposite of control. It's the foundation of sustainable scale.

Action: Define what must stay standard, and what can safely vary. Make this distinction visible to every team. With the new tool you are driving behavior and thereby process, so leave little room for subjectivity on the tool itself, and let your tool be the framework for questions and discussions that will lead to a positive impact.

AUTOMATE REPEATABLE TASKS WITHOUT LOSING TRUST

In both organizations, automation played a role, but only after trust had been built.

Claudio's team introduced auto-generated dashboards that visualized team capability levels. These were used to support planning and identify skill gaps. However, before releasing them, teams had input on design. Supervisors helped define how the data would be used. That early involvement ensured the output was trusted, not questioned.

In Guyana, the software replaced paper-based workflows, saving hours of manual effort each day. But automation wasn't pushed as an efficiency tool; it was framed as a safety and alliance enabler. Teams still had control to override or comment on tasks, and human review of digital input remained as part of the core process. Automation was made possible as both the processes were fully digitized.

Insight: Digitalization and automation accelerate adoption when they support, not replace, good judgment. Note, because your workflows turns digital, you must consider process and behaviors which should be adjusted accordingly.

Action Move: Involve frontline users in defining automation triggers and review points. Build confidence before scale. Map your current state process – where are your pain points, have repetitive tasks or copy/paste activities been automated? Digitize and automate a future state process.

DESIGN FOR ECOSYSTEM INTEGRATION FROM DAY ONE

Claudio's team began hearing from partners: could vendors align their training to the matrix? Could contractors use the same capability definitions? Anticipating future needs, the team designed the next iteration of the matrix with ecosystem use in mind: a simplified external version, clear language guides, and usage boundaries. The organization and its partners now spoke the same language.

In Guyana, external coordination was a requirement from the start. Contractors, service partners, and vendors all needed access to the same live data. The platform was built as a SaaS[2] model with secure external access, permission tiers, and integration pathways. This didn't just scale internally, it enabled the entire ecosystem to coordinate more effectively. This included partners located thousands of miles away in remote operating centers, who could suddenly see real-time offshore operations.

Insight: Show the power of your solution to the ecosystem. Do not wait for an invite. Do not talk about conceptual ideas – show them value through action. If you wait until others ask to connect, you're already behind.

Action: Build tools as if you know others will need them. Design for integration before it becomes urgent. Satisfy a current need, but keep in mind that you will enable the future through your solutions.

FUTURE-PROOF FOR LONG-TERM SCALABILITY

Both leaders understood that what works now might not work next year.

Claudio's matrix wasn't just scaled, it was future-proofed. Roles changed, new projects emerged, and cross-functional capabilities were added. Because the system was modular, it absorbed this growth while remaining usable.

Guyana's software architecture was designed to evolve. New features, such as AI-based recommendations and reporting enhancements, were rolled out gradually. The team ran small pilots of future functionality in low-risk environments before scaling across offshore drilling rigs.

Insight: Scaling isn't the end, just the end of the beginning.

Action: Build systems with the next two stages of growth in mind. Pilot quietly. Evolve visibly.

Technology is a powerful enabler of scale, but only when it's built with the work in mind, not layered on top of it.

In both cases, design decisions weren't made in isolation. They were shaped by the people doing the work, and led by teams who understood that scale isn't about adding more. It's about making more possible, **without losing control, trust, or clarity.**

Framework for Step 2: Design and Leverage Technology for Scale

Key Action	*Case Insight*	*What to Do as a Leader*
Build flexible systems with clear limits.	Claudio locked matrix content but let teams change layout. Guyana used permissions and modular workflows in digital system. In both cases, it was built on modular basis and easy to transfer to updated versions/systems.	Define what's fixed (e.g., capability language and workflows) and what can flex (e.g., visuals and notifications). Document rules. Train on boundaries.
Automate repeatable tasks with care.	Claudio's dashboards auto-calculated capability levels. Guyana automated job sequencing. Both co-designed with users. Automated flow of lessons learned further enhanced the collaboration and eliminated common pain points related to gathering and integrating lessons learned.	Identify two to three repetitive tasks. Co-create automation. Measure time saved per task (e.g., –40%), reduction in manual errors. Don't automate anything people don't trust. Embed improvements/ lessons learned in future work.
Design for integration from the start.	The new digital system enabled vendors to view tasks and timelines. Further, it would integrate vendor solutions and thereby eliminate a number of systems and physical screens – instant value add. Claudio created a matrix version for contractor onboarding.	Choose systems with role-based access, open API, and multi-user views. Define three use cases where partners interact. Test in one. Track friction and fix it.

(*Continued*)

Key Action	*Case Insight*	*What to Do as a Leader*
Future-proof platform and architecture.	Claudio scaled the matrix with evolving roles. Guyana tested AI features on a single rig before wider release.	Identify one long-term requirement (e.g., partner data sync, analytics, and AI). Pilot with one team or site. Measure adoption and impact before investing further.

Step 3: Embed and Resource for Scaling

Key Question: How Do We Transition from Project to Operations and Sustain It at Scale?

Scaling without embedding is just rollout. And rollouts generally don't last. Too often projects and digital transformation are successful during project stage, especially during planning and execution phase as there is high focus, motivation, and resources available, yet fail to transition from project to operations!

Both Claudio and the Guyana teams learned this early. Once their systems started expanding, the matrix across new business units, and RigFlow™ across drilling rigs and functions, early enthusiasm was no guarantee of long-term impact. What mattered now was whether the system would hold under pressure, evolve with growth, and stay useful as complexity increased.

This step is about making scaling real: Turning initial success into operational infrastructure.

TRANSLATE INNOVATION INTO OPERATIONAL MODELS

In Claudio's case, what began as a people-centered development tool risked becoming a static HR artifact parked on a Microsoft SharePoint™. Claudio and his team responded by translating the matrix into working templates, onboarding guides, and conversation tools that made it easier to use in real settings, creating a hook and anchoring it into daily workflows.

In Guyana, the software had replaced paper job packs. But when rolled out across rigs, teams needed clear guidance on who was responsible for the task entry, how updates would sync between onshore and offshore, and what escalation looked like. The team documented operational handbooks within the system, embedded use cases into onboarding, and adjusted workflows where needed. Extensive use of visual management onshore and offshore contributed to making the new digital system an integral part of daily workflows – not just integrated, but an essential part of operations.

Insight: If people need to be reminded to use it, or require long sessions to understand it, it's not embedded.

Action: Document what works in practice, not just what was designed. Make tools that live where the work happens. Create your hook, anchor it deep in daily workflows and promote it via visual management and/or through continuous communication.

RESOURCE THE SCALE, INTENTIONALLY

According to research done over the years, the majority of transformation efforts fail, and the failure rate for digital transformation is even higher.[3] Transformation failures are often based on the initial assumption that once something worked, say a successful pilot or proof of concept, others could just take it and run with it. They could not have been more wrong.

In the Guyana example, a "sustaining" project phase was defined and executed as the project was transitioning from project to operations. This is how you gain lasting success.

Claudio's team underestimated the support required as the matrix was adopted across sites. Supervisors needed more than a template; they needed coaching. Some teams lacked facilitation capability. So internal resources were reallocated: a few skilled leaders became regional enablers. Time was carved out for rollout and training. The matrix became part of performance reviews. Budget followed later, but resourcing began with people.

In Guyana, success in one location led to fast requests for expansion. Deploying RigFlow™ to multiple rigs meant new onboarding demands, offshore tech champions, and tighter data coordination. This meant that the project now had several parallel tracks: by the time execution began on drilling rig number two, planning was already underway for rigs three and four. Rig number one had entered the sustaining phase, with execution fully completed. A series of structured actions ensured a smooth handover: the project team transferred ownership of tasks, new end users were onboarded using customized training materials, and it was embedded into daily operations, not by outsiders, but by the very people who had implemented it. This success led to another project in early 2025, where the alliance was expanded to include a fifth rig.

Insight: Systems don't scale on intent. They scale on capacity.

Action: Map what's required: support, time, people, cost. Don't scale until you've modeled it, and resourced it.

DESIGN THE ORGANIZATION TO SUPPORT SCALED DELIVERY

New roles and new behaviors often emerge when systems scale. Claudio's matrix created a need for local stewards, people who understood the language of capability and could guide others. These weren't new hires. They were experienced team leads, recognized informally, and equipped formally. They were identified by using the matrix and as all had more clarity on their responsibilities, people became more efficient and were able/willing to take on additional responsibilities.

In Guyana, the scaled use of a digital system required clearer accountability. Offshore teams needed go-to support without defaulting to IT. Local champions were trained to manage first-line troubleshooting and feedback collection. Onshore planners were included in design sprints, creating a bridge between operations and new product development.

Insight: If no one owns it, it drifts. If everyone owns it, it dilutes.

Action: Assign roles, not just responsibilities. Make delivery part of someone's actual job, with time and support to do it well.

CLARIFY WHAT'S CORE VS. ADAPTABLE

As both systems spread, in both cases the teams naturally adapted them. Some of that adaptation improved effectiveness. Some of it introduced noise.

Claudio's team responded by making the distinction explicit: What's non-negotiable? What can flex? They kept capability levels and development paths fixed, but allowed local teams to redesign how they visualized and discussed them.

In Guyana, the core digital workflows remained standard while customizations were available. Onshore teams could customize dashboard views, and the people responsible for improving operations could see lessons learned across the fleet, notification settings, and offshore handoff routines. This flexibility made adoption easier, without compromising the integrity of the system.

Insight: If everything's open to change, nothing scales.

Action: Make it clear what must hold across the organization, and where teams are free to adapt.

Both Claudio and the team in Guyana show that success doesn't come from adding more layers; it comes from aligning the structure with how people already lead.

When systems are documented, supported, owned, and respected, they stick.

And once they stick, they can start to scale for real.

Framework for Step 3: Embed and Resource for Scaling

Key Action	*Case Insight*	*What to Do as a Leader*
Translate innovation into daily routines.	Claudio converted the matrix into onboarding kits and 1:1 tools as part of employee performance reviews. The new digital system was embedded into performance, safety, and daily operations among teams onshore and offshore.	Turn the system into one onboarding guide, one planning template, and one coaching prompt. Quality check its use regularly. If it's not in daily routines, it's not embedded.

(*Continued*)

Key Action	*Case Insight*	*What to Do as a Leader*
Resource the scale intentionally.	Claudio trained internal facilitators. Guyana assigned leads and champions onshore and offshore. Further, this was anchored in continued remote support for both technical and operational issues that the end users might face.	For every three teams, assign one enabler. Budget 20–30% time for support roles at start. The time allocated will decline over time and also depend on how often you onboard new people, how often you add new features, and how often you make changes to your workflow.
Adjust roles and org structure.	New roles and/or responsibilities appeared in both orgs: capability stewards, onboarding champions for engineers and supervisors, as well as onboarding responsibilities.	Identify two to three critical support roles that didn't exist before. Write short role scopes. Assign people. Give time. Track if issues decline in those areas. Understand who it makes sense to assign the responsibilities to. Someone the new end users are already meeting? Someone with mandate? Someone with "street credit"?
Define the core vs. what's adaptable.	Claudio listed matrix elements as "must hold" or "can flex." Guyana did the same for workflows, regulations, and custom features that end users can toggle on/off, without interfering with core workflows.	Make a simple two-column "Core vs. Custom" guide. Use it in all rollout briefings. Audit deviations quarterly. Correct drift quickly.

Step 4: Align Ecosystem Partners for Amplified Impact

Key Question: Who Do We Need to Bring in to Make an Impact beyond Our Own Boundaries?

Systems that scale often cross organizational lines before anyone plans for it.

In both Claudio's and the Guyana team's cases, the internal solutions worked, but the real shift came when external partners noticed and asked to participate. In fact, the real impact came when the wider ecosystem participated.

That's when the leadership challenge changed. It wasn't just about delivering the system to new teams. It was about inviting others in, without losing clarity or control. Scaling through an ecosystem requires trust, coordination, and just enough structure to make shared value possible, without creating bottlenecks.

MAP THE ECOSYSTEM AND ALIGN EARLY

In Claudio's case, readiness came from the field. But expansion came from the edges. Contractors began asking for access to the matrix. A major client reviewing performance management practices asked if the same framework could be extended across vendor teams. HR and training vendors raised their hands to align their content to the capability structure.

That prompted the leadership team to map the full ecosystem – not just internal users, but adjacent actors who influenced how work was done, how teams were trained, and how expectations were set.

In Guyana, the need to align came even earlier. The onshore team depended on input from service partners, whereas the offshore drilling rig performance relied on coordination with contractors and support vendors. Once the digital solution gained traction, it became clear: without bringing partners into the platform, the system would stall at the organizational boundary. This is the time when a more granular approach to the roles and permissions started. When the main team members had full access, some vendors would have just view access, or be able to input their comments.

Insight: If you're scaling in isolation, you may not be unlocking the full potential and thereby limit your impact.

Action: Identify who else touches the system, and who needs to believe in it for it to succeed. Don't wait. Bring them in early. Think of who else could be invited in to add value.

BUILD TRUST THROUGH CONSISTENCY AND TRANSPARENCY

Ecosystem engagement only works if partners trust what they're being invited into. Claudio's team didn't pitch the matrix, they demonstrated it. Contractors were included in onboarding sessions. Capability expectations were made visible. Teams used the same language across internal and partner staff.

In Guyana, platform access was expanded carefully. Vendors were shown how a digital system supported safer operations with more reliable planning. There were no promises, just performance. Offshore coordinators were given clear documentation, aligned expectations, and support when needed.

Insight: Trust isn't just a communication strategy. It's earned through consistent, shared experience and results.

Action: Share what's real. Be transparent about goals, limits, and what's expected. Trust follows when others see the system work, not when they're told or promised it will.

DESIGN PARTNERSHIPS FOR MUTUAL PERFORMANCE

Claudio's matrix wasn't handed to vendors as a requirement. It was shared as a resource. Partners who aligned their training and assessments saw reduced onboarding time, fewer misalignments, and more predictable delivery. The benefit wasn't theoretical, it was operational.

In Guyana, ecosystem collaboration reduced manual data entry – in short, *people could focus on their jobs with reduced administrative tasks.* When everyone saw the same schedule, shared the same task logic, and had aligned responsibilities, things moved faster, and with less stress.

Insight: People adopt what helps them perform, not what helps you scale.

Action: Define the mutual win. Make clear how adoption improves their efficiency, coordination, or delivery. Then build joint metrics around it.

PUT THE RIGHT AGREEMENTS IN PLACE

As the systems crossed company lines, both Claudio and Guyana needed light but effective governance.

In Claudio's case, shared access required agreements on data visibility, updating protocols, and responsibility for system upkeep. A simple role-based access model was enough to enable collaboration without legal friction.

The Guyana team worked with developers and vendors to create the correct access levels, whitelisting of URLs, and integration of existing data streams.

Insight: Good governance doesn't slow things down, it prevents things from falling apart. It might seem tedious to start with, but if you want success in the long term, you must do the groundwork from the start.

Action: Co-create agreements. Understand access and permission needs. Protect what matters. Enable what's possible. Make it easy to start, and clear how to sustain. Challenge existing ways of collaborating and show how the new tool can facilitate new and enhanced ways of working together.

Both cases prove that scaling beyond the organization doesn't happen by accident. It happens when leaders make space, and structure, for others to join.

The systems didn't grow because of mandates. They grew because people wanted in, and had a way to do so without breaking what worked.

Framework for Step 4: Align Ecosystem Partners for Amplified Impact

Key Action	*Case Insight*	*What to Do as a Leader*
Map the ecosystem and align early.	Claudio mapped training partners and vendors. Guyana opened up the system for vendors and service partners by creating new roles and access permissions. These new roles created a new level of transparency and the collaboration unlocked additional value.	List top 5 ecosystem partners by influence or interdependence. Meet with three of them. Ask what would help them use your system better.

(*Continued*)

Key Action	*Case Insight*	*What to Do as a Leader*
Build trust through consistency.	Claudio's partners saw teams using the matrix before being asked to join. Guyana's contractors got early access.	Open your rollout meetings to partners. Show real data, real results. Use transparency to build pull, not pressure. Get their inputs.
Co-design for shared performance.	Claudio's vendors saved onboarding time by aligning to the matrix. Guyana reduced revision control and document handling by designing roles in the system purely for ecosystem partners.	Identify one metric your partner cares about (e.g., onboarding speed and planning accuracy). Improve it together. Share credit and results.
Use lightweight governance to protect value.	Claudio used non-binding agreements with partners. Guyana used SLAs and phased rollout agreements.	Create one-page agreements: what's shared, what's protected, who supports. Keep it simple. Review after the first three months. Adjust if needed.

Step 5: Measure Success to Refine and Sustain

Key Question: How Do We Measure Success in Scaling to Ensure a Sustained Positive Impact?

At scale, what matters isn't whether the system is in place. What matters is whether it's still doing what it was built to do.

With both Claudio and Guyana, the systems didn't succeed because they were implemented. They succeeded because they continued to deliver real value, and because the team's leading the efforts during and post project phase had the discipline to monitor, adapt, and improve without drifting.

To be clear, this step isn't about reporting. It's about having meaningful data in place that will help guide you. It's about listening to what the system is telling you, through people, through data, and through impact. It is a continuous improvement.

ESTABLISH CLEAR OWNERSHIP AND ROLES POST-SCALE

In Claudio's case, as the matrix was adopted more widely, performance began to vary. Some teams continued to evolve and apply it with purpose. Others stalled. The difference? Ownership. The teams that had named matrix stewards, usually operational leads who were trained and resourced to maintain and adapt the tool, sustained progress.

In Guyana, success offshore depended on having someone locally responsible for usage, updates, and feedback. Teams that embedded this role saw continued coordination improvements. Teams that didn't start reverting to older habits.

Insight: With the digital system and the matrix, you suddenly have context for the data! Measurement only works if someone is responsible for what comes next.

Action: Assign clear responsibility and accountability for sustaining the system across functions. It can't be everyone's job, or no one will do it.

EMBED ROUTINES TO PROTECT QUALITY AND RELEVANCE

In Claudio's world, the highest-performing teams ran monthly check-ins to review how the matrix was used. Were levels being applied consistently? Were development conversations improving? Were people using the matrix more fulfilled? Did they now have an overview of capabilities and future needs? These weren't audits, they were routines that reinforced ownership.

Guyana's teams implemented short learning loops: shift leads held brief end-of-week reviews to flag friction, highlight good use cases, and feed small fixes back into the platform roadmap. Safety responsible held RigFlow™ briefings when new people landed on the drilling rig. Visual management was reinforced.

Insight: What gets reviewed, gets reinforced.

Action: Build lightweight operating rhythms, not one-off reviews. Feedback and reflection should be part of how the system lives, not just how it was launched.

SECURE LONG-TERM RESOURCES AND SUPPORT INFRASTRUCTURE

Sustaining progress requires investment. Not large, but intentional.

In Claudio's company, the matrix team secured training budget for local facilitators and protected time for periodic calibration across business units. They didn't build a new department, they kept the structure lean but funded.

In Guyana, platform success led to internal requests for feature upgrades, additional integrations, and partner enablement. The rollout team worked with leadership to include ongoing support in operating budgets.

Insight: If no time or money is allocated, it will be challenging to sustain your efforts.

Action: Secure resources, whether it is time or money. Ensure tools, time, and people are available to support scaled delivery, even after the initial wave of momentum fades.

KEEP LEARNING LOOPS ACTIVE AS AN INTEGRAL PART OF "BUSINESS AS USUAL"

Claudio's team didn't stop collecting input after implementation. They set up ongoing feedback loops, both at a site level and across regions, not just to catch issues, but to improve the system as teams used it in new ways. One result: the capability matrix was updated to reflect real-world use, including new cross-functional roles that emerged as the tool was adopted beyond its original scope. In Guyana, quarterly partner sessions with offshore and onshore users helped identify future needs, leading to better planning tools and smarter deployment sequences for future rigs. A "product council" was established to gather end-user feedback and jointly prioritize new developments and upcoming pilots.

Insight: If you're not learning, your system will become obsolete.

Action: Run regular reviews that involve the people using the system, not just those who built it. Set weekly, quarterly, and/or yearly reviews. Make it creative and enable co-design as per design thinking principles. Create a space where honest feedback can be provided and will enable even closer relationships.

TRACK LONG-TERM IMPACT, NOT JUST ACTIVITY

Claudio's team didn't celebrate usage statistics. They looked for signs that the matrix was driving the behaviors it was meant to enable: capability-based staffing, clearer development conversations, and increased workforce agility.

In Guyana, success wasn't about how many plans were created in the digital system. It was about increased safety, procedural compliance, reduction in manual work, fewer coordination delays, and improved offshore decision-making, with confidence in the data behind those decisions.

Insight: True scaling requires measuring what matters: impact on behavior, decisions, and capabilities, not just activity levels.

Action: Clearly define and regularly update meaningful metrics focused on behavioral change, decision quality, and organizational capability. Continuously monitor and realign your approach to sustain impactful outcomes.

Framework for Step 5: Measure Success to Refine and Sustain

Key Action	*Case Insight*	*What to Do as a Leader*
Assign ownership post-scale.	In both Claudio and Guyana, sustained progress depended on having named, empowered individuals responsible for maintaining and evolving the system.	Name an owner per site or function. Measure: usage rate, support requests, and feedback quality. No owner? No accountability.
Embed regular rhythms for quality at scale.	High-performing teams ran recurring reviews, not audits, to reinforce relevance and resolve friction early, creating a culture of shared stewardship.	Implement a monthly system health review: data and discussion. Include one user voice. Track 2–3 quality indicators.

(Continued)

Key Action	*Case Insight*	*What to Do as a Leader*
Secure support, funding, and time.	Both cases secured lean but dedicated support: training, tools, and operating budget, not large, but consistent and embedded in ops.	Move budget from "project" to "operations." Lock in % of FTE or contractor hours to sustain rollout. Show value in cost avoidance or adoption gains.
Keep learning loops active.	Claudio built in-site and regional feedback cycles. Guyana created a user council to co-design updates. Learning became part of how the system lived.	Run quarterly learning sessions. Collect feedback anonymously. Choose one change to implement each quarter. Communicate it widely.
Track long-term impact (not just usage).	Success of Claudio and Guyana was measured by behavior change and better decisions—not dashboards, but real-world improvements.	Define two outcome metrics tied to the original problem (e.g., onboarding time, safety, and team mobility). Use them to guide future investments.

Claudio didn't set out to build a system for scale. He set out to bring clarity and fairness to how people grow. But when the matrix worked, when teams started owning it, improving it, and using it to make better decisions, the question changed. It wasn't, *can we sustain this?* It was, *can we take this further without breaking what made it work?*

In Guyana, the goal wasn't to roll out a "just another digital tool." It was to solve a real operational problem, manual planning that wasted time. It was to enhance safety and to enable and strengthen a growing alliance between multiple partners, vendors.

RigFlow™ worked because it helped people do their jobs better. And when offshore crews started asking for it, using it, and improving it, the same question emerged: *Are we ready to grow this without losing the trust it took to build it?*

This is the work of scaling and amplifying impact.

It's not about spreading a product. It's about growing a system that people will actually use, believe in, and want to contribute to.

If you've built something that's delivering value, something your people trust, that works in the real world, then the next challenge is not, *what to do*, but how to do it. You have seen how!

You've seen the frameworks. You've worked through the leadership moves that matter, understanding the How!

Up next is the story of Esben and Michael, two leaders who helped spin out a corporate startup and scale it into a global player, all while navigating the balance and tension between innovation and operations – one still ongoing to this day! It's not just a case study, but a blueprint for what bold, grounded leadership looks like under pressure.

Then we'll meet Lucy, an offshore petroleum engineer and digital transformation leader in one of the world's most complex industries. Her approach? Lead with heart, decide with clarity, and build relations with people. Her story reminds us that real, lasting impact, starts with how you show up for your people.

NOTES

1 In Agile methodology, a *retrospective* is a regular team meeting, typically held at the end of a work cycle, to reflect on what went well, what didn't, and how to improve moving forward. Claudio held these weekly based on agile principles to review what worked well and what needed improvement.

2 *Software as a Service (SaaS)* is a cloud-based delivery model where users access software via the Internet rather than installing it locally. It enables scalable, subscription-based access, centralized updates, and secure collaboration across organizations. For more information, see www.docschlosser.com.

3 See Bonnet, D. (2022). *3 Stages of a Successful Digital Transformation*, Harvard Business Review. The article cites studies showing that failure rates for digital transformations range from 70% to 95%, with an average of 87.5%.

Chapter 11

Balancing Operations and Exploring Future Business

The Horizon56 Journey

Esben Thorup's words highlight the innovative side of this book's core argument: how to make things happen. With an entrepreneurial mindset, he helped spin Horizon56 out of a legacy organization, seizing opportunities, challenging norms, and building something from scratch. To balance Ebsen, Michael Olesen brings the discipline required to scale: structured, detail-focused, and operationally grounded. While Esben leans into disruption, Michael ensures consistency, quality, and control, together embodying the balance that next-generation leaders must enable.

Leaders like Esben and Michael enable lasting impact. This chapter illustrates how they did it, using the Enablers presented throughout this book: striking the right balance – or imbalance – to drive meaningful change through transparency, structures, ecosystems, technology, transformation, and scaling. Through an honest dialogue, they reveal how they navigated these complexities in a rapidly growing technology company within the energy sector.

I introduced Horizon56 in Chapter 10, where I detailed its extraordinary growth and enabling digital transformation for super majors. This chapter tells that story through the voices of those who led the journey, Thorup Esben and Michael Olesen.

I had the opportunity to work directly with both Esben and Michael during our time at Horizon56. I chose to include their voices in this chapter not just because of that shared experience, but because their leadership under pressure, their balancing of innovation and operations, and scaling of a digital startup to becoming a driver for digital transformation for super majors of the world offer rare, real-world insight into what it truly takes to build and scale something meaningful.

Esben Thorup, CEO, comes from an engineering background and spent several years leading major projects in a global engineering, architecture and consultancy company. Esben recently relocated to Houston, TX from Denmark. Esben

DOI: 10.4324/9781003638551-12

transitioned into the energy sector, assuming multiple leadership positions, all related to innovation and technology.

Michael Olesen, COO, brings close to 20 years of experience from offshore drilling operations, starting his career as a mechanic, and then becoming a mechanical engineer by education. Originally from Denmark, Michael has worked internationally throughout his career. His talent was recognized early on when he was selected for the shipping company Maersk's prestigious offshore talent development program.

As you can see, Esben and Michael are complete opposites: Esben is the face of innovation, loves variance and takes risks: "Visionary leaders who champion innovation are crucial to overcoming this natural inaction. Without sustained, long-term support from leadership, innovative initiatives rarely survive."

Michael, on the other hand, does what he can to reduce variance, reduce risks and focus on process and stability: "I hope we don't see the same expansion as the last couple of years. We need stability to ensure we don't lose control of what we've built."

Esben and Michael were not alone in leaving their stable careers and predictable working hours, to drive the digital future in the energy sector. Therefore, before we dive into the interview, I would like to share this conversation I had with Mikael Skov. I am sharing it with you because it truly shows how the company was fully focused on exploration and innovation in a market where no such products existed. This will also give you an understanding of the balancing act the leadership team constantly has to navigate – how much focus on innovation and how much focus on operations? The company is based on innovation, the success came from innovative product design and development. The success demanded a project and operations team to be established, countering the explorative culture!

Here is how Mikael put it to me word for word. I am sharing this with you because it shows the passion and that despite it being years since the early days, the culture and the drive are still there!

When I write about Horizon56, it is critical to understand that early journey with all the ups and downs, because it is so defining for the culture as a company. We kept on pushing through all these obstacles even though we were on the brink of closing so many times. However, we had a belief in our product that was so strong that we managed to find a way every time. This culture is what still stands today and what keeps us going in the rough times.

In 2025, I was posted in Houston, Texas, and Mikael came to visit as part of joint client meetings. One evening before dinner, I told him about my book project and despite having worked together, I never heard the story on how he got involved with Horizon56 and from there, the conversation took off.

Mikael leaned back, and started telling me a story that captured the raw spirit of those first years.

"This company almost didn't make it," he said.

Back in 2018–2019, Horizon56 wasn't even a company; it was still an innovation exploration project. It was just an idea born out of a collaboration between a major offshore drilling contractor's innovation team and a North Sea operator's push to move beyond the old paper-based process. Mikael, then with another digital provider, teamed up with the contractor's innovation team to chase it through a tender. A tender is the formal bidding process that decides who gets the contract, if any. Win the tender and the idea gets the fuel to grow. Lose it, and the spark goes out.

When that bid collapsed, so did the momentum. For months, it felt like the project was finished before it had even begun. This is how so many corporate innovation experiments end, quietly, with no announcement, just a slow fade as resources drift away. Innovation inside big companies doesn't usually die because the idea is weak; it dies because it never gets the backing to stand on its own feet.

Those months dragged on. Every week without progress felt heavier. Market conditions weren't helping either. After setback on top of setback, I remember thinking, *this is it,* Mikael told me, *The project we had put so much energy and belief into was dead.*

Then came a phone call.

In the summer of 2019, Esben called Mikael and asked if he could build the product from scratch. Mikael agreed, but only if he could set the team himself. That's when he asked Marius Hjelmervik (Marius who also took part in the tender) to continue his design work and in addition brought in Christoffer Jacobsen and Øystein Hopland Brattetaule – all three of whom are still part of Horizon56. By October 2019, they were officially underway. Remarkably, by April 2020, the first version of the system was ready for a rig test pilot program.

Then COVID hit. Everything froze. Projects were slashed across the sector. Mikael told me bluntly, "We thought we had to totally shut down."

But they didn't.

Instead, he, Craig, and Esben kept grinding with another operator, week after week, pushing for an opening. Mid-2020, they managed to pilot the system on a rig in the North Sea, running it alongside the operator's in-house procedure system. Later that year, they deployed on another rig.

It still wasn't smooth sailing. Integration with one of the major systems failed, and again it looked like the end. But in the background, Mikael, Marius, and Craig together designed and developed a tool for creating operational instructions. The first to test it wasn't even their main customer, but another international operator. Soon after came the breakthrough: a contract with a supermajor that gave Horizon56 its pivotal moment.

What you see in this period is pure exploration turning into innovation: chasing what the market needed, turning ideas into working prototypes through rapid design and development. The team was an unlikely mix, offshore veterans, a software developer, a designer, a front-end programmer, and two engineers, working shoulder to shoulder with end-users, co-designing, and testing at speed. That combination of passion and pace paid off, leading to a breakthrough contract. As Mikael told me, "That's when I realized we were going to make it."

He laughed when he said it, but it was clear how close they had been to collapse. What kept them alive wasn't perfect plans or secured funding, *it was belief.* Belief in the product and the positive impact on the end-users, belief in the team, belief that if they just kept pushing, and did not back down, they would find a way through.

And that deep belief and determination became culture. Today, the persistence, the determination and exploration is still what the management team and the employees are known for.

That era was 100% innovation and exploration.

Now, it's time to dive into the interview with Michael and Esben and how they today balance innovation and operation, while staying true to the culture forged the early days. Trying to understand how Esben and Michael, two opposite profiles, are so successful together?

It is like the center of our model, operations and innovation – the dynamic finds the balance. Personally, I can tell they both have what I would call a *pitbull mindset* (you are right, they do not come across like that, but don't be mistaken, they are persistent like few are) – and they want to get the job done no matter what. They value people more than anything and they both understand the objectives, also when the road is unclear.

Esben and Michael openly discuss their journey below, offering authentic insights into how they balanced the complex dynamics of building and maintaining operational excellence while driving innovative exploration. This conversation provides rare transparency into the real-life application of strategic frameworks, the challenges and rewards of building effective structures, cultivating robust ecosystems, leveraging cutting-edge technology, and successfully scaling an innovative enterprise.

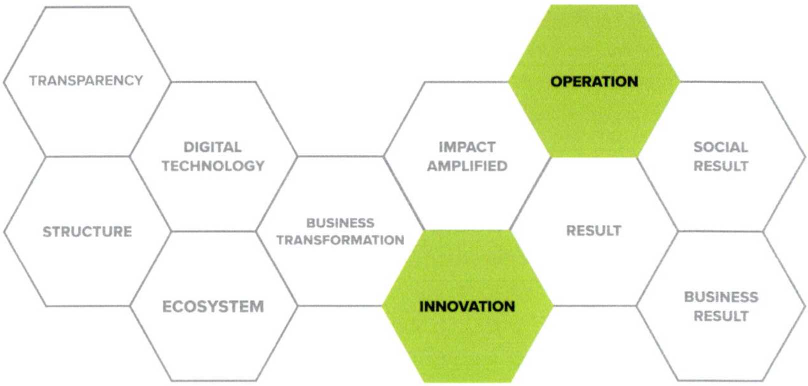

Figure 11.1 Balancing Operations and Innovation

As you engage with their dialogue, consider reflecting on your own organizational experiences and see how these Enablers are at play in your environment. The dialogue will encourage you to think critically about your own approach to leadership, innovation, and organizational growth.

Below, you will find the honest reflections and lessons learned from Esben and Michael, offering practical examples of how to navigate and thrive amid complexity and rapid change.

Before we dive into this dialogue, I want to draw your attention to our transparency and empowerment Enablers. Throughout this conversation, you'll notice how Esben and Michael consistently describe the empowerment they received, the trust, autonomy, and ownership that enabled them to succeed. Just as crucially, you'll see how they passed on that empowerment to their teams, fueling passion and high performance through radical transparency.

Horizon56's success was made possible by **two levels of empowerment:**

1. **From the owners:** Long-term funding, autonomy to run the business, and access to top talent from the parent company, allowing Horizon56 to operate and innovate freely.
2. **From Esben and Michael to their teams:** Staying true to who they are and where they came from – not trying to fit into a corporate box. Handpicking the right people, trusting them to take ownership, and using transparency to align everyone around a shared vision.

KEY THEMES TO LOOK OUT FOR:

- **Vision & Backing** – Owner's trust and funding enabled long-term innovation without immediate pressure for profits.
- **Building the Right Team** – Horizon56 strategically selected top talent, including key hires from the parent company.
- **Empowerment** – Esben and Michael fostered ownership, skill development, and autonomy in execution.
- **Transparency and Alignment** – Open communication clarified roles in operations vs. innovation and kept everyone on the same page. Esben used extreme transparency to share cash flow and deals which were won. But also when key deals were lost, Esben openly expressed his views, the impact on the company and how they all could move ahead from such loss.

INTERVIEW WITH ESBEN THORUP AND MICHAEL OLESEN

Kristian: What does it take to lead innovation when operations, originally a secondary focus, is now a rapidly growing core responsibility?

Esben: When I think about balancing core business and exploring new ventures, I see it like managing a legacy, a stable, well-running operation, while simultaneously looking ahead to innovation and expansion. Take our example with Noble Corporation:[1] we have established, reliable operations, yet we're constantly seeking ways to expand and innovate. But it's tricky," he admits, "there's inherent conflict when you're balancing the certainty of operations against the unpredictability of exploration.

Kristian: That's exactly right, Esben. Your story fascinates me precisely because Horizon56 began within Maersk as an internal innovation team. Then, for specific reasons, reasons that I'm genuinely curious about, you decided to spin off and become your own separate entity. Initially, you continued as primarily an oil and gas exploration unit. But as you grew, operations inevitably came into play, and that's when Michael entered the picture.

Esben: Now, Horizon56 itself embodies both exploration and operations. It's fascinating to see how scaling introduces different cultures, behaviors, and tensions between these two dimensions. Early on, exploration might dominate, but eventually, structured processes and operational excellence become crucial to maintaining cash flow and sustainability.

Kristian: Could you talk more about those early days, before Horizon56 even existed as we know it today?

Esben: Absolutely. I often picture it like climbing stairs. Initially, you have a large established business, like Maersk Drilling, and you consider spinning off a new venture. As you successfully do this, your new business grows, eventually becoming substantial enough that you end up with a structure resembling your original starting point.

He paused,

Every spin-off story is unique. However there are certain foundational enablers, critical things that absolutely must align. To be honest, I struggle to single out one dominant factor behind our success because, in reality, it wasn't one thing. There were many smaller, interconnected elements.

Esben continued,

First and foremost was visionary management support. In large organizations, there's often a resistance to innovation, new ideas are perceived as wasteful or unnecessary. Visionary leaders who champion innovation are crucial to overcoming this natural inaction. Without sustained, long-term support from leadership, innovative initiatives rarely survive.

Kristian: What does it actually take to make a corporate spinout succeed?

Ebsen: Then there's clarity about your focus. You must pick something relevant, substantial, and aligned with your core strengths. It's not enough to just have an idea; you need a real value proposition. You must identify your unfair competitive advantage. In our case, Horizon56 benefited tremendously from Noble's deep industry experience and unique access to resources. These assets and resources are unique and a pure startup wouldn't easily access or afford these.

Esben continued,

Assets and resources like deep offshore drilling knowledge, talent and HR support, funding, access to offshore units globally, and a team of executives who supported with their experience and network to help Horizon56 reputation within the sector

Kristian: Esben, can you speak to how you enabled and benefitted from the ecosystem?

Ebsen: Yes, customer connections are vital. Early engagement and establishing an ecosystem, enabled by their relationship with

> Maersk, provided credibility. There's always resistance to adopting new solutions in conservative industries like offshore energy, companies typically want proven solutions. A startup might have the perfect idea, but without trusted pathways, they'll struggle. Our established connections and industry experience allowed us critical early proof points.

This is fully aligned with ecosystem thinking and Esben, with support from Noble, understood the value of leveraging the ecosystem:

Kristian: What other resources or capabilities are you tapping into?
Esben: Funding is another key. Building a business-to-business operation isn't something you achieve in a few months, it takes sustained investment over several years. Accepting this reality upfront is essential. This is a critical point which has been raised by several leading researchers referring to this as "timeframe to be profitable."

Often owners and investors give too little time for the exploration unit to become successful and turn a profit. This links back to what Esben mentioned in the beginning about "visionary leadership" and how the owner kept funding and supporting Horizon56 for several years before the company turned a profit – it took years to break even. Imagine the trust from leadership, the board and investors who year after year must pour cash into this new, blue ocean, startup:

Kristian: So, what makes the difference when everything else is uncertain – processes, funding, timing?

Esben highlighted what he believed was perhaps the most important enabler of all:

Esben: People. The right people, those committed deeply to the journey rather than just performing a job. To be honest, I don't fully understand how we managed this perfectly early on, but we did. Software and innovation are inherently people-driven businesses, and without strong people, you simply won't succeed.
Kristian: Michael, Esben mentioned something crucial, getting the right people in early. You came directly from offshore drilling, where conditions are both lucrative and stable. How did Horizon56 manage to persuade you?
Michael: Well, I believe there's always an element of stars aligning. Most startups fail because something goes off track early on. But we had support, 'a big brother' watching over us. Without Noble's backing us financially and structurally, we likely wouldn't have survived those critical early years.

Michael's reply captures something every next-generation leader should recognize: success doesn't come from vision alone, it's about having the right enablers in place, early and consistently. What he described wasn't just good fortune. It was **ecosystem**, the presence of a stable, trusted partner offering financial and operational support when it mattered most. It was **structure**, not in the org chart sense, but in the clarity of roles, decision rights, and the space to operate with autonomy. And, above all, it was **empowerment** and **transparency**, committed individuals who believed in the mission before the business had fully proven itself. That's how transformation takes root, not through heroic effort, but through a system designed to enable impact:

Michael: Initially, I wasn't that interested. Esben called me when I was assigned elsewhere. I redirected him to Craig, who was eventually hired by Esben. Somehow Craig and Esben kept pulling me back into their orbit. Then the pandemic hit, which changed everything. Offshore work meant quarantines and disruptions, and suddenly, helping Horizon56 seemed more feasible. (*Michael smiled, still somewhat amazed*) I agreed to help deploy just one rig. That was four and a half years ago.

REFLECTIONS:

- What you see happening here is that Michael is being brought in by Esben to deploy the software for the very first time. Until now it has all been experiments in controlled environments. Now, Michael has to deploy the technology on an offshore unit and this will be the first step in starting, what today is a large operations division within Horizon56 – note, until this point, Horizon56 was pure innovation with design, experiments, prototypes and had never been in operations.
- Sometimes, successful innovation hinges on the flexibility to recognize and seize unexpected opportunities. Has your organization experienced unexpected circumstances that presented unplanned yet valuable opportunities?

I listened intently, fascinated by how small details could shift an entire trajectory.

Kristian: Michael, your involvement seems almost coincidental, yet clearly instrumental. How important do you believe luck and timing are, compared to strategic planning, when starting something new?

Michael: You absolutely need both. Strategic clarity and planning are essential, of course. But no amount of planning can fully account for timing and luck. Sometimes, the stars must align, as they did for us.

He paused,

We've been fortunate to reach this point. Even when you have a strong project and the right people, success isn't guaranteed.

Kristian: Espen, earlier, before Michael joined, Horizon56 was heavily focused on exploration and innovation. Michael's role was crucial, transitioning innovation into operational reality. Could you comment?

Esben: I can clearly remember my initial phone call with Michael. But I genuinely can't remember if we discussed how long you would stay?

Michael: Yes, we did. It was supposed to be just three months (*he responded with alacrity*).

Esben: I thought it might extend beyond three months, but I genuinely didn't know how long it would take. It wasn't a deliberate deception, more like a sincere underestimation. You know, recruiting for this kind of role requires someone willing to step away from traditional career paths and take risks. It's not easy to find such passionate individuals. We've been fortunate in many cases, though there have been exceptions.

Michael: True. We've seen high-profile hires that just didn't fit. Sometimes throwing money at talent doesn't guarantee success. We've experienced this firsthand, especially during scaling and in locations which were new to us. We brought in highly qualified individuals who simply weren't suited to our pace and style of working.

Esben: Exactly. Early on, we hired consultants who, on paper, looked great but were ultimately ineffective. They lacked alignment with our culture and objectives.

REFLECTIONS:

- Think of a situation where someone on your team stepped completely outside their role, took ownership, and solved a problem. How did it feel for the team afterward? Did you celebrate this openly? Imagine the effect on your team if such moments were the standard, not the exception.
- Picture your own CEO or senior manager performing tasks usually considered "too small," perhaps troubleshooting an issue, joining the frontline workers, or personally handling customer feedback. How would witnessing that action change your perception of leadership? How might it influence your own willingness to go the extra mile?

Kristian: Finding the right talent seems central yet tricky. Esben and Michael, your roles in operations demand structure and consistency, quite different from the innovative side of Horizon56. How do you balance bringing in the right people for each side without creating an 'us versus them' mentality? Have you witnessed friction between operations and innovation?

Esben: Yes, absolutely. It's natural that there's some friction. Everyone at Horizon56 understands we're on a continuous journey, change is inevitable. Yet, from an end-user perspective, stability is preferable. People appreciate applications that remain consistent over time. However, innovation inherently means continual improvement, adding new features, and accepting temporary instability. Balancing these two desires, stability and advancement, is complex but essential.

Michael: Ideally, people want both stability and innovation simultaneously. The challenge lies in prioritizing effectively. When introducing improvements, initial instability can occur. We must accept this as part of our growth.

I pressed Esben to provide a concrete example.

Kristian: Esben, could you share a recent instance where you had to navigate this delicate balance? Perhaps something involving resource allocation or funding decisions?

Esben: Certainly. Our experience with our clients illustrates this perfectly. They preferred stability, sticking with proven technology, which we recently deployed. Meanwhile, we aimed to upgrade our platform significantly – an upgrade which is client driven. Initially, we underestimated the complications of managing two parallel systems simultaneously, dealing with diverse user expectations. It quickly became evident how challenging balancing innovation with operational stability could be.

REFLECTIONS:

Now, let us revisit our technology Enabler. What I want you to truly grasp here is the critical lesson Horizon56 learned from their global technology deployment with a major client. Horizon56 initially spent over two years rolling out their digital solution worldwide. That first deployment was timed perfectly, introducing technology at a "high" level, significantly reshaping workflows and routines. People embraced the solution, although naturally it required significant adaptation.

However, when Horizon56 introduced subsequent upgrades, even though these were "lower-level" incremental enhancements, the timing created challenges. The upgrades arrived concurrently with the tail end of the initial rollout, overwhelming end-users who had just begun to feel comfortable. Users still adjusting to the initial deployment found the simultaneous introduction of new features and interfaces challenging.

The key takeaway here, and something you should reflect upon, is the importance of timing and sequencing when managing technological change. Even simple upgrades, if poorly timed or overlapping with ongoing changes, can overwhelm teams. Horizon56 discovered that the perceived simplicity of new technology matters less than how and when it's introduced to end-users.

As you consider your own organization's technology strategy, ask yourself:

- How carefully are you timing and sequencing your technology deployments?
- Have you considered how concurrent deployments might impact your team's capacity and morale?
- Could you create clearer separation or staging to ensure technology introductions feel manageable rather than overwhelming?

Kristian: Michael, I'm curious about your perspective on designing and managing Horizon56's global structure. Earlier, Esben covered how Horizon56 was spun off. Since then you have built teams in Denmark, Norway, India, and the U.S. On top of this, you're running projects in Africa, the Middle East, Australia, Central Asia and South America. How do you manage this distribution and resource allocation?

Michael: You're intimately familiar with our approach, having been a key part of it. Initially, I handpicked individuals we trusted deeply, forming a core team with strong, proven capabilities. Unlike my past offshore experience, where we couldn't choose our team members, Horizon56 gave us the rare chance to select precisely who we needed. It created a high-performance environment, crucial during our rapid growth and also crucial as we were doing something no one had done before. Without our owners' belief in us we would never have had the funding to bring consultants and offshore leadership folks on to our payroll. However, as we expand globally, it's becoming very difficult to maintain such an approach. We must accept some variability in performance, relying on strong local leaders to uphold standards and guide newer team members.

Esben was quick to expand on Michael's point:

Ebsen: Managing global teams significantly amplifies structural complexity. If we were a traditional company in a single location, communication and coordination would be simpler. With teams spread across multiple time zones, clear and structured communication becomes critical. There are undeniable advantages, like global talent recruitment and easier regional expansion. Yet, we also face significant downsides, like communication gaps and reduced personal connections.

Michael: Not everyone thrives in remote work environments. Our global structure demands careful hiring, emphasizing people who can effectively communicate and operate independently. It's an ongoing balancing act.

REFLECTIONS:

Reflecting on Horizon56's structural Enabler, several insights emerge from Esben and Michael's experiences. Horizon56 was purposefully spun out from Maersk Drilling to create a distinct, autonomous space specifically dedicated to innovation, allowing rapid decision-making free from bureaucratic barriers and conflicting priorities of the core business.

To facilitate swift growth, Michael adopted a matrix organization combined with project-based teams who would lead projects in different parts of the world, what I would refer to as "project nomads." These structures provided critical flexibility in resource allocation and supported high autonomy levels necessary for rapid market responsiveness. On a strategic level, this was achieved by relocating members of the original core team to key growth locations. For instance, Michael relocated Kristian to Houston to drive strategic U.S. market expansion and effectively embed the company's culture and operational expertise locally.

Esben and Michael underscored the strategic necessity of clearly separating exploratory units from operations to foster innovation without disruption to established business routines – yet not losing the key link between operations and innovation. Operations are close to end users, know the clients and therefore can provide valuable inputs to innovation initiatives.

- Have you strategically separated your innovation activities from operations to ensure each can thrive without hindrance?
- Do you have a clear and balanced resource allocation strategy that prioritizes both exploratory innovation and operational excellence?
- How effectively does your organization leverage key personnel relocations to drive strategic growth and embed organizational culture in critical markets?

Kristian: Michael, with Horizon56 operating across different geographies and teams, how did you ensure alignment and fast decision-making in such a dispersed setup, especially during high-pressure deployment phases?

Michael: All the years I've spent offshore drilling have ingrained the importance of clear, constant communication. Consider having six crews in Norway – if something happens with one crew, it's essential that everyone else knows immediately, including those who are off duty. We've always prioritized strong communication, especially during deployment phases. Often, when challenges arose, we wondered why certain crucial information hadn't reached everyone. But in our case, we've managed to build an environment where knowledge sharing is key, making use of digital platforms and ensuring everyone remains aligned and informed daily. That's been critical to making our global structure work effectively.

I now wanted to shift our conversation toward the impressive scale achieved by Horizon56:

Kristian: Considering how rapidly Horizon56 has grown, I find it intriguing because scaling an exploration-focused unit is notoriously difficult. Research doesn't typically highlight successful cases of rapidly scaling such innovative entities. So, what's been the real driver of growth? Is it primarily about the people, expanding the global footprint, or are there critical customer and partner integrations at play?

Esben: Fundamentally, the driver behind our growth has been the strong market demand, a clear platform where our solutions and services meet a genuine customer need. But growth isn't always linear. For instance, during the early COVID period, we had resources but not enough deployment activity. In hindsight, we were somewhat inventing work to keep busy, a common pitfall in larger organizations.

He continued,

> Real growth occurs when there's a clear pull from the market, enabling us to respond proactively or reactively by scaling our capabilities. Yet scaling rapidly brings complexity. As we add more people, information sharing and alignment on projects become exponentially more complicated. Roles and responsibilities often overlap or, conversely, fall through the gaps. Clear delineation becomes challenging because what we anticipated even six months ago might not align with our current reality. Ultimately, it comes down to effective planning, forecasting demand, understanding organizational needs, and structuring accordingly. But even the best-laid plans are adaptable, revised regularly as new challenges emerge.

Kristian: Michael, in terms of scale, if we were to revisit this conversation a few years from now, what would you hope to see for Horizon56?

Michael: Looking ahead a few years, I hope our rapid growth stabilizes somewhat. We've expanded so aggressively that now might be the right moment to pause, to consolidate, and ensure our foundations are solid. I'm not suggesting we halt expansion completely, because new opportunities might emerge. But right now, my priority would be to achieve stability, making sure we're not simply scaling for the sake of growth. We must maintain quality and purpose in everything we deliver.

Michael continued,

> It's critical that we don't become overly consumed by rapid expansion and lose sight of our core competencies. I believe firmly in providing practical, efficient solutions that truly benefit operations, rather than just mass-producing products for growth's sake. Doubling our current size without carefully ensuring this alignment wouldn't necessarily be beneficial.

Kristian: So, you're emphasizing a period of foundational stability. It reminds me of what we spoke about earlier during this interview about the challenges we faced with software upgrades, where unforeseen pushback underscored the need for a stable foundation.

Michael: Exactly. It's crucial to have that balance. If you were discussing this with our head of development, their perspective might differ, likely favoring rapid advancement. But stability and innovation must coexist carefully. If we neglect stability, we risk failure; yet, if we stop innovating, we risk becoming obsolete.

Kristian: It's almost like true balance involves intentional shifts between innovation and stability, sometimes leaning more heavily in one direction to address current needs.

Michael: Absolutely. We've begun shifting towards stability after intense growth. A concrete example is our customer support. Initially, we underestimated the importance of robust post-deployment support. Over the past year, we've invested significantly to strengthen this area. Effective support is vital, particularly in our sector where operational downtime can be incredibly costly. Our clients consistently remind us that while innovation is exciting, reliability is essential.

If we look at our Enabler scaling and amplify, Horizon56 didn't just respond to demand, they created it. Initially, the pull came from one client who believed in their solution based on a need from their organization. Now, through targeted expansion, Horizon56 has made its technology known to the industry globally and after several years of hard work, a global pull came from the super major players.

Esben and Michael scaled by strategically embedding their platform into client operations, proving its value onshore and offshore, and securing long-term buy-in. They leveraged deep industry connections, first by drawing talent from their parent company and later by partnering with key clients to refine and expand the product. Capacity was built methodically, not just by hiring but by relocating trusted core team members to strategic locations, ensuring cultural alignment and local execution.

However, rapid scale brought growing pains. Information silos, shifting priorities, and overlapping roles threatened efficiency. Horizon56 tackled this through agile restructuring, adjusting teams, refining responsibilities, and continuously aligning resources to client demand. Instead of blindly expanding, they maintained tight operational control while amplifying their impact on end users.

I then wanted to understand how Horizon56 works with clients and partners:

Kristian: Listening to Esben, it almost sounds as though Horizon56 has evolved and has become the innovation department of key clients, thereby enabling an even closer relationship?

Michael: Yes, we're deeply integrated and often co-develop solutions directly with our customers.

Kristian: Would you say we've become an extension of the clients' exploration capabilities?

Michael: Absolutely, especially in the digital space. Many of our clients rely on us to test and refine their innovative ideas, making operations safer and more efficient. For example, one of our major clients brought us the initial concept for of one of our solutions, Rig Plan™. Rather than our client developing this on their own, they partnered with us and used our design and development expertise, enabling their future and digital vision. Therefore, they invested in its development to see if we could create something valuable – and together we did. Our client acquired a new digital capability, and we developed a new product we could offer our other global clients. Initially, five years ago, our clients had vague ideas, and it was largely up to Esben and the innovation team to define and shape these into practical solutions.

Kristian: That's a significant shift, from shaping the client's ideas to now co-owning the roadmap. It sounds like you've moved from being a vendor to a strategic partner and enabler of their digital journeys.

Michael: Now, we've advanced to a stage where clients have clear visions for further enhancements. They're actively participating in shaping our product roadmaps, reflecting a deeper integration and partnership. Today, we have a long backlog of new features which have been requested by our clients and their end users. This is a unique position to be in; we can now design and develop what the market needs.

Esben: Historically, large organizations attempted to develop their capabilities internally. Many times, these projects resulted in expensive failures. Nowadays, companies are more inclined to partner with specialists like us rather than risk internal development. It's strategic: our clients recognize that Horizon56 is uniquely positioned to innovate efficiently, making us their preferred partner for digital transformation.

Kristian: So how would that look in Horizon56?

Esben: To facilitate this, we have created a quarterly product council where we invite representatives from each of our clients. This is unique as clients, who normally are competitors, fly in from around the world to align on a digital roadmap, delivered by us. Moreover, we have created strategic partnerships with software developers who can support our Chief Technology Officer Mikael Skov's team.

Kristian: Michael, given your role and proximity to end-users, how do you effectively advocate for resources within the stakeholders, especially when others might prioritize exploration and innovation over operational stability?

Michael: Clear communication and evidence-based advocacy have been essential. I've even brought direct feedback and recordings from customer interactions to executive meetings, clearly illustrating where we needed improvement. Highlighting these real, frontline experiences made the need for action undeniable. Fortunately, our leadership, especially from Esben, has been responsive, understanding, and willing to allocate resources accordingly.

Kristian: So, it's about using evidence and transparency to create urgency, making sure both internal leadership and external stakeholders truly see the challenges faced by frontline teams and clients.

Michael: Exactly. Transparent communication has always been a cornerstone for us. Every team member, regardless of their role, feels empowered to speak up. If something seems off, it's our duty to highlight it openly. This culture ensures continuous improvement and accountability.

Horizon56 has mastered ecosystem thinking, transforming traditional client relationships into strategic partnerships that fuel both innovation and scalability. Unlike conventional setups where companies develop technology in isolation, Horizon56 has positioned itself as an extension of its clients' exploration capabilities. By co-developing solutions with major industry players, clients who would typically be competitors, they've created a dynamic innovation loop where market needs drive product evolution.

A standout example is RigFlow™, initially a client's concept that Horizon56 designed, developed, and ultimately scaled into its product portfolio and adopted across the industry. This model of shared innovation means clients invest in the digital roadmap, ensuring new developments are relevant, valuable, and immediately deployable. Rather than merely selling products, Horizon56 integrates deeply with its clients, shaping their future operations while securing long-term business.

To formalize this approach, they established a quarterly product council, where competing companies align on shared digital needs. This level of cross-industry collaboration is rare, yet it accelerates adoption and ensures Horizon56 remains central to the industry's digital transformation. Additionally, key software partnerships enhance their ability to scale efficiently.

Imagine a small startup bringing together the industry's biggest players, competitors who now align on a shared digital roadmap. This isn't just about technology; it's a testament to the credibility Horizon56 has built through the culture and values the entire Horizon56 team live by and by leveraging the ecosystem to its fullest.

To conclude the interview, I shifted the conversation toward a more personal dimension:

Kristian: Before we wrap up, I'm genuinely interested in hearing about your personal journeys. Esben, you've transitioned from an innovation department lead to the CEO of Horizon56. Michael, your journey brought you from offshore drilling operations into the role of COO at a rapidly growing company, surrounded by uncertainty. How have you both personally adapted to these significant changes?

Esben: That's an important question. Honestly, we're not the same people we were four or five years ago. If someone were hiring for our current position based purely on past experiences or resumes, we probably wouldn't meet the qualifications. However, our true strength comes from the deep, hands-on understanding we've gained along this journey. We've grown into these roles through direct experience, fueled by pride and passion for what we've built.

Michael: I've often mentioned in our management meetings that perhaps with more time, formal training might have better prepared us for the roles we hold today. Initially, we were very hands-on, deeply involved in operations or specific design tasks. The jobs we have now are radically different from what we were originally hired for. Everything we've learned has been through on-the-job experience and constant adaptation.

Michael pauses briefly before reflecting deeper,

> I sometimes wonder if, given more structured training or guidance, we could have avoided certain challenges or pitfalls. Not to say it would have drastically altered our trajectory, but a little more preparation might have smoothed some bumps. Nonetheless, our ability to adapt, learn quickly, and rely on each other carried us through.

Esben: That's true, though we also have a leadership team of people who often wouldn't prioritize formal training even if offered. In retrospect, taking dedicated time to regular structured guidance, perhaps a week every half year, might have benefited us. But there's also something valuable about our organic growth. We've developed authentically, facing challenges directly, which gives us genuine credibility.

Michael: Absolutely. From the beginning, the original Horizon56 team had a unique quality and resilience. These were people willing and able to shoulder significant pressure without buckling. They were driven to continuously improve, learn from challenges, and do better each day. This resilience became our backbone, especially during high-pressure periods.

Esben: I also think there's something powerful about our less traditional backgrounds. We aren't overly polished or textbook-driven managers. Instead, we bring authenticity to our roles, and people respond positively to that transparency.

Balancing innovation and operations isn't a one-time decision, it is enabled by leadership awareness. Horizon56 began as a bold spinout chasing new ideas. Esben and Michael show us what it takes to hold both: to test the uncertain while scaling the proven. It's in that dynamic space, where structure meets experimentation, that the most meaningful outcomes emerge. Not just smoother processes or smarter tools, but measurable gains for clients, teams, and society.

In the next chapter, we focus on how leaders drive results that go beyond efficiency or growth, results that create lasting business value *and* deliver real social impact.

NOTE

1 Noble Corporation is a leading offshore drilling contractor for the oil and gas industry, known for its fleet of advanced drilling rigs. In 2021 Horizon56 was spun-out as a separate company, still fully owned by Noble Corporation. As of early 2026, Noble Corporation is still the owner of Horizon56.

Chapter 12

Lucy Blount

Achieving Business Impact Through a Social-First Approach – The Art of Seeing the Whole Person

In this chapter, we will explore how business results are driven, not despite a focus on people, but because of it. I'll provide several examples that show you how this is done in practice.

Figure 12.1 illustrates how balancing the Enablers through leadership connects people, purpose, and performance. Through Lucy's story, this chapter shows how shared ownership, inclusive dialogue, and visible wins can drive both social impact and business results.

Through an interview with Lucy Blount[1], a digital transformation leader, we'll uncover how seeing and supporting the whole person at work creates clarity, trust, and momentum. By the end of the chapter, you should understand that empathy is not a soft skill – it's a strategic approach.

Figure 12.1 Achieving a Positive Impact on Business and Social Results

DOI: 10.4324/9781003638551-13

I want to start with a statement by Lucy, one that has stayed with me, and I believe captures the essence of leadership. It's something I've witnessed firsthand while working with Lucy, and it reinforced a core truth that underpins this book: we enable others to create a positive impact:

> I grew up listening to my mom take pediatric surgery calls from our house, always calm, always composed. She'd hang up, have a plan, and walk out the door to help someone. That's where I first saw what real leadership looked like.

For Lucy, leadership was never about authority; it was about impact. That is the core message of this book. As leaders, we carry a responsibility, not just to deliver results, but to shape the environment around us. To impact people and uplift the next generation, with intention, knowing the business outcomes will follow.

This chapter is about achieving real business and social impact. It isn't about choosing one over the other, it's about learning to lead in a way that delivers both. In the early days, we drove profit, not because we didn't want to create impact beyond the bottom line, but because we didn't know how to do it. Today, we've learned that leading through people is the bridge between performance and purpose.

Lucy Blount is an experienced engineer and leader currently specializing in digital transformation initiatives within the energy industry. When I asked Lucy what first drew her to engineering, she smiled and said, "Honestly? I was fascinated by how toothpaste flows from the tube." We both laughed, but she wasn't joking. Lucy, who holds a degree in chemical engineering from Georgia Tech, has always seen the world through a lens of curiosity and practical problem-solving. It's a mindset that continues to shape how she leads today.

Her career began at an International Energy Company (IEC), where she completed multiple cooperative education rotations, immersing herself deeply into structured thinking, logical problem-solving, and operational excellence. Her experiences at IEC set the groundwork for a disciplined approach to complex industry challenges.

Following her graduation, Lucy joined another International Energy Company, where she has spent the past 12 years progressing through various engineering and operational roles, including significant experience working offshore. Approximately three years ago, Lucy transitioned into IEC's[2] Wells Digital team, driven by a personal motivation to make a meaningful impact beyond traditional engineering roles. Her career trajectory has consistently reflected her philosophy of turning side projects into central initiatives, positioning herself as a key leader in digital enablement and technology adoption within the company.

It was Tuesday evening, around 4:15 PM. Lucy was wrapping up a long day at the Houston office while I was working from Guyana. After quickly catching up, I wanted to explore what drove Lucy's natural inclination toward positively impacting people, something I'd noticed clearly in our previous interactions.

"Lucy, why don't we start by you sharing a bit about yourself, something from your early life or family that influenced your desire to create positive impacts beyond just business success?"

Lucy paused thoughtfully, a gentle smile forming as she reflected. "Well, I suppose it goes back to my upbringing. My mom was chief of pediatric surgery, and my dad was a cardiologist working with the CDC. Growing up, I constantly observed their calm and purposeful leadership."

Lucy's personal reflections resonated deeply with what I'd already observed about her calm approach to tense situations at work. Curious about how these early influences translated into practical leadership decisions, I asked her if there was a moment at work where she felt she made a meaningful impact on someone. She paused for a moment, then smiled.

"There was this one time," she said, "where I spent 45 minutes helping a colleague set up his iPad."

She laughed at the memory, not because it was funny, but because of how unremarkable it sounded. "This wasn't a big strategy session or a massive rollout. Just me, him, and an iPad."

But then she walked me through the issue. Her colleague was completely unfamiliar with tablets. A quick guide or a helpdesk link would've left him stuck, and likely left out of the broader digital transformation happening. So, Lucy pulled up a chair. For the next 45 minutes, they sat together, walking through the basics: setting up an Apple ID, choosing a password, and figuring out which screen swipe did what. They grumbled about the terrible UX design, shared a few laughs, and slowly, step by step, he started to understand how the machine worked.

"That was one good leadership moment I've had," she told me. "And it wasn't about tech – more about confidence. He felt seen. Supported. Capable and empowered."

That moment of care paid off. He didn't just use the new tools, he stuck with them. Lucy called that moment, "sweat equity," the idea that when someone has your back during a hard or unfamiliar moment, you're more likely to lean in, not opt out. That's what empowerment looks like, in its most everyday form: not loud, not formal, just one person taking the time to lift another into the future.

What makes this story a model is not just the empathy or the time spent, it's how that empathy translated directly into business results: faster adoption of new digital tools, smoother operational workflows, and a stronger culture of learning and trust.

From a metric perspective, this looks like improved time-to-adoption rates, higher employee digital engagement scores, employee NPS, and reduced first-time error rates on new systems while unlocking efficiency gains by using the new system.

This is the Empowerment Enabler at work, building individual capability and confidence, combined with the Technology Enabler, recognizing that successful technology adoption depends on meeting people at their level and matching it to the level of technology you are adopting.

She continued,

> It's easy to forget that adopting new technologies isn't just about implementation; you cannot forget about understanding the human side. People aren't resistant because they dislike change; they resist because change can feel intimidating. Leaders must repeatedly meet people where they are, again and again.

I wanted to dig deeper into the intersection between social empathy and tangible business outcomes. "Lucy, how have you seen these empathetic approaches translate directly into business results?"

Lucy responded confidently,

> When people feel seen, heard, and supported, their willingness to embrace new tools skyrockets. This speeds up technology deployment, boosts efficiency, and ultimately contributes to bottom-line performance. If I help one person gain confidence in new technology today, tomorrow they're better equipped to innovate and drive results.

I wanted to shift the conversation toward a different kind of leadership moment. One that doesn't come with any applause or slick presentations. The kind that quietly defines a leader's integrity.

I asked her, "You once told me about a project you decided not to move forward with. That you shut down entirely. Would you walk me through that again?"

"We didn't fail," she said, "we chose not to scale something that wasn't right. That's a success."

She nodded, and I could tell that this was a story that still sat with her, not because it was dramatic, but because it mattered. Because it was a decision that was made with people in mind.

She explained to me that the project had started the way so many promising ones do, with momentum. The software came highly recommended, the kind that ticks every executive box: streamline operations, boost collaboration, deliver measurable efficiency. Lucy's team had done everything right. Stakeholders were aligned, the rollout was structured, and there was genuine energy in the room.

Lucy smiled as she told me about the early days, half proud, half amused. "You know that feeling when everyone's nodding, the slides look good, and you think, *this is the one?*"

But then her face changed, eyebrows lifted, the smile now wry. "And then," she said, leaning back slightly, "we started doing behavioral gymnastics."

She let the words hang there.

It wasn't broken, but it wasn't right either. Her team found themselves creating workarounds, bending processes, reinterpreting their own ways of working to accommodate the tool. The software was slowly becoming the focus, rather than acting as the enabler of positive impact. What was meant to save time was now consuming it. Still, no one wanted to say it out loud.

"It's that sunk-cost trap," Lucy said. "You've spent months on it. Hours. People's reputations are quietly wrapped into it. And the pressure is to just keep going, to salvage something."

But Lucy made the call: **stop the project**.

What you see here is a great example of how you can evaluate your project at a very early stage. By setting measurable outcomes upfront, Lucy avoided wasted effort, preserved team morale, and freed resources for higher-value initiatives. This translated directly into business results: faster project cycle time, reallocation of capital expenditure (CAPEX) budget to more promising opportunities, and sustained operational efficiency. From a metric perspective, this shows up as reduced sunk costs and improved project return-on-investment (ROI) rates. Remember that acting decisively on clear success metrics not only protects your people, but it also protects your strategic capital and accelerates better outcomes.

I should reiterate that her decision wasn't a suggestion. It wasn't a pause. She shut it down completely. And in doing so, she did something rare in corporate environments: she created clarity. "A lot of people wanted to just simmer it, put it on the back burner in case it got better," she explained. "But that back burner becomes a source of stress. Of second-guessing. And I knew it would erode the team."

She wrote up the findings. The lessons learned. She framed the decision not as a loss, but as a smart pivot grounded in data and well-defined success criteria they had agreed upon at the outset.

And the response? Unexpectedly, it was gratitude.

A colleague, someone who hadn't even been part of the core team, approached her at the water cooler one day. "I heard about that decision," he said. "Thank you. Too many times we keep pushing tools that don't fit, and then everyone's frustrated. You saved us from that."

Lucy smiled as she told that part of her story. It mattered. Because leadership isn't just about championing wins, it's about shielding people from avoidable failure.

That moment wasn't just about software. It was about protecting her team's energy, morale, and focus. About reinforcing a culture where stopping something is just as valuable as starting it, if it means staying true to impact.

What made the decision possible, Lucy explained, was that success had been clearly defined from the very start. Before the trial began, the team aligned on what good would look like, what outcomes would signal a green light to scale, and what red flags would mean it was time to stop. That upfront clarity gave her the framework she needed to evaluate things objectively when the trial started to drift off course.

"We hadn't hit those criteria," she said simply. "It was clear."

And because it was clear, she acted.

She also understood something many leaders overlook; that **not making a decision is, in itself, a decision**, often one with hidden and negative consequences.

"If we had just said, 'Let's put it on the back burner,'" she told me, "that would have been a choice to keep everyone in limbo. And that uncertainty creates stress. People don't know whether to invest energy, or walk away, or wait. It erodes focus."

By making a firm call, she gave the team clarity. Relief, even. There was no more second-guessing or quiet frustration. Just a shared understanding that they'd learned what they needed to learn and were moving on.

That kind of decision-making doesn't just protect resources. It protects people. It models accountability. And it builds trust, because when you make a hard call for the right reasons, people remember.

BRIDGING A PEOPLE-FIRST APPROACH WITH BUSINESS IMPACT

I wanted to bridge the impact she made on people with business results. I asked Lucy directly, "How does your people-first approach show up in the hard stuff, financial performance, efficiency, shareholder value?"

"The reality is, we operate in businesses where profitability and shareholder value are non-negotiable. Leaders are accountable for outcomes, not just good intentions."

She didn't hesitate. "Efficiency. That's how it shows up."

Lucy explained that while cutting costs and overhead has its place, there's a floor. You can only cut so much before operations begin to suffer. The real unlock, she argued, is in improving efficiency through better, faster technological adoption, and that only happens when people are engaged and capable.

"I can't walk up to someone who's barely comfortable with a laptop and ask them to start using artificial intelligence. That just won't work," she said. "We haven't done the groundwork. They don't know how it works, they don't see the value, and they certainly don't trust it. That's not resistance, it's a leadership gap."

For Lucy, digital transformation is not a plug-and-play event. It's about consistent investment in digital literacy, trust, and human connection. That's what accelerates time-to-value. That's how you reduce the lag between introducing a new tool and seeing business results from it. It's not just a matter of installing systems, it's about preparing people.

When that preparation is in place, she explained, two key roadblocks vanish: lack of understanding and lack of perceived value. And once those are removed, deployment speeds up, adoption increases, and ultimately, the business benefits, whether through reduced downtime, more consistent processes, or lower resistance to future innovation.

This wasn't theoretical. Lucy pointed to real-world examples where teams were able to scale digital tools faster, precisely because of the trust, support, and groundwork already laid.

We paused for a moment. It was one of those moments where the silence said as much as the story. Lucy had shown how clarity, courage, and care for her team could result in stronger operational outcomes, not in spite of people, but because of them.

It made me consider that, this wasn't just how Lucy led projects. Her enabling showed up everywhere.

INCLUSION ISN'T A POLICY. IT'S PRACTICE

I'd heard about Lucy's outreach work, how she carved out time to visit universities, support early-career professionals, and advocate for women in energy and STEM. None of it was part of her job description. But it was clearly part of how she made an impact:

> Lucy, I know you do a lot to support women in the industry, especially in offshore roles and engineering fields where diversity still lags behind. Why is that work so important to you? And how do you see that kind of social investment coming back around, for people and businesses?

"When I mentor students or speak to young women about engineering, it's not about checking a box," Lucy said. "It's about shifting culture, creating spaces where people don't feel like they have to shrink themselves to belong. I didn't even think of myself as a 'woman in energy' until someone pointed it out," she said. "I was just doing the job."

But there was a moment – offshore, out on rotation in the Gulf of Mexico – when she realized how subtle exclusion can feel. She was the only woman on the rig. She wasn't looking to make a statement. She was just doing her job, like everyone else.

And Then They Delivered Shirts

She explained that the operations team had recently hit a milestone, and to celebrate, they'd ordered custom polo shirts, nice, branded ones, the kind of shirt you wear with pride when heading back onshore or walking into HQ. Lucy got hers with the rest of the crew.

"It was a men's small, and technically it was the smallest size they'd ordered," she said, laughing.

"But when I put the polo on, it was obviously not made for me. The shoulders were too wide, the cut was wrong, it was baggy and awkward. I tucked the shirt in and made it work. That's just what you do, right?"

She wore the polo anyway, because that's what people did offshore. You wore the team shirt. You showed up.

Until her supervisor saw her wearing the baggy shirt.

"Where the hell did you get that shirt?" he asked, half-serious.

Lucy blinked. "You bought it for me," she said.

He paused. Looked at her. And then, without making a big deal, he said, "Come with me. We're fixing this."

He sat her down with the catalog and asked for her size. He ordered a proper set of women's polos, five of them, because the supplier had a minimum, and handed over three that actually fit her.

This wasn't about a DEI policy or part of a campaign, nor rules written on a wall. It was positive action.

"He wasn't trying to make a statement about inclusivity," Lucy told me. "He just saw something that wasn't right and fixed it."

But in doing so, he made a much bigger impact.

That moment, that gesture, sent a message louder than any memo: You belong here. You matter. *You don't have to shrink yourself to fit in*. And that, Lucy explained, is how cultures shift, not with giant moves, but through dozens of small decisions that quietly say, "You're seen."

For Lucy, the decision wasn't just about a better-fitting shirt. For the rest of the team, it's a reminder: culture isn't shaped by slogans or policy. This was about correcting something that was obviously not right. And next time, you might be the one to make that moment happen.

Because what's the cost of not doing that? High turnover. Lower engagement. Lost trust. Talented people walking away.

This was also about being able to do your job without discomfort or second-guessing. And when people feel empowered and included, they do better work. They stay longer. They invest more.

That's the return on inclusion. That's where social impact becomes business impact, with one well-fitting shirt at a time.

TEAM TURN AROUND – A MICRO LEADERSHIP APPROACH

One of the clearest examples of Lucy's people-first leadership came through a team she didn't even manage directly. She was brought in as a stakeholder, someone to guide the work and help deliver results on a digital transformation initiative.

But what she saw was a group that had been overlooked, under-coordinated, and quietly written off.

"They were seen as underperforming," she told me. "No one really knew what they were working on, or why they were still on the project."

Instead of stepping in with a top-down directive, Lucy took a different approach. She listened.

First, she asked what the team believed they were meant to deliver; their reply, they were not sure. Then, she worked with them to clarify expectations. They sketched out a one-month milestone, something achievable, but fast enough to create energy. When the team estimated it would take three months, Lucy challenged that. "What would it take to get it done in one month?"

It turned out they just needed one more person. Someone who was about to roll off another assignment anyway. Easy fix.

With the right structure in place, Lucy let the team take ownership. They chose the cadence of meetings. They chose who would run the check-ins. She made it clear she wasn't there to micromanage, just to clear the path and celebrate progress.

Every week, she checked in, not with pressure, but with curiosity. "What do you need from me?" she'd ask. "Who do I need to call to make something easier for you?"

And every week, they moved faster.

The energy shifted quickly and the team began delivering ahead of schedule. Other managers took notice. One even pulled Lucy aside and said, "I've never seen them this motivated."

The secret wasn't some management hack. It was empowerment, a slight restructure with clear expectations, and genuine support. Lucy recognized the value in people that others had overlooked, and by treating them like they mattered, they started acting like they did too.

She told me, "You don't have bad teams. You have teams without expectations. Without belief. That's something you can fix."

And in doing so, she didn't just improve a team's performance, she modeled the kind of leadership that creates lasting, scalable impact.

Once again, a very powerful example of how, *through a people first focus, you will drive business results.*

Establish clear business and social metrics upfront before scaling any initiative. Prioritize high-leverage impact areas, safety, retention, and integration, to generate genuine value. Track success through customer, operational, and workforce indicators to ensure measurable, sustainable business outcomes.

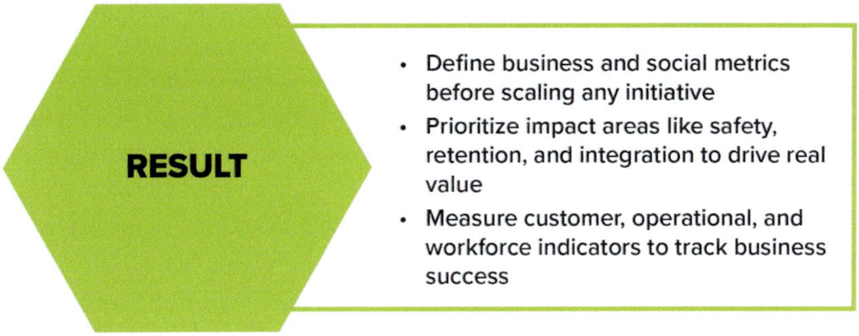

Figure 12.2 Results: Scaling with measured impact

SUPPORT THE WHOLE PERSON, NOT HALF

As our conversation began to wind down, I could tell Lucy was still holding on to something important. We'd covered projects, decision-making, inclusion, outreach, all vital leadership territory. But I sensed she had one more insight to share, one that came from a deeper place.

I asked her, "If you could give one piece of advice to a future leader, someone who really wants to make an impact, not just in business but in people's lives, what would that be?"

She took a breath. Thought for a moment. Then leaned forward.

"You have to support the whole person," she said. "Not half."

She didn't mean wellness perks or a motivational poster in the hallway. She meant real, lived empathy. Leadership that acknowledges that people come into work carrying their full lives with them, ambitions, pressures, anxieties, relationships, identities. And if those things are ignored, performance suffers. Morale drops. Culture becomes shallow.

"In the medical field, there's something called a *duty of care*," (a legal responsibility to act with reasonable care and caution to avoid causing harm to others, ensuring their safety and well-being) she said. "We need something like that in leadership, too. A duty of care for the *whole human*, not just the worker who shows up at 8 AM."

Lucy talked about how small actions ripple through a person's life. If a manager dismisses someone's stress, piles on pressure without context, or ignores basic needs like schedule flexibility, that employee doesn't just carry it through the day, they carry it home. To their partners. To their kids. To their mental health.

"And if we're bad coworkers," she said plainly, "people go home and become bad parents. Or bad spouses. Or they just burn out. That's on us."

Then she told me a story that brought it all into a clear focus.

She'd once joined a team that held recurring morning meetings, very early – sometimes 6:30 or 7:00 AM. It wasn't unusual in operations, but it was brutal for working parents, especially those with young kids to drop off at school.

"People were missing the call or showing up frazzled, and no one wanted to say anything," Lucy explained. "They didn't want to be *that* person asking for special treatment."

She didn't have kids herself, but she'd been paying attention. And one day, she spoke up.

"I said, 'This early morning call doesn't work for me, I go to the gym in the morning.' Which, at the time, I did," she said with a grin. "But that wasn't the point."

The point was that someone needed to take the heat, to *normalize* the ask. And sure enough, after a bit of back-and-forth, the call time was pushed back. A small change. But the relief? Immediate. Parents could drop their kids off without panic. Mornings felt manageable again. People showed up more focused.

Several coworkers later pulled her aside and said thank you. Not because she'd changed a meeting, but because she'd seen them. She'd removed the tension that was quietly wearing them down.

"These decisions seem small," she told me, "but they create clarity. Stability. Psychological safety. And if you're not actively creating those things as a leader, then you're passively allowing stress to accumulate."

Lucy paused again, then added something that really stuck with me.

"People don't always want you to solve their problems. Most of the time, they just want to feel seen. Heard. That what they're going through is valid."

And when that happens, when people feel safe, acknowledged, and supported, you don't just get loyalty. You get energy. Creativity. Accountability. You get performance.

Social results become business results.

HAVE YOU EVER HEARD OF CURB-CUT DESIGN?

Then Lucy introduced a metaphor that stopped me cold. "Have you ever heard of curb-cut design?" she asked.

I hadn't.

She smiled:

> It's this idea that started in cities across the U.S. When wheelchair ramps, those little sloped cuts in sidewalks, became mandatory, people thought they were just for a small group of users. But what happened next? Suddenly, *everyone* benefited. Parents pushing strollers. Delivery guys with carts. Travelers with suitcases. Kids on bikes. Those ramps helped people move through the cities more easily. Not just the group they were designed for.

She let it hang there:

"That's how I think about leadership," she said. "You make one thoughtful change, something that helps someone on the margins, and suddenly the whole system starts working better. It lifts the floor."

Then she paused.

"People don't want to stand out. Most won't ask for help. So, when you build something that quietly includes them from the start, it changes everything."

I couldn't help but think back to every story Lucy had already shared: shifting morning meetings for parents, helping someone set up an iPad with patience and empathy, the purchase of shirts that fit women on offshore rigs. Each of them was a curb-cut moment. A small adjustment that, while seemingly minor, changed how people felt about themselves, their teams, and their work.

"Those little decisions, those actions?" Lucy said. "They shape culture. They build trust. And eventually, they show up on the bottom line."

Leading through people does not distract from business results. It is how you drive them. When you empower individuals, define success clearly, and support the whole person, you accelerate adoption rates, protect your capital, improve operational efficiency, and build a resilient culture ready for future challenges.

Focusing on people shows up in business results you can measure faster time-to-adoption for new technologies, higher project ROI, reduced turnover costs, increased productivity rates, improved safety – both psychological and physical – and stronger operational margins.

NOTES

1 Lucy Blount, P.E., is a petroleum engineer and digital transformation leader in the energy sector. Known for her people-first approach, she has led high-impact initiatives in a global energy company, advocating for inclusive leadership, mentoring, and sustainable digital adoption. Her story in this chapter is based on an in-depth interview conducted by the author in April 2025.

2 This IEC. It is one of the oil and gas "supermajors" and one of the world's largest companies measured by revenues and profits. With the purpose to deliver energy to the world, today and tomorrow.

Chapter 13

A Milestone Is Set

This book's cover is green. It's not meant to blend in. Neither are you.

When I began the process of writing this book, I was very aware that that too often, business books had nothing useful to offer on when it really mattered and was kept high level. The questions from coworkers, partners, and students kept coming, asking why there were no textbooks that could answer the questions of *how* to execute strategies and tactical actions.

Let me be very clear, I'm not discounting the *why*. It gives purpose and motivation. But if you can't turn that motivation into action, then the initial passion becomes empty words, slogans written on a whiteboard or promises on a website, but they are rarely executed. That is a lot of wasted time and energy.

GETTING BACK UP FROM OUR DEEP DIVE

We've been deep-diving into each of the Enablers and their impact. This final chapter zooms back out. Leadership demands both views, by zooming in on the details, then enabling your team, yourself, and your stakeholder ecosystem.

But you also need to zoom out to see the bigger picture, then hold the overall objective in focus, and connect today's decisions and actions with tomorrow's outcomes. That is what your new Enabler framework will give you. The ability to understand why, and when, and what to do, and the very difficult but necessary *how* to do it! You should know how to focus on the details, but your framework also allows you to keep the big picture in view, enabling you to focus on the objectives of running today's business while innovating for tomorrow.

Without this, the risks become blatantly obvious: if you get lost in the details then you'll you lose direction. If you stay too far above then you'll lose relevance. However, when you master these movements, you'll be able to shift seamlessly between the ground level and the big picture, knowing when to go deep and when to pull back. You will know exactly how, with the right people, to ensure cash flow and create the positive impact needed today. At the same time, you'll also understand that you need to drive innovation through exploration of, for

DOI: 10.4324/9781003638551-14

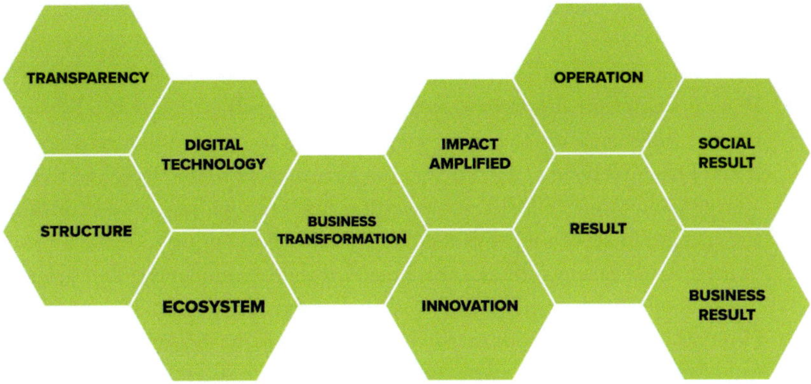

Figure 13.1 Enablers for You to Apply and Lead for Positive Impact

example technologies, and how you plan, develop, then corporate them into your core business.

The Enablers give you all that and more. They help you work on the part of a team, division, or business that needs attention. They also let you step back, see the whole, and understand the consequences of your actions, good or bad, by adjusting each one. That is how you stand out, whether you're deep in the weeds solving a particular issue, or cruising at 30,000 feet.

On a personal note, I can say that in my career, I've been lucky to witness all kinds of leadership in action all over the world. On offshore rigs in Guyana, where crews worked 12-hour shifts in the sweltering heat, leadership showed up in the way supervisors set the tone for safety before the day even started. In corporate boardrooms in Barcelona, leadership showed up whether decision rights were clear, or if the upper management circled around the same debate for weeks while projects stalled. In Japan, I saw how cultural context shapes every interaction, where respect and hierarchy matter, but so does finding the right way to encourage new voices. In the United States, while working with the biggest players in the energy sector, I witnessed the constant push to be at the forefront of innovation. I also learned that technology only sticks when leaders win hearts and minds, and when they bring street cred: the skill to get hands-on with their people, meeting them where they are, and carrying it forward with empathy and endurance long after the launch spotlight has moved on.

These experiences taught me something simple: leadership doesn't travel as a fixed model. What works in Denmark doesn't transfer to Tokyo, Houston, Perth or Bangkok.

What is clear: the demand for leaders who understand "the how" is growing. Leaders who can execute, understand details and the big picture are in demand. The time for cute or trendy statements but no accompanying action has passed.

In addition, these questions keep coming up and you should consider them as well:

- How do you run operations with the discipline that keeps the business strong, while creating the space for innovation to scale? While writing this book, I had just returned from a trip to Japan. I was invited to Tokyo to visit a large conglomerate. All their attention was on how they could continue to innovate in all of their business units, while continuing to make a profit in their stable business lines. I was hosted at their headquarters and brought out to their clients to help them answer this exact question.
- How do you deliver profit on the bottom line and, at the same time, create impact for your people, your customers, and the societies your business depends on? In a recent project in Australia, this was the highest priority on the agenda. The first question was answered by bringing in new technologies to conservative operations. Then the following questions constantly needed to be addressed: How do we create a positive impact beyond profit and shareholder value? Demand from employees, from government, and local associations?

As you may understand, I am constantly on the move. There is a bottomless supply of new projects, new innovations, and new clients working in many cultures. What I have learned and is that wherever I worked, whatever the culture or company, three things always mattered: **be reliable, be predictable, and be useful**.

We explored this in Chapter 5, and I encourage you to revisit it if needed. Those qualities are what people look for in the structures you create. But as a leader, the demands run deeper. It takes time to build and for the first days, weeks, or months, everything is fragile. Knowing the Enablers helps me to speak a language everyone is inspired by. If you can help your people zoom in on their specific business opportunity (or problem as some may prefer to say), then bring them back to understand the big picture, I can confidently state, clarity is something that is appreciated anywhere I go.

This is why I built the Enablers framework. To give you the clarity and upper hand from the get-go.

THE WORLD YOU'RE LEADING INTO

The future of leadership won't slow down for anyone. It will get faster, more demanding, and more visible.

Even while I was writing this book, artificial intelligence moved from a topic we debated in conference rooms to being built into almost every project I'm involved with. In the company where I work, we have established a dedicated

AI research team and implementing AI in our solutions. With this, you can say that the company has added a long-term exploration unit. We already have a very active innovation department. How fast do we need to move? When we made the decision that it was critical to invest in AI research, now, only a few months later, we are implementing the findings from our research in our core products!

Colleagues of mine who run businesses are figuring out how to make AI part of their work. For me? I had to get on that train myself, or risk becoming obsolete. That's why the Enablers matter even more now. At the same time, sustainability and social impact are no longer optional. Regulators demand it. Communities demand it. Employees demand it. Hitting financial targets is never enough if the way you get there erodes trust, weakens culture, or damages the environment. The leaders who will be remembered are the ones who deliver results and impact together, not one after the other, but side by side. It is how to create the positive impact that will make you stand out. Do it at the core of your business. Make it business as usual.

What you've read in this book didn't come from strategy sessions alone. It showed up in real-world experiences. In project meetings, client visits, field visits, over coffee, and in many hallway conversations.

It came from engineers, senior leaders, support staff, and partners and executives.

It came up when I gave lectures, during boardroom debates, and in real-world delivery reviews. These weren't edge cases, this was daily business life.

Questions like these were always at the core of our conversations:

- What does empowerment look like when a team is stuck, and no one knows who is supposed to make a decision?
- What happens when a decision isn't made at all?
- What does it take to deploy a new technology and actually get people to use it?
- How do you scale a business without losing your values in the process?
- How do you keep going, year after year, driving change, pushing uphill, and still show up with empathy?

I listened. I researched. I asked people who didn't just talk about leadership, but enabled it. They found ways to make others succeed, and they could explain how.

We looked at how to develop people and systems. How to amplify what works. How to collaborate without losing speed or focus.

We broke apart the false trade-off between operational results and social value.

We treated ecosystems as real structures, not buzzwords.

We examined technology as a tool to use, not a trend to follow.

We showed that transformation was not a launch event but something you stay with long after the spotlight moves on.

I hope you now see how to create results that matter, both social and business.

As a final digression, I was once working on a new digital offshore project with Michael Olesen, who you'll remember from an earlier chapter. When that rig finally came online after months of work, he turned to me and the other stakeholders. He said just one line: **"A milestone is set."**

That was it. The project had succeeded. Nothing more needed to be said. The actions had already spoken for themselves. The project had been carefully mapped and has laid the foundation for how we now deliver successful major digital transformations.

That phrase has stayed with me, because every milestone is both an ending and a beginning. Leadership is the same. You never arrive. You set milestones, and then you keep moving forward.

The question remaining, is how will the Enablers change over time? The framework and tools I've set out are not set in stone. I am fully aware that we live in extremely dynamic times. However, many businesses do not realize this.

There are many business schools using the same 50-year-old frameworks to teach competitive advantage – I am not kidding you! When you consider that fact, this may be part of the answer as to why so many businesses and leaders are failing.

A close friend of mine came to me while he was studying for his MBA, at a reputable business school. He asked for help with an assignment. He told me how the school taught competitive advantage through a well-known framework. What he did not know was that this was developed in the 1970s. My friend told me that they are looking through the lens of "industry" – my question to him was, what is an industry? Classification buckets made up by statisticians. Let me offer some thoughts: The framework does not include the firm, does not include you/the individual, and is always static. How can reputable business schools get away with teaching this? This means there is a lack of guidance for firm- and individual-level decisions. Did my friend learn about how capabilities change? Dynamic resources and the impact of technology in the context of competitive advantage – no, he did not! Tell me how can anyone graduate from an MBA class today and this is what they pay for? I can tell you what I think: because it does not require the teachers to reinvent themselves and it is easier just to let the students fill out a few boxes and then tell prospective employers, "They are prepared to create a competitive advantage for their company."

The first MBA program was created to meet the increasing demand for business leaders to be able to keep up with the Industrial Revolution. We should not forget why and it may be time to rapidly update how MBA programs are taught.

FINAL THOUGHTS

The chapters of my next book will be written by leaders like you – leaders who've led innovation, faced the pressure of conflicting priorities, disruption, carried people through change, and connected business results with social impact in ways others thought couldn't be done.

If you've lived it, built it, enabled it, I want to hear your story. My next book will be built from your examples.

So when you set your milestone, don't keep it to yourself. Share it with me. Reach out at **docschlosser.com** and be part of enabling what comes next.

A MILESTONE IS SET

The next one is yours. Share it with me, and let's shape what comes next.

Bibliography

Alstrup, Nis. 2024. Interview by Kristian Pultz Schlosser. Denmark, May 2024.

Babenko, Konstantin. 2024. "30% Less Overstock and Stockouts? How Predictive Analytics Helps Optimize Inventory for SMBs and Enterprises." *LinkedIn Articles*, September 30, 2024.

Blount, Lucy. 2025. Interview by Kristian Pultz Schlosser. Houston, Texas, May 2025.

Bonnet, Didier. 2022. *3 Stages of a Successful Digital Transformation*. Harvard Business Review.

Caputo, Claudio. 2025. Interview by Kristian Pultz Schlosser. Online, June 2025.

Goleman, Daniel. 1995. *Emotional Intelligence: Why It Can Matter More Than IQ*. New York: Bantam Books.

IDEO. 2024. "Design Thinking." IDEO. Accessed August 16, 2025. https://www.ideo.com/thinking

Kotter, John P. 1996. *Leading Change*. Boston: Harvard Business Press.

McKee, Annie. 2017. *How to Be Happy at Work: The Power of Purpose, Hope, and Friendship*. Boston: Harvard Business Review Press.

Olesen, Michael. 2025. Interview by Kristian Pultz Schlosser. Denmark, July 2025.

O'Reilly, Charles A., and Michael L. Tushman. 2013. "Organizational Ambidexterity: Past, Present, and Future." *The Academy of Management Perspectives* 27: 324–338.

Schlosser, Kristian Pultz, Tatjana Volkova, and Aivars Spilbergs. 2023. "The Effect of Ambidextrous Strategic Leadership and Digital Technology Adoption on Creating Shared Value." *European Research Studies Journal* 26 (3): 73–94.

Schlosser, Kristian Pultz. 2024. *The Impact of Strategic Leadership on Creating Shared Value*. PhD diss., RISEBA University of Applied Sciences.

Skov, Mikael. 2025. Interview by Kristian Pultz Schlosser. Houston, Texas, August 2025.

Thorup, Esben. 2025. Interview by Kristian Pultz Schlosser. Houston, Texas, July 2025.

Index

Note: **Bold** page numbers refer to tables and *italic* page numbers refer to figures and page numbers followed by "n" refer to end notes.